HIGHLAND RESISTANCE

HIGHLAND RESISTANCE

The Radical Tradition in the Scottish North

Iain Fraser Grigor

EDINBURGH AND LONDON

First published in Great Britain in 2000 by
MAINSTREAM PUBLISHING COMPANY (EDINBURGH) LTD
7 Albany Street
Edinburgh EH1 3UG

ISBN 1 84018 265 2

A catalogue record for this book is available from the British Library

Typeset in Giovanni Book and Manson
Printed and bound in Great Britain by Butler & Tanner Ltd, Frome and London

contents

Preface   7

1 An Emotive and Political Thing   11

2 Rehearsal   24

3 The Growth of Resistance   36

4 The Road to Glendale   52

5 Braes and the Napier Commission   67

6 The Land League Grows   83

7 Crofters' Party, Crofters' Act   99

8 The Mass Movement in Action   116

9 The Movement Reforms   139

10 A New Land League   154

11 War and the Promise of Land   174

12 Avoid Lawyers, Continue Ploughing   192

13 The Cat Stroked is Meek   209

14 The Land for the People   224

Further Reading   239

'MY PEOPLE HAVE BEEN ON THIS LAND FOR CENTURIES.
IT IS OUR LAND, AND WE MEAN TO HAVE OUR LAND.'

ALLAN MACRAE, ASSYNT, 1992

PREFACE

The subject of this book is the record of opposition to landlordism – and the political and cultural overtones associated with it – which characterises so much of the last two hundred years of Scottish Highland history. This record is put in a modern context. The first chapter considers landlord-centred disputes from the 1970s and 1980s, while the final chapter examines some similar disputes from the 1990s. The intervening chapters concern themselves broadly with the story of anti-landlordism from the aftermath of the final Jacobite rising to the Knoydart land-raid in 1948. This record is discontinuous and the focus on it, of the text, is therefore discontinuous too. But the effort is made, so far as it is possible, to put those people involved in the anti-landlord tradition at the centre of their own history.

This is not a point of view that would have recommended itself to all writers on Scottish affairs in earlier times. As early as the 1730s, with the ink scarcely dry on the Treaty of Union, George Buchanan's great Latin histories of the country were alleged as unfit to be 'put in the hands of our Scotch youth while at school, now there is an Union between the two Kingdoms, for fear of awakening that Old National Grudge, that should now be sopited [suppressed as discreditable] and industriously forgotten.'

In the second half of the same century the government's censors extended this animosity to the theatre. The Lord Chamberlain's office refused a licence for the performance of Duval's *Prince Charles Stuart*, for instance, and granted permission only to plays which portrayed the Scots as quaint pastoralists or as comic characters, and which ridiculed Scottish manners, character and speech. And by the middle of the following century, with the Knoydart Clearances satisfactorily completed, *The Times* could assert that 'Scotland is a country manifestly in want of a grievance. She labours under the weariness of attained wishes and the curse of granted prayers. Good fortune has joined her inseparably to the richest and most enterprising nation of modern times. Never was a territory north of Latitude 55 Degrees so favoured before.'

An echo of these sentiments is still, it may sometimes be thought, found with reference to the modern Highlands. Consider, for instance, a humorous item in the *Daily Telegraph* in the autumn of 1981. '"Clackies," as these small, tough, unusually ferocious dogs are called in Scotland, tend to bite anyone they can get at on sight. They were formerly used by landlords' agents to evict crofters in the West Highlands. A couple of "clackies" down the chimney would soon have the crofters and their families outside and running for their lives.'

This item was judged so excessively funny that, with admirable economy of effort, it was reprinted fifteen months later in the same column: 'In the days of the Highland clearances, they were used by landlords' agents for evicting obstinate crofters. A couple of "Clackies" down the chimney had the wretches out in seconds, running for their lives in the direction of the nearest port where they might hope to get a boat for Nova Scotia.'

The same sort of pertinaciously generous humour was detectable at the Isle of Eigg 'Games' in 1984. The festivities commenced the evening prior to the Games themselves with a cricket match (for which the proper gear and costume was plentifully supplied) on that island beach where once the Norsemen hauled their longships for respite from the Minch, and across which at dusk rang cries in tones appropriate to such spirit as these Games, in such a location, may be thought to represent. The following morning, things got under way with a suitable seriousness:

> The McVaugh family had flown in from Philadelphia despite imminent business meetings in Tokyo and Paris. Distant German cousin Axel von Schellenberg had arrived that morning from Frankfurt, chartered a helicopter at Glasgow airport and landed on the croquet lawn. The 'Clanranalds' (led by Ranald MacDonald, Chief of Clanranald and Hereditary Chief of the Western Isles) wore kilts during the windsurfing. The Great Eigg Campaign re-enacted the bloody struggles between the Hanoverians and the Jacobites. Barbour jackets and wine-bottles littered the verandah. Dimly I could see a figure under an enormous white pith helmet, standing in a jeep which proudly bore the Union Jack flag.

Or consider the proud opinions attributed to an interviewee by *Vogue* magazine in the same recent period: 'My father's family have all the qualities traditionally associated with west-coast Highlanders. They're sloppy and dirty. They lie. They are fantasists with a babbling loquacity and an inability to look people in the eye.'

Or again, as another observer of this 'traditional' Highland scene informed the readers of a local newspaper in 1990: 'Local people do not want to work. They are unreliable. It is outsiders who achieve things here, not your Highlanders and Islanders. The women gossip too much. Apathy pervades the place. Be less anti-English, without us, you would have drifted off into the Atlantic by now.'

And yet, and yet: the record of popular struggle, of popular aspiration to some sort of cultural and national integrity, will not lie down, will not be written, or humoured, or patronised, out of its own history. Many Highland writers have born witness in recent years, and in a very direct way, to this tradition of struggle.

Derick Thomson has recalled, 'There was a small inner harbour behind my grandfather's house on which the Established Church was built. It was here that the Revd Donald MacCallum, the famous Land Leaguer, preached to his small flock, and my grandfather acted as precentor, though he never committed himself sufficiently to join the Church. He and MacCallum were good friends. MacCallum had a large glebe and ran it as a farm with the help of his brother Dughall. Later this glebe was raided and the village of Keose Glebe built on it. One of the raiders was my uncle Willie, and my grandfather must have derived real satisfaction from seeing his youngest son staking his claim to Keose land that had been denied himself so many years before.'

The folklorist Calum MacLean wrote of his meeting with a former anti-landlord activist from Sutherland: 'Hector Sutherland is one of the few surviving Gaelic speakers in the district and a most intelligent and discerning old gentleman. In his younger and more active days he was prominent during the time of the crofter and Land League agitation.'

James Shaw Grant also recalled a similar meeting: 'I remember, as a young university student, meeting one of the leaders of the Sutherland crofters of that era, in my uncle's office in Inverness. Joseph MacLeod from Kildonan was a very old man by that time, but still active and full of fun. He looked like an Old Testament patriarch . . . My uncle spoke of him almost with reverence, because of his standing in the north during the Crofters' War . . . His technique was to go to a village, call a meeting, and deliver an address . . . He could then send an account of the meeting to the local press, reporting his speech in full . . . Other nearby villages, not wanting to be undone, would invite him to speak to them, and the snowball – perhaps I should say fireball – of land-reform was rolling through the district.'

Many others, in the closing decades of the last century, could also claim a direct connection with the anti-landlord struggle of earlier times. John MacKay, who died as recently as 1989, could transmit in perfect detail the oral record of the destruction of his family's community in Strathnaver in the early nineteenth century. Aonghas MacNeacail has recalled in print the story of his great-aunt's imprisonment for her anti-landlord activities on Skye. The *West Highland Free Press* has reported, as piper at a Harris Sound wedding in 1976, the man who played the pipes at the Balranald land-raid in 1919. The *Press and Journal* has profiled another of the men who took part in that same raid, unrepentant at eighty-four years of age. Meanwhile, John Macrae MacLellan has described in print his memories of his grandfather, John MacRae, secretary of the Ross-shire Land League. And Rob Gibson has established a direct link with the Land Leaguer

Donald MacKay through his daughter Joan Fraser, and with the Land
Leaguer Donald MacRae through Alexander Robertson.

The *West Highland Free Press* has also told the story of Donald Beaton
of Skye. He was just three years old, with his father in gaol in Inverness
for Land League activities, when the remainder of his family were evicted
from their home in Waternish. The furniture was thrown out of the hovel
and its entrance secured. Neighbours fed them at night, though could not
offer shelter for fear of a similar fate; but Irish sailors on the coast at the
time broke into the house and re-instated the family. Beaton died, as the
paper recorded at the time, as recently as 1979.

And as late as the early 1980s, I myself interviewed a very elderly
resident of Glencalvie. He could remember back to when he was a small
boy and two of his neighbours were very elderly sisters – one of whom
was crippled as a result of having been involved as a child in the
Greenyards eviction riot of 1843.

In this respect, as in others, the land question in the Highlands is not just
a matter of history. It remains a living issue for the Highlands, and the
Scotland, of our own present times. This is so in both economic and
cultural terms.

In a large and largely rural area like the Highlands, land-ownership
could hardly fail to be a matter of economic importance. It significantly
governs patterns of land use and land management (though good land
management is never the exclusive property of any one form of land
ownership). It governs issues such as crofting, ecological conservation
and popular access to the 'wilderness area' that constitutes much of the
Highlands.

This is not, of course, the only issue of importance in the Highland
economy. Enterprise in a whole range of activities largely unconnected
with the land is central to the Highland future. But the land cannot be
ignored. And the past cannot be forgotten. Nor should it be. The question
of the ownership of the land in the Highlands is central to the cultural
integrity of Scotland in this new century. Indeed, the long record of land-
centred struggle in the Highlands may be said to have contributed – in
conditions of unassailable Imperialist Unionist hegemony – a struggle,
albeit by proxy, for precisely that cultural (and political) integrity.

In other words, a vibrant, democratic, culturally confident Scotland
demands a modern and democratic system of land-ownership in the
Highlands. The Scottish Parliament can make that sort of framework
available. The rest is up to the people.

Iain Fraser Grigor
March 2000

ΟΠΕ

ΑΠ ΕΜΟΤİVE ΑΠD POLİTİCAL ΤΗİΠG

'These people typify a breed of greedy, grasping nuisances who contribute nothing to society and who usually exert a positively malign influence on the communities that they inflict themselves on.'

—⊸⊚⊚⊸—

The land question in the Highlands commands as much significance and interest in Scotland today as at any time in the past. What is the reason for this continuing significance and interest?

Developments during the 1970s and 1980s may help explain. In these years, public attention focused in particular on the concentration of ownership of great stretches of the Highlands, the operation of the game laws with regard to deer and salmon, and often-grotesque levels of speculation in landed estates.

As far back as the mid-1970s, John McEwen was publishing material in respect of this concentration of ownership:

> One hundred and forty individuals or companies own just under half the Highlands. Four individuals own just under half a million acres. Seventeen individuals or companies own sixty-nine per cent of the land of Caithness. Thirty-eight own eighty-four per cent of the land of Sutherland. Eighty own fifty-seven per cent of Inverness-shire; sixty-seven own fifty-eight per cent of the land of Argyll; seventy-six own eighty per cent the land of Ross and Cromarty; and sixty-three own sixty-two per cent of the land of Perthshire.

And in the early 1980s a report on land ownership and use in the Highlands and Islands identified aged and absentee landlords as a major factor in the under-utilisation of land in the area. It added that the popular image of the Highland landlord as the product of an English public school, followed by perhaps Oxbridge or the Services, was accurate. About half of the landowners in the north of Scotland could be regarded as absentee. Of those of who were listed in *Who's Who*, more than two-thirds had attended public schools – and of the forty-six who had attended university, Oxford was almost the exclusive choice. Many landowners had a background which included some military training and almost one-third still retained their military titles. No less than half of the estates which had had titled owners a full century earlier remained in the possession of the same family.

An opinion poll conducted shortly afterwards showed that seventy-seven per cent of Scots were in favour of some form of control over the amount of land that could be privately owned in the country. No less than sixty-three per cent of the respondents favoured limitations on the amount of land that could be owned by any single individual, and fifty-eight per cent felt that there should be control over how much land was owned by any company or institution. A similar percentage wanted controls on land ownership by anyone who was not Scottish by nationality, while sixty-eight per cent also thought it 'very important' that remote communities should survive in Scotland.

These revelations, and their implications, did not go unnoticed.

Some years earlier, indeed, the Western Isles Council had announced that a land-register delineating the possessions of the principal landowners in the islands was to be compiled. And shortly afterwards the council's crofting committee was calling for unused and under-used land to be transferred to public ownership. A year later the Highlands and Islands Development Board (HIDB) launched its 'comprehensive strategy' for agriculture and land use in the Highlands, which strategy was to include compulsory powers of land acquisition. These powers, however, would be no more than a 'final string to the bow,' as ownership of land was an 'emotive, political thing.'

Just how emotive – and political – this final string was would soon be apparent. By the following Christmas, the MP for the Western Isles was asking in the House of Commons whether the government was 'aware that there is great disappointment in the Highlands that the HIDB has never used its existing powers with regard to land? The Highlands requires legislation to wipe out the curse of landlordism once and for all.' The appropriate Conservative minister replied that he disagreed 'totally with this sort of socialism.'

Given this sort of lead from its political masters, the Board was quick to back off from the emotive and political thing. At the 1983 conference of the Scottish Landowners' Federation speakers, including Keith Schellenberg and Lord Burton, took very strong exception to any HIDB plan to take a leading role in land ownership.

The assembled landowners were also addressed by the HIDB's chairman. Mixing metaphors with some *élan*, he noted that the land question was 'one of the hottest potatoes on the Board's table, on which I don't want to get drawn into too much debate because I'm sure I'll put my foot in it.' He then announced that he did not subscribe to the view that changing the system of land-ownership would solve the problem. The conference chairman promptly congratulated the Board on 'breeding' a new kind of chairman: practical and down-to-earth rather than the impractical ideologue-type of the past.

And the clout of the landlords was not confined to government and its development agencies. They also exerted a remarkably dominant influence with regard to forestry policy, against the background of a debate on the extent to which trees might constitute a worthwhile agricultural crop in an era of European food surpluses. The controlling principle of this influence was tax-break schemes for the very rich. In the 1980s, prevailing forestry schemes were criticised by, among others, the North East Mountain Trust, which claimed that many of the schemes were 'barely competent.' Of some proposed plantations, the trust added that it was 'difficult to avoid the conclusion that they are simply thinly disguised deer shelters financed, in considerable measure, out of the public purse.' One calculation put it like this:

> The gross cost of afforestation work before tax relief of grants is up to £1,000 per hectare spread over the first six years. Of this £1,000 per hectare, the Forestry Commission gives a grant of £240. The rest, £760, is your business loss for the year, and under tax schedule D you can claim it against tax which you are paying at 60 per cent. This means that sixty per cent of the £760 comes back as tax relief, which means that something like seventy per cent of the total cost – excluding the price of the land – is paid for by the taxpayer. After a relatively small number of years – perhaps ten – the investor can then sell to an institutional purchaser like a pension fund, who have no tax incentives to plant bare land, but are prepared to buy plantation land to invest in the physical growth of the crop and the inflation of land and crop values. The investor can sell at £1,000 a hectare, which means that he gets back £1,000 on land for which he originally paid about £300.

These, and similar, entrepreneurial efforts did not go unnoticed or uncriticised, although the criticism was something that at least some landlords affected not to understand.

For those landlords, the problem was one of image. At the 1981 conference of the Scottish Landowners' Federation, one speaker suggested that it was 'particularly important during the current recession, when people are being asked to make real sacrifices, that the lairds make a greater effort to dispel their image of champagne-swilling and pouring whisky down their throats and doing very little for it.' The truth was entirely to the contrary. According to the Duke of Buccleuch and Queensferry (whose great-grandfather had been the federation's first-ever president in 1906): 'We have been far too reticent over the years in letting it be known that we are doing a helluva good job. I think we should be flying the flag a bit more.'

On crofters, however, the landlords have expressed less fulsome sympathy. During the parliamentary debates in the mid-'70s on the reform of crofting law, for instance, Lord Burton – a member, it might be thought, of one of the world's smallest and most pampered minorities – was attacking crofters from his seat in the House of Lords: 'There was no reason why crofters, a small section of the community, should be pampered.' He also asked of his peers why a crofter should receive 'enormous' privileges in grants and subsidies while at the same time paying tiny rents. In that same debate Viscount Thurso nostalgically regretted that 'no longer would they see a peasant form of existence, with crofters scraping a living from a few rough acres.' And Lord Balfour, owner of 105 crofts in Sutherland, complained that, 'some rents had been fixed in 1888 and [were] unchanged because landlords were sympathetic to the difficulties and struggles of crofters.'

The precise nature of this sort of sympathy was evident a few years later in Caithness, when some employees of the Langwell estate were bold enough to approach their MP, with regard to the management style of the estate. It was then in the ownership of one Lady Anne Cavendish Bentinck, possessor of a personal fortune worth an estimated £50 million (It had come from her father, the Duke of Portland, otherwise known as 'Chopper,' according to his obituarist in the *Daily Telegraph*, on account of his prowess in the woodworking shop at Eton).

Bentinck reacted to this insubordination most decisively, and wrote in stern terms to her employees' (elected) MP. He had sent her a letter stating that he had been approached by her employees at Langwell, who felt she might not be aware of what had been decided about their 'perquisites.' She declared that she was, of course, aware of the decision – 'I am not a puppet' – and that there was nothing whatever to prevent the employees from approaching her personally. But they chose to go behind her back, she said, 'which to my mind is the height of disloyalty and disloyalty is something which I have never been prepared to tolerate in anyone.' She went on to state her intention to place Langwell and Braemore on the market without delay, hoping, as she put it that the employees 'will find their new employer more generous than they consider I have been. In view of this, I shall not be returning to Caithness, either now or at any future time.'

But it is in the cause of the game laws that the landlord class in the Highlands has been most incorrigible. Even in the 1976 parliamentary debates on crofting reform, the game laws were perceived as central to the matter. Lord Burton, for instance, was so worried that sporting rights could be taken compulsorily from landlords that, 'it would be better to be a tenant than a landlord.' Lord Kirkhill had to reassure the peers that the government, 'had made adequate provision for cases where shooting and fishing rights would be materially affected.'

The same obsessions with the protection of private interest regarding the game laws were also evident in 1982, when the House of Lords debated the Deer (Scotland) Bill – a debate 'remarkable even by parliamentary standards for the naked parading of vested interests.' The central preoccupation of this private Bill was to penalise poachers further. It was intended to lead to the licensing of venison dealers and the empowering of the police to inspect their records. It would also lead to the tightening-up of the law on night shooting and out-of-season shooting, these last provisions serving as eloquent testimony to the paranoia of the landlords with regard to deer-poaching (That is, the unauthorised shooting of beasts that infest the Highlands, that are not owned by anyone in law, but the shooting of which is reserved for the landlord over whose acres they roam).

The names of those who took part in the debate are eloquent testimony too. Viscount Thurso, owner through a family trust of 52,000 acres of Caithness, thought the whole thing would be 'an enormous step forward against the poacher. The higher sentences proposed will really put the skids under the poacher in a way that has not happened since the Deer (Scotland) Act was first enacted.'

A second speaker was Viscount Massereene and Ferrard (19,000 acres of Mull). After Eton, John Clotworthy Talbot Foster Whyte-Melville Skeffington – as his obituary in *The Times* records – farmed, raced, shot and was president of the (very) right-wing Monday Club. He had introduced the 1963 Deer Act into the Lords. On another occasion he told the peers that unemployment was not as bad as it seemed: he knew this from his own experience when he had been unable to obtain an under-gardener for Chilham Castle. As to proposals for a transport tunnel under the Channel, he hoped, 'that the ventilation arrangements will not stick up a long way above the sea because that would obviously interfere with ships.' Now he told the Lords, 'Poaching has grown appallingly in the last few years. With due respect to crofters and farm tenants, my experience has been that they know very little about deer.'

And down from his castle outside Beauly, Lord Lovat (76,000 acres of Inverness-shire) thought it an excellent Bill, but urged its sponsor, Lord Glenarthur, to ensure that night poaching was made a much more serious offence than it had been before. Serious, of course, because it is relatively easy for someone to shoot at night an out-of-season beast beside a more-or-less remote roadway; although any man who does so for money or food must be judged desperate for one or the other.

In Glenelg, meantime, a seventy-year-old man was threatened with eviction from his tied estate-house because the landlord suspected him of poaching. He was ordered to quit the house in question, along with his family, on New Year's Eve. The tenant involved had lived in the district for over thirty years but the landlord felt his 'generosity abused' when he began to suspect that 'his' deer were being poached.

This particular landlord went to his tenant's house. Though there was no one there at the time, he felt himself justified in searching it, until he found venison in a refrigerator. He did not, however, call on the services of the police. But he did 'feel very sad, very angry about the whole matter. I liked Kenny very dearly for many years, but after this I just couldn't let him stay on.' According to the thirty-five-year-old amateur detective, whose address was given in court as a castle in Warwickshire, the tenant could get a council house in the district: 'People on social security can get houses, so why can't he?'

Similarly, the subject of salmon enormously excites the proprietorial instinct, and in particular the nightmare of poachers acquiring 'their' fish. And in turn, nothing demonstrates better the continuing tradition of antipathy to landlordism in the Highlands than the sport of taking a landlord's fish; for a point, unspoken or not, has always been made by it. It is not a crime so much as a 'moral duty,' in the words of a former MP for the Western Isles.

By its nature, salmon-poaching is shy of publicity. But in the 1970s and 1980s, there was a rash of press reports relating to salmon-related disputes in the Inner and Outer Hebrides. Protests were made to Stornoway police as a result of alleged harassment of locals in the Uig area of Lewis. In Skye four men were fined an extraordinary £800 on charges of poaching the River Snizort; while at the same court a nineteen-year-old, unemployed for a year and in receipt of less that £16 a week in benefit, was fined £150. That same month estate-owners on Skye 'declared war' on poachers. Under an obscure law dating from 1862, they planned to establish a district fisheries board which would give them sweeping powers: 'Such a board would be able to appoint water bailiffs, constables and river watchers, with the powers of search and arrest if illegal fishing is suspected.'

At around the same time, the chairman of the Northern Joint Police Committee thought it appropriate to condemn his chief constable's practice of offering private landlords help in arresting poachers. 'I personally do not think the police should be doing this job,' he said, following reports that a sergeant had been sent under cover to Lewis to assist estate servants in protecting their masters' fish.

In Lewis the Loch Roag district salmon fishery board issued a bailiff's card in the name of a convicted murderer 'despite the very substantial powers that go with the office.' In Lewis three young men, two of them in receipt of £22.50 a week unemployment benefit, were fined £150 each on charges of salmon poaching and contempt of court. In Harris, a doctor swimming in the bay at Amhuinnsuidhe Castle was told that he could not swim there as 'it was private,' and that if he didn't get out of the water, 'he would be shot like a seal.' And in Harris again, soon afterwards, water bailiffs were witnesses against two local men: 'Police officers said that when one of them was arrested and charged, he had given his occupation as poacher. In the police vehicle taking him back to Stornoway he had been singing Gaelic songs, and saying that as soon as he got out he would be poaching again.' Despite this splendid bravado and despite one of the accused having suffered a broken jaw at the hands of the bailiffs, fines totalling £600 were imposed.

But the most publicised location for anti-landlord conduct with regard to the game laws during the '70s and '80s was the Grimersta estate and river system in the west of Lewis.

One early incident involved a Stornoway man found not guilty of a charge of breach of the peace outside the under-keeper's house at Grimersta. The court was told that the accused had shouted at the under-keeper, 'Are you The [expletive deleted] Commando?' When asked whether he was often known as The Commando, the under-keeper modestly informed the court, 'No, very often I was referred to as The [expletive deleted] Geordie.' A little later, the legal authorities dropped charges against a Grimersta bailiff who had, armed with a shotgun, approached a 16-year-old youth, knocked him to the ground, and smashed his (legal) angling tackle. The authorities refused to discuss the decision with the press.

In another local poaching case, one of the witnesses for the prosecution was Lord Biddulph, a member of the syndicate which owned the water in question. A second witness, one of Biddulph's bailiffs, told the court of his encounter with the accused: 'There was a lot said. He asked me, "why are you working for the English? We've been fishing salmon here for years." You couldn't even go to a petrol station without someone shouting abuse at you.'

Another report, following a summer of fierce conflict in the district – during which the fishery launch *Omsk* was deployed – claimed that the quote in question was, 'Why are you working for these English bastards? We have been fishing here for centuries!' The accused was arrested on shore by the Northern Constabulary's 'poaching liaison officer' who had been staying plain-clothed at various estates in the district incognito, and had been aboard the *Omsk* at the time of the incident. The sergeant in question, said the estate afterwards, had been 'exceedingly helpful'. The accused claimed he was fishing for flat-fish; 'expert witnesses' told the court that a five-inch gill-net was not, however, suitable for such a purpose.

In another case in the same court, a not-proven verdict on a charge of breach of the peace was returned on a frogman-suited swimmer arrested in the mouth of the river. The sheriff concluded that any state of alarm – the precise nature of the alarm was not specified – among the lodge residents as a result of the frogman's presence had been self-induced.

The following summer there was 'acrimony and violence', with the Stornoway procurator fiscal ordering the weekend detention of two men arrested on suspicion of poaching. A week later the dispute took a farcical turn, when the chairman of the company owning the Garynahine estate was arrested by bailiffs for alleged poaching. Meanwhile a house and boat belonging to the fiscal, who had been attending a royal garden-party in Edinburgh, were vandalised. Referring to the alleged need for bailiffs the chairman in question, a London company director, drew on his extensive knowledge of a phenomenon hitherto undetected by European historiography: the shocking poaching problem in Nazi Germany. 'We are afraid our guests could be attacked by thugs. This is like Germany in 1934.'

And in the autumn of 1983 the Grimersta fishery manager appeared in court from custody on charges including assault and breach of the peace. He denied three charges of the former and two of the latter, as well as a charge of wilfully damaging a van. 'The offences occurred after he had unlawfully stopped the passage of vehicles on the public highway when carrying out his duties as water bailiff for the estate,' it was reported. He had been charged with assaulting one youth by striking him in the face with a truncheon, and another by forcibly removing him from the van and striking him on the face with his fists.

When the court convened the procurator fiscal announced that several charges already outstanding against the accused had been dropped; but that he would now plead guilty to what remained. For the accused an Edinburgh advocate offered a lengthy plea in mitigation, to the effect that a high degree of ill-feeling existed in the Grimersta area: 'A constant state of war existed between poachers and the estate, which had led to a long history of violence.' The wife of the accused 'can barely walk through Stornoway without having abuse hurled at her,' he claimed.

The sheriff then admonished the accused. It was, no doubt, entirely irrelevant that the sheriff himself came from a wealthy background in Sutherland, had been educated at the universities of Grenoble and Cambridge, and shared membership of Edinburgh's New Club with at least two members of the Grimersta syndicate.

The following month, it was revealed that the Lord Advocate had been consulted before it was decided to prosecute the fishery manager. And that revelation was by means of a written parliamentary question, to which the Solicitor General for Scotland replied curtly, 'The Lord Advocate was consulted. I have no further statement to make.' Two months later the same sheriff was again dealing with the 'problem' caused by poachers; and fining two (local) men £550 or ninety days, and £200 or thirty days.

For the full glory of narrow class interest masquerading as the majesty of the law, there is no better example than the parliamentary debates surrounding the passage of the 1986 Salmon Act. Introduced by Lord Gray of Contin, it was one of only three specifically Scottish measures in that parliament. Its principal provision was to force salmon dealers to have a licence and so remove the 'main outlet for illegally-taken salmon'. In a masterly under-statement, the then shadow Scottish secretary Donald

Dewar said that it was 'pathetic that a clamp-down on poaching is the government's main piece of Scottish legislation in the current parliamentary session'.

But its reception in the Lords pressed hard on the boundaries of ecstasy. Of the twenty peers who spoke, at least fifteen had vested interests as the owners of salmon fishings. Lord Burton made no less than thirty-two contributions, and commented, 'How nice it would be if in the future one could say, look how good our fishings are, thanks to the Bill that Lord Gray introduced in 1986.' In October 1986 the Bill finished its passage through parliament and became law the following month.

Above all, however, it was the abuses of ownership of stretches of the Highlands which drew most critical comment during the 1970s and 1980s.

Affairs on the island of Raasay were brought to national attention in the early 1970s following the refusal of one Dr John Green – who scarcely ever visited the island – to allow a sliver of his land to be used for a much-needed pier to service a ferry to Skye. In 1961, the Department of Agriculture had offered for sale to the highest bidder ten and a half acres of the island, along with Raasay House Hotel and various other properties. Green got the lot for £4,000, with time to pay. Raasay House, in which Boswell and Johnson had dined so richly in 1773, was allowed to fall into ruins. When plans were launched for a very modest ferry, on which HIDB proposals for the island rested, Green blocked them.

Subsequently, the Secretary of State for Scotland confirmed Inverness County Council's compulsory purchase of a small area of land to serve as a ferry terminal. Dr Green had objected to this at the outset, forcing an inquiry. And on a decision being reached which was unfavourable to him, he announced that he would appeal to the Court of Session. In the Commons, meanwhile, the local MP Russell Johnston had forced an adjournment debate on the issue, noting that, 'Nothing in nine years experience of representing the constituency of Inverness remotely compares with the bitter frustration I have had in trying to get something done on the island of Raasay.' Dr Green's actions, he thought, had been 'evasive, delaying or downright obstructive of anything proposed for the island's benefit.'

The row is recalled in the words of the celebrated stage play *The Cheviot, The Stag and the Black, Black Oil*:

> Dr Green of Surrey
> Is in no hurry
> For a ferry to cross the Sound.
> You want a pier?
> Oh no, not here –
> I need that patch of ground.
> This island she

Belongs to me
As all you peasants know –
And I'm quite merry
For I need no ferry
As I never intend to go.

A second row concerned a proposal to build with public funds a bypass round Amhuinnsuidhe Castle on the western side of Harris. The house and 62,000 acres of associated land had been bought in the 1960s by Sir Hereward Wake, who objected to the very occasional car to be found on the public road which passed in front of the house. Both he and the chairman of the roads committee of Inverness-shire County Council, Lord Burton, had been at Eton. The council decided to spend £40,000 on a bypass: a decision which occasioned a huge uproar, and forced the council to reverse its opinion. Another outcry followed Wake's attempt to sell his castle and estate in 1975 to a syndicate of Americans. After just nine years of ownership, he was asking for the estate three times what he had paid for it.

A brochure issued by the selling-agents (Period Houses of Wisconsin Avenue, Washington), announced a plan to convert North Harris into a vacation haven and a sporting retreat for the investors, although a 'good profit' was also assured. The main residential property on the estate was Amhuinnsuidhe Castle, a Victorian property built in 1867 for the Earl of Dunmore; but the syndicate was intending to increase the accommodation potential by the construction of 'other castles.' For a rateable value of less than £800, the investors were to get 35,000 acres of deer-forest, 22,000 acres of common pasture and 4,500 acres under crofting tenancy, along with 174 registered crofts. According to the agents, the estate was particularly attractive because 'it is remote and uncontaminated, so rich in unpolluted natural resources that they have never been overused. We mean to keep it this way indefinitely.'

In the event, the estate went elsewhere: though exactly where elsewhere was not immediately known. As one commentator observed:

> Sixty-two thousand acres of North Harris have now been sold. The vendor is an obscure Northamptonshire squire and the buyer is an anonymous continental. An Edinburgh estate-agent protects the secrecy of the client's identity. The people have no right in law to know who owns the land they walk and work. In due course they may discover which parasite upon society has bought the right to call himself their landlord. These people typify a breed of greedy, grasping nuisances who contribute nothing to society and who usually exert a positively malign influence on the communities that they inflict themselves on.

Around the same time, Skye was the centre of attention, with the Strollamus Estate on the market for £100,000. Comprising 2,000 acres and a 'fine, old stone-built house,' the land had been bought only seven years earlier for £1,600 – but as the owner announced, 'I have never lost on a deal involving land.' The following year, 1976, was a brisk one for similar speculators in Highland landed estates. In January a planning application to build a holiday village in Torridon revealed that for some months past, the greater part of the Ben Damph estates' 18,000 acres had been in the ownership of a consortium of Dutch businessmen. They were hoping to build holiday chalets over 200 acres of a designated area of great landscape value, as well as a proposed national park.

A month later it was revealed that an investment fund manager had a twenty-year lease – at a cost of £3.70 a week – on Skye's Glendale Estate. This involved the year-round tenancy of a twelve-room lodge, its one-acre walled garden, wooded policies, 20,000 acres of rough shooting, exclusive trout fishing on a hill loch and free salmon fishing on the Hamera River. Naturally free exterior maintenance of the lodge was required too, from local crofters. That May, the three Lewis villages of Valtos, Kneep and Reef were for sale – along with the rest of their 20,000-acre crofting estate, for £45,000, through a company registered in the Isle of Man.

In August, public attention focused on an attempt to take out of crofting legislation part of Skye's Strathaird estate at the bidding of its owner, a 36-year-old Londoner. Britain's second-richest property dealer, he had purchased its 15,000 acres in 1973 for £720,000, had visited the estate once, and had since auctioned-off the contents of its lodge. The following month, the Dutch owners of the Ben Damph estate in Torridon let it be known that their project there was 'no more than a foothold in the Scottish market' and that they were 'already seeking further sites for development.' In November ownership of the Uig estate on Lewis was being transferred to Isle of Man companies by one Timothy Proctor of Holland Park and Belgravia. As the year drew to a close, there were complaints about the 'appalling record' of absentee landlords at Inverinate in Wester Ross.

A year later, Skye's Horace Martin was offering for sale house-sites, at a cost of £6,000 per acre, on land that he had bought nine years earlier at a cost of 50 pence per acre. And in Lewis the Uig estate was to be broken up into patches of three-fifths of an acre each, at a cost per patch of $100, though each buyer was also promised an 'elaborate vellum scroll' proving title to this 'heritage;' while the 30,000-acre Morsgail estate was being offered through the London estate agents of Savills for around £750,000.

Further publicity followed the proposed sale of the Island of Eriskay's 1,740 acres, home to a population of 181 people. South Uist Estates, owners of the island, comprised a syndicate of nine families headed by Colonel David Greig, and had acquired the property in 1960 from the merchant banker Herbert Anton Andrae. The selling agents Knight, Frank and Rutley described the island as an 'exceptional property; we expect a great deal of interest, not only in the United Kingdom but from abroad as well.' The asking price, it was reported, was upwards of £250,000.

Just two months later, in Lewis, the Morsgail and Uig estates were offered for £750,000 – the latter now being in the ownership of an Irish syndicate, whose spokesman noted: 'The return on this kind of place is on capital appreciation rather than from projects that might be undertaken.'

Not long afterwards, ten-day shooting holidays were on offer from South Uist and Garynahine, Lewis, estates in a joint package costing £2,500 per person. Johannes Hellinga (a Dutch speculator who had been heavily involved in buying and selling parts of Skye) was in gaol on charges of currency forgery. Conservationists and the armed forces were squabbling over the sale of the Knoydart estate. And on Skye the Dutchman Jannes Wolthuis, who had bought the Fasach part of the Waternish estate from his incarcerated countryman, was offering it for sale to local crofters – for a sum of £385,000, or four times its estimated actual market value. Five months later Mr Wolthuis' company, Intrad Developments, was seeking planning permission to 'develop' Fasach, while the local district councillor observed: 'We all know about the rape of the Waternish peninsula. It is a disgrace, but these are the laws of the land.' The Dutchman's offer was equivalent to £650 an acre, when prime farmland in Perthshire was selling for £500 an acre (though this might not be entirely surprising in an estate of which parts had been bought and sold five times in four years following Hellinga's acquisition of it in 1978).

On the mainland, meanwhile, the owner of the Inverinate estate in Lochalsh was attempting to curb local rights of way. Sheik Mohammed bin Rashid Al Maktoum, defence minister of the United Arab Emirates, denied however that there was any concerted attempt to thwart public access to a beauty spot in the ownership of the National Trust for Scotland. And at much the same time, the uninhabited island of Scarp off the west coast of Harris was being improved too – by its owner, Nazmu Virani, a former Ugandan Asian and owner of a string of hotels. Mr Virani, it transpired, had acquired the 'freehold' of the 2,200 acre islet, and was planning to build 'a few residential units in the quarter-million to half-million price range'. Virani claimed to know that the island was entirely under crofting tenure and added that he had already 'bought-out' some of the crofters involved. A spokesman for the Crofters' Commission said that this transfer of responsibility was 'news' to him and added, with marvellous restraint, that 'in any case things aren't that simple with land in crofting tenure.'

And so it went on. And on. By 1990, the heiress to the Sears fortune had bought herself 19,000 acres of the Highlands for £2.5 million. The Mar Lodge estate near Balmoral had gone for £7 million to a woman described as an American society hostess – which may, or may not be the least inelegant description of a one-time pornographic 'model.' Nearly 30,000 acres of the Lovat estates, along with a stretch of the salmon-rich Beauly River, had gone to a timeshare property development company. And in Ross-shire, a stalker at Kinlochewe had been in dispute with the wealthy southern owners of the estate. He was sacked after falling out with Mrs Cathy Whitbread over window panes that she had wanted installed in dog kennels. Part of an out-of-court settlement was that the stalker would be re-housed. Speaking from her principal residence in Suffolk, the brewer said, 'The house in Gairloch is only 20 miles away, so it's not really far. I think we are being perfectly reasonable. Mr McLellan was very rude to me.'

And by 1990 Scotland continued to be home to the most concentrated pattern of private landownership in Europe, with half of the country owned by less than 600 people and an élite thirteen owning ten per cent of it. As the *Sunday Times* reported in July of that year, 'The sporting estates of Scotland continue to defy almost every other sector of the property market with rising prices and continuing demand. Sporting estates have risen consistently in value since the early 1970s, as wealthy London businessmen have ploughed money into Scotland's Highlands for their own amusement.'

And so the critical attention of the Scottish public – much resented though it is by the landowners – goes on, and on, too. Why is this? Why do people still care? A little history might now be in order.

two
REHEARSAL

'Look around you and see the nobility, without kindness . . . to
friends; they are of the opinion that you do not belong to the soil.'

◆━━◆

The impact of crudity exists in direct proportion to its grasp of the
essential. Therefore:

The unions of the English and Scottish crowns and parliaments in
1603 and 1707 (the disconvention of the latter so lately overturned)
respectively established a unitary ship of national state with its decks
cleared for imperial expansion on an international stage. But Jacobitism
in the Scottish Highlands remained at the very least an irritant to this
process, with risings taking place on one scale or another in 1689, 1715
and 1719.

The final one came along in 1745. The following year saw an end to
the nonsense, however, and the Highlands were subject to first a military
and then a commercial (and shortly, recreational) colonial occupation.
The chief features of this were, or would become, clearance and
emigration; the exploitation of natural resources through sheep-farming
and deer-afforestation; the exploitation of population resources through
military recruitment; the smashing asunder of the traditional society and
its established class relations; the divorce by force of the common people
from the occupancy of a land they looked upon as their own; and the
invention of a tradition today identified as the cult of Balmorality.

The process was crude – so, indeed, were the times – but it represented
for the government a very firm grasp of the essential. The characterisation
of the process may have been crude too, in that it did scant justice to the
subtleties involved. But it also commanded, apart from the virtue of
brevity, a sure sense of the essential. As the Gaelic poet John MacCodrum
wrote, 'Look around you and see the nobility without pity for poor folk,
without kindness to friends; they are of the opinion that you do not
belong to the soil, and though they have left you destitute they cannot see
it as a loss . . .'

The common people did not wait long to feel the effects of the process.
If they would not join the services of the Crown (in which, to quote

24

Wolfe's celebrated phrase, it would be 'no great mischief if they fall'), they could be emigrated, that their hardy characteristics and imaginative minds might otherwise contribute to the construction of Empire. And removal from their homes was the first stage in this, their improvement.

The process has been widely documented, and not only by factual writers. No less a novelist than Stevenson, for instance, attributes the following to a character (in *Kidnapped*) on the shores of the sound of Mull:

> In the mouth of Loch Aline we found a great sea-going ship at anchor. As we got a little nearer, it became plain that she was a ship of merchandise; and what still more puzzled me, not only her decks, but the sea-beach also, were quite black with people, and skiffs were continually plying to and fro between them. Yet nearer, and there began to come to our ears a great sound of mourning, the people on board and those on the shore crying and lamenting one to another so as to pierce the heart. Then I understood this was an emigrant ship bound for the American colonies.

His barely-fictional scene would be in reality replicated time and again in the years to come.

Emigration too has been documented. Occasionally less predictable material comes to light, as in the memoirs (*Jail Journal*) of the exiled Irish patriot John Mitchel:

> We have ridden to a lonely region, known as the Blue Hill, being a succession of small hollows lying westward of a high mountain which bounds our valley at one side. Went up to the first settler's place we came to, a rather humble wooden house and was received most joyfully by the proprietor, one Kenneth MacKenzie, an ancient settler, from Ross-shire. He brought us in, sent our horses to the stable, introduced me to his wife (one of the MacRaes), a true Gaelic woman of tall stature and kindly tongue, who speaks Gaelic better than English, though thirty years an exile. As we sat round the table tall youths and maidens came in, and were addressed by such names as Colin, Jessie and Kenneth. Here is a genuine family of Tasmanian Highlanders, trying to make a Ross-shire glen under the southern constellations.

What the common people thought of this improving emigration, or said of it amongst themselves, was not recorded – unless behind the cautiously illuminated veils of their poets. And such attempts as these common people may have made to halt the process are poorly documented too. Yet, from the closing years of the eighteenth century, there were signs of popular disaffection with the new order of things in the Highlands, scattered and unsynchronised though these signs were.

By the middle of the eighteenth century there were reports of 'widespread disaffection' from Argyll, where ambitious landlord plans were frustrated by a spirit of popular resistance. And as early as 1782 there was an attempt to stop sheep farming in its early and destructive tracks in the Great Glen. Only the government and legal authorities, in the shape of the Home Office and the Lord Advocate, preserved its memory in durable fashion. They record that during that spring two prospective Great Glen sheep farmers, one from the southern Highlands at Breadalbane and the other already a sheep farmer in the Borders, brought themselves to the inn at Letterfinlay on the eastern shores of Loch Lochy in Inverness-shire.

These men had come to look at part of the lands of George Cameron of Letterfinlay with a view to leasing it as a sheep farm. Intelligence of their coming had clearly, however, spread among the people of the district. Their opinion of sheep-farming, and the forces it represented, can readily be assessed from what ensued. On the evening of 28 May John Cameron MacInnes, 'Dark John' as he was known in the area, along with a group of local people (many of whom, and not for the last time either, were women) set upon the would-be sheep farmers, beating them severely in the process. The following day too, as the farmers were making their way back down the glen towards the government stronghold of Fort William, MacInnes appeared from behind a wall and after threatening and abusing them, 'fired several shots at them.'

Soon afterwards, at Strathoykel on the border of the counties of Sutherland and Ross, there were signs of further and more serious dissent, with reports of a 'combination' of recently evicted indigents formed to 'steal and destroy the sheep and lambs' of a tenant-farmer originally from Perthshire and currently leasing land from Sir John Ross of Balnagowan Castle. The aim of the combination was to force the tenant, Geddes, to give up his sheep farm, thus forcing Ross to return it to its previous occupants.

Ross was a former vice-admiral who had arrived at Balnagowan in 1762: indeed, he was the first landlord to come to the north of Scotland with the specific intention of exploiting the region by sheep-farming. Soon after his arrival, therefore, he began to organise the importation of sheep to the district, along with south-country shepherds. This did not impress the native population, as Sir George Steuart MacKenzie was to observe in his general survey of the county a few decades later. These shepherds 'found themselves very disagreeably situated, amongst a race of people who considered them as intruders; whose language they did not understand; and who used every cut to discourage them, and to render their lives miserable.'

They had, Sir George observed, to struggle against the prejudices of the people, 'which were inveterate against the new system', and it was with great difficulty that the people of the district had been restrained from acts of violence. The precise nature of that restraint is nowhere recorded. But considerably more is known about another, and much greater, surge of direct-action opposition which was centred on Kildermorie in 1792 and which has since become known as the Year of the Sheep.

A long time afterwards, the minister of Rosskeen was to observe that prior to that year, the minds of the people had been 'irritated by recent occurrences.' And he went on:

> As the sheep-farming system was progressing in every corner of the Northern Highlands and the people driven year after year from the fields of their fathers, their minds were exasperated at what they deemed oppression, and thus were ready to adopt any course, however violent, which they foolishly thought would rid them of sheep and sheep farmers.

At the centre of the dispute was the conduct of two farmers who had come to the district in or around 1790, leasing land for sheep from the owner, Sir Hector Munro (MP for Inverness Burghs for the previous 24 years). Their arrival was greeted with alarm by the natives of the distict. As Sir George Steuart MacKenzie noted, 'strong symptoms of opposition began to appear about this time, among the lower orders of the people.' Nor was this opposition entirely isolated in nature, events far beyond the Highlands having induced 'the lower classes inhabiting the low country to make common cause with the dispossessed Highlanders.' It was rumoured, for instance, that a Gaelic-language edition of Paine's *Rights of Man* was spreading rapidly through the Highlands. In public affairs a well-rooted rumour can command amazing strength, and sedition in an unknown language must surely be counted by any propertied élite as a danger most doubly poisonous. In any case, with these 'rights of man' as the watchword of the tumultuous events then under way in revolutionary France, the very idea of such a book can only have struck terror into the hearts of the land-owning class in the Scottish north.

Therefore 'at the unfortunate time when the spirit of revolution and revolt was fast gaining ground over the whole Kingdom,' an 'open insurrection' broke out in 1792, with the aim of simply driving the newcomers back whence they came. The conduct of Sir Hector Munro's tenant-farmers, Cameron brothers from Lochaber, served as the spark for this insurrection. They complained to Sir Hector that the cattle of the natives were being allowed to graze on land they had leased for sheep; and soon enough the Camerons began to impound such cattle, demanding a fine as a condition of their release.

In May of that year all the cattle belonging to the people of Strathrusdale, the glen immediately to the north of Kildermorie, crossed on to the Camerons' land – where they were at once impounded by shepherds and penned at the western end of Loch Moire. The owners of the cattle sent a messenger to the people of Ardross, further down the glen, to ask their assistance in recovering the stock by force rather than fine. The joint party of Strathrusdale and Ardross people were then led to the pen by one Alexander Wallace, where they overpowered the Camerons and took re-possession of their cattle. Wallace himself disarmed one of the Camerons of a firearm and a foot-long dirk (which, a century later, was still in the possession of Wallace's grandson).

Thereafter the seizing of cattle was discontinued. But the Camerons turned instead to the law. Four months later, at the Inverness Circuit Court, Lord Stonefield tried eight men of Strathrusdale, including Alexander Wallace, on charges of 'riot, assault, and battery, by assembling with a number of other persons, and forcibly relieving from a poind-fold certain cattle confined there, and, at the same time, assaulting and beating the gentlemen and his servants.' The good jurors of the town, though, found the defendants not guilty and they were released to return to their glen.

Kildermorie had by then sparked much greater developments, however. Having reclaimed their cattle, the people of Strathrusdale went on the offensive with a vengeance some weeks later that summer. At the end of July they gathered for a wedding in the area. Given the rural nature of their community, such a meeting was rare for these people, rather than an everyday event. Nothing is now known about that wedding; and written history is, in any case, a grotesquely incompetent means of recovering the currents of popular consciousness in conditions of social repression. But between the whisky and the dancing and the matchmaking, what did the people talk about? What did they know of events in the wider world? Had the sentiments of the radical press in the south filtered to the north of Scotland? What might they have thought of the spirit of that scandalous and revolutionary sentiment (expressed in the contemporary radical newspaper *Black Dwarf*): 'The earth is the common property of man. In its produce we have a common right as a means of preserving our existence – and he is a robber and murderer, who would prevent me from obtaining that subsistence'?

Had the people of Strathrusdale followed the great events shaking France over the previous three years?

There, in July 1789, the capital had fallen to the mob, which had promptly looted 30,000 muskets from the Hôtel des Invalides and stormed the Bastille – a hated symbol of former tyranny. And that season, an impromptu army of peasants left across the blue summer sky a languorous trail of smoke from the castles and manor-houses that they had burnt. Then at the end of August the Assembly, still at Versailles, had adopted the Declaration of the Rights of Man and Citizen, with its implicit approval of the 'right of rebellion.' In the following three years the destruction of the nobility had gathered pace; and the royal family was dragged back from Varennes to Paris in the hot June of 1791, prisoners of the people in arms. (Louis XVI would be executed in January, 1793.) Is it credible that the people gathered at that wedding knew nothing of these great – and hopeful – events in France? Is it likely that the storming of the Bastille as a symbol of tyranny inclined them to think of similar symbols rather closer to home? Did the notion of the Rights of Man strike a common chord as the celebrations gathered pace that day?

We do not know now, and never can do in detail. But we at least know that at that wedding the leaders of the people plotted to drive away all the sheep, and by implication all the sheep farmers, in the entire district. Two days later they issued a proclamation to that effect, distributed to all the neighbouring parishes. Soon afterwards hundreds of people were gathering at Strathoykel.

Their plan, which they quickly began to effect, was simple: to drive south all the sheep they could find in the parishes of Lairg, Creich and Strathoykel itself. Within days of this drive getting under way, another 200 men, from the Balnagowan estate, had joined them and were also driving sheep southwards. By the end of that first week, perhaps 10,000 head of sheep were on the move. The authorities took immediate fright. The sheriff-depute of the county, Donald MacLeod, wrote to the Lord Advocate Robert Dundas, asking that a force of the Black Watch be sent north to crush what MacLeod saw (with some reason) as rank sedition and open rebellion.

The Lord Advocate wrote to the Home Secretary to report that sheep farming was very unpopular in the Highlands, as it 'tended to remove the inhabitants from their small possessions and dwelling houses.' The Home Secretary replied to the effect that it was 'indisputably necessary that the most vigorous and effectual measures should be taken for bringing these daring offenders to punishment' – and ordered troops to proceed north with all despatch.

By now, muskets were reported to be in the possession of men involved in the drive, while the local landlords believed that some of the seditious drovers had recently been visiting Inverness for the purpose of purchasing gunpower. In Edinburgh serious accounts of the rising began to circulate. The *Evening Courant* reported that 3,000 sheep had been drowned by 'people rendered desperate by poverty.' The sheriff-depute wrote again to the Lord Advocate: 'Not one constable had ventured or dared apprehend' any of the men taking part in the sheep-drive. The men of property in the district were now, he reported, 'so completely under the heel of the populace that should they come to burn our houses or destroy our property in any way their caprice may lead them, we are incapable of resistance.' He also wrote to his opposite number in the county of Inverness:

> You can be no stranger to the tumults, commotions, and actual

seditious acts that are going on in this country . . . The flame is spreading . . . I understand a force of about 400 are now actually employed in collecting the sheep. I have the Lord Advocate's orders to proceed against the insurgents, should it be necessary, to the last extremity.

In the event, this final extremity involved a joint attack at midnight some days later by the local gentry on horseback, along with the soldiers sent by the Lord Advocate, upon the drovers' ranks. Unsurprisingly or otherwise, the drovers scattered – an excellent outcome, and a timeous one, in the view of the sheriff-depute, for the spirit of sedition was afoot in the hills. As he noted later:

A regular plan for a general insurrection was formed . . . The spirit of violence was carried so far as to set the civil power at defiance; the laws were trampled on; there appeared no safety for property; and the gentlemen of the county seemed to be subjected to the power and control of an ungovernable mob [which was] linked by solemn ties and engagements . . . The first object of their united exertions was to banish and drive off all the sheep from the hills of Sutherland and Ross.

The lower orders of these counties had been infected with a turbulent spirit of anarchy, and had talked of other 'improvements' as soon as they had banished the 'noxious' sheep.

Had the sheep-drive been allowed to continue for just another week, the sheriff-depute added, a force of 2,000 soldiers would not have managed to suppress 'the insurrection which would ensue not only in this but in the counties which surround us.' Therefore, in September, the ringleaders of the drive appeared in court in Inverness, charged with 'advising, exciting, and instigating persons riotously and feloniously to invade, seize upon, and drive away from the grounds of the proprietors flocks of sheep,' thus daringly insulting the law, disturbing the public peace, threatening property, and placing its owners 'at the mercy of a lawless and seditious mob.' Unsurprisingly, they were all found guilty. Two were sentenced to transportation to Botany Bay (Scotland's loss, it might be thought, as Australia's gain); while other sentences included life imprisonment, banishment and various terms in gaol.

Subsequently, all the prisoners escaped from their captors and disappeared from history, at least so far as it was recorded by the authorities of the time. And if their people, or their descendants, knew what became of them, they took good care not to speak about it.

In this silence, they had good reason. In the half century after Culloden (April 1746), the economic basis of the old Highland society was increasingly challenged on two fronts: first, the demand for wool from the growing manufacturing centres of the southern cities; and second, the demand for industrial products made from seaweed, import of which products had been stopped by the wars with revolutionary and, later, Bonapartist France. The booming demand for wool forced up its price to unprecedented levels at the turn of the nineteenth century, and served strongly to encourage the growth of sheep farming in the Highlands, for spectacular profits were waiting to be made by landlords and sheep farmers alike. As a result, huge areas of the Highlands were earmarked for 'development' into sheep farms (once the native populations had been evicted), while 'the competition for farms became excessive, and rents were given which were often extravagant.'

As for the newcomers, whether mere tenant farmer or speculative landlord: these were therefore good years for the established, and increasingly Anglicised, propertied class in the Highlands. By August, 1807, for instance, the coming-of-age of the eldest son of the Marquis and Marchioness of Stafford was celebrated at Dornoch with two companies of the Sutherland volunteers to 'fire volleys after each of the leading toasts'; while the following summer the *Inverness Journal* was able to record that the Highlands were becoming 'a holiday resort for southern gentlemen.' A year later, the *Journal* could note: 'This place for some days back has been the resort of an immense number of persons of rank and fashion who at this season of the year generally visit the north for the purpose of viewing its beautiful and romantic scenery' – another stepping-stone to the coming cult of Balmorality, for not many years earlier the Highlands and everything associated with them had been perceived as a barbarian swamp of intrigue and sedition.

The times, however, were less easy for the natives of this so-newly romantic land. Already, some thirty or forty vessels were arriving yearly in London with Hebridean kelp. For this vastly profitable trade the common people paid in the way of eviction from their land, or semi-enslavement on the sea shore in harvesting the seaweed. For a time, indeed, the landlords did their best to prevent emigration. That way they secured for themselves emptied sheep-farms in the interiors of their estates, while retaining on their margins the recently-evicted inhabitants of these interiors – now improved to the status of a cheap labour force for the gathering of kelp.

Emigration nevertheless went on. From Thurso, for instance, 130 natives were shipped out, bound towards Pictou across the Atlantic Ocean. Although they made the passage within a matter of weeks, they did not land in Canada, being wrecked off Newfoundland, and all being drowned. From Leith the following spring the *Pampler* sailed, with an emigrant cargo from the parishes of Farr, Lairg, Creich and Rogart: she too foundered, and all were lost.

Unsurprisingly, those who remained were as determined as before in their opposition to these new forces over which they commanded so little control. There was another sign of determined anti-landlord feeling, under guise of a religious grievance, in eastern Ross and Sutherland. The appointment of local clergy was in the gift of the landlords; but trouble broke out when the Marchioness of Stafford imposed a new minister on those who remained in Creich. Consequently the minister was presented under protection of the military, 'when a riot ensued in which Captain Kenneth MacKay of Torboll had his sword shivered to pieces by stones thrown at him by an old woman of seventy.' According to a memoir of the time, published many years later:

> The people were opposed to him, and his settlement was one of those violent ones. The parishioners rose *en masse*, and barred the church against the presbytery, so that the Sutherland Volunteers were called out to keep the peace. The people never afterwards attended Mr Cameron's ministry . . .

In 1813 there was further violence in the area, on a much larger scale. It was associated once again with the Sutherland family – along with their commissioner James Loch, their agent William Young, and their prospective sheep farmer Patrick Sellar. The head of the family, George Granville Leveson-Gower, was Duke of Sutherland for just the last six months of his life. When he was 27 he married the 19-year-old Elizabeth, Countess of Sutherland. She brought to the union two-thirds of the county, 1,735 square miles of the Highlands, along with the rents of the 25,000 people who inhabited them. Throughout their marriage they were to enjoy an annual income of around £300,000 and an expenditure to match. In one year alone, £30,000 was spent on Stafford House, while other establishments were maintained at Lilleshall in Shropshire, Trentham in Staffordshire, and at Dunrobin Castle on the coast just north of Golspie. This wealth derived largely from the efforts of the coal miners that Sutherland employed in Staffordshire; for in 1803 he had inherited his father's marquesate and estates in both Staffordshire and Shropshire, along with the huge fortune of his uncle, the Duke of Bridgewater.

During the turbulent war which was shaking Europe at this time, the countess raised from her indigenous tenants a force of soldiers by the simple expedient of directing five hundred of them into her 'volunteer' Sutherland Highlanders: the sort of men of whom Eckermann was thinking when he described to Goethe, 'the Highlanders as he saw them that June day on the field of Waterloo, stepping forth erect and powerful on their brawny limbs, so physically perfect that they looked like "men in whom there is no original sin".'

In the absence of these tenants from Sutherland, however, great changes were under way. They were accelerated by the arrival there of Patrick Sellar and William Young. Sellar, a lawyer possessed of all the fabled vision of his trade, had spent the previous three years as a procurator in Moray: but he really wanted to make some serious money. Young, on the other hand, was on his way north at the invitation of the Sutherlands, to take up the post of estate manager for them. Two years earlier, in 1807, the countess had written of her husband that 'he is seized as much as I am with the rage of improvements.' It was in pursuit of these improvements that Young had recruited Sellar as his assistant.

And within two years of arrival Young and Sellar had indeed improved the people in the parishes of Dornoch, Rogart, Loth, Clyne, Golspie and Assynt. As the anti-landlord stone-mason and historian Donald MacLeod wrote later, 'A large portion of the people of these parishes were in the course of two or three years, almost entirely rooted out.' Seventy years later old men could still recall, to the Royal Commission into crofting conditions in the Highlands, the names of forty-eight settlements cleared of people in the parish of Assynt alone.

When the same Commission visited Helmsdale its first witness, Angus Sutherland, recalled:

> In the year 1815, when many natives of the parish were fighting for their country at Waterloo, their homes were being burned in Kildonan Strath by those who had the management of the Sutherland estate. The people of the parish of Kildonan, numbering 1574 souls, were ejected from their holdings, and their houses burned to the ground. These burnings were carried on under the direction of Mr Patrick Sellar, who was at the time under-factor on the estate, and who was also tenant of the land from which the people were evicted, and which their ancestors had held from time immemorial.

Underlying these evictions was a clash of attitude that can still echo quietly in the Highlands of today. Sellar's view of the native inhabitants of the county was clear. As he wrote to the Lord Advocate, 'Lord and Lady Stafford were pleased humanely to order a new arrangement of this Country. It surely was a most benevolent action, to put these barbarous hordes into a position where they could advance in civilisation.' Young described the people of Kildonan, who were in due course to be burnt out of their homes, as a 'set of savages,' adding that they were no better than *banditti*, implacably opposed to their eviction, and who could only be turned out by force. Young also complained to Earl Gower, later second duke, of their 'unaccountable prejudices,' and wrote to the countess herself to complain that 'a more provoking lawless set of people than many of the Kildonaners never inhabited a civilised country.'

The background to these bitter complaints lay in the refusal of the people of Kildonan to be 'improved.' In 1812 they had been given notice to quit. At the end of that year the land they had indeed occupied from time immemorial was divided into three sheep farms, while eighty tenants were to be transplanted to plots beside the coastal seashore. In January of the following year, agents for the intending sheep farmers arrived to inspect the land in question, but were met by a crowd who told them that if sheep 'were put upon that ground there should be blood.' A shepherd was also cursed as 'one of these English devils come to the country,' and warned, that 'before Easter every shepherd's house would be set on fire and burned to the bare walls.' Another two shepherds (not for the last time) were force-marched to a meeting and insulted, interrogated, threatened – then released with a warning to quit the district.

At an all-night meeting in the Kilearnan mill, the suggestion was also put that 'the men of the Strath of Kildonan ought to rise' to stop the farmers, and 'that both sides of the strath ought to rise.' Young wrote to his superiors in alarm, that 'the natives rose in a body and chased the valuers off the ground and now threaten the lives of every man who dares dispossess them.' He believed that the eyes of the Highlands were on them, 'to see how the war will end,' and added that 'all our movements are watched and everything we do is improperly construed.' Civil warrants instructing the people to get out were obtained in the courts and agents sent to serve them. But they were followed by a hostile and threatening crowd and were 'apprehensive of their lives.' The sheriff-substitute, with Sellar and Loch, met a crowd of 150 men in the Kildonan schoolhouse, and were told that the people had a right to the land because of promises made to them at the time the Sutherland Highlanders had been raised. Sellar replied that the assurances only ran until 1808 and were therefore void – though those who had enlisted on the basis of the promises were still on active service abroad.

Young later told his employers: 'Their answer was, it may be so but we will hold the land until the men are delivered to us again.' Sellar also wrote to the countess, reporting:

> I returned on Tuesday night from the parish of Kildonan where I am sorry to say we did not succeed in our endeavours to make peace with the rioters. That is to say, the most daring fellows being entirely hostile the people refused to sign a Bond retracting their threats and obliging themselves to keep the peace, and their orators declared that they were entitled to keep possession of their grounds and would allow no Shepherd to come to the Country. At same time the Eyes of the people of the other parishes are watching us. We find Spies hanging about our dwellings from Lairg, Rogart and from Assynt. Could there be any hope of success in so desperate a project, I am satisfied that the rioters would find friends in every Quarter.

The people later attempted to reason with Young and the estate authorities, sending a messenger with a letter of proposals to the sheriff-substitute. Having delivered it, however, the messenger was promptly gaoled at Dornoch. At once there was talk of rescuing him and there were rumours that 1,800 men from the Reay country in the north-west, and also Caithness, were going to 'assemble and drive the sheep out of the country.'

Sellar wrote again to the countess, having 'ascertained that the whole population feel desirous of success to the rioters, knowing that they have one common interest in the exclusion of strangers'. He continued, 'Even the people of Armadale, finding that our purpose is to cram the property full of people, make common cause with the rioters, and have their communications with the people of Kildonan.'

Once again the services of soldiers were called upon. The Sutherlands told Loch that they were 'fully sensible' of the propriety of the 'very fair, just and liberal arrangement which you proposed for the settlement of the people,' and asked him to go cautiously before he had 'recourse to the last extremity of forcing them into submission.' They also, however 'gave their Authority and approbation to any measure you may hereafter find it necessary to adopt to carry your proposed arrangements into full and complete effect.'

The people petitioned the Prince Regent, sending with the petition a delegate, William MacDonald, who was a former recruiting sergeant for the Sutherland regiment. Young wrote to the countess, asking that she use her influence to prevent MacDonald getting access to the Regent, and also to make sure that his army pension be withdrawn from him – for 'it will not be MacDonald's fault if a rebellion does not follow.'

While MacDonald was in London, however, the soldiers arrived, and the leaders of the people were arrested. Understandably enough, opposition collapsed. By the end of March, 1813 the soldiers were withdrawn, those people arrested were released and proceedings were dropped. Sellars explained that if a judical enquiry had followed, the results would have been 'more unpleasant than anything at present before us.' Defeated, 700 people applied to emigrate and by July more than 100 had left the estate. The removals went ahead and within two years around 100 men from the strath were working as fishermen out of Helmsdale. Kildonan was given over to sheep: its native people lived on the barren shores of their county; and on the banks of Canada's Red River, near Winnipeg, in an area which is still called Kildonan to this day.

And in 1815 one James Sutherland led another party of people from Kildonan and Upper Farr to the Red River. His great grandson was to be Angus Sutherland, the Land League leader of years to come, and one of the 'Crofter Members' elected to parliament in the great anti-landlord agitation of the 1880s. By 1815 therefore, a pattern of resistance had been set. But there were many years of conflict – and defeat – still to come.

THREE

THE GROWTH OF RESISTANCE

'Hardly a gentleman present or soldier came back without being
hurt and several severely. One woman was shot and it is supposed
mortally, another was badly wounded in the mouth and eye by a
bayonet, and a young lad was shot in the legs. Their principal force
of reserve, it was said, were armed and reported to be about five
hundred.'

Fourteen hundred feet above the village of Golspie, on the eastern shore
of Sutherland, stands the monument to the first Duke of Sutherland.
Quarried over four years from the side of the hill's red sandstone, the
plinth and pedestal stand seventy-six feet tall, while the duke (in a stone
toga) rears another thirty feet. Together, they are visible for eighty miles.
The monument was, according to contemporary press reports, designed
by Burns and modelled by Sir Francis Chantrey, with construction
entrusted to a Mr Theakstone.

The stone duke faces out over the sea with his back to the empty glens
of Sutherland. In this sense at least the monster memorial is a fitting
tribute to events in the nineteenth-century Highlands; and the carnival of
land-trading and Balmorality so characteristic of those years.

In the spring of 1812, for instance, the Duke of Gordon's 14,000-acre
Glenfeshie forest was offered, 'adapted either for a summer-grazing to
black cattle or for shooting-ground to a sportsman who might wish to
preserve the tract for deer'. Little more than a year later a number of new
sheep farms on the Glengarry estate were being advertised to let. Shortly
it would be announced that the first sheep and wool market at Inverness
had been a glowing success; while it would also be reported that sheep
farming was growing so rapidly in the Highlands that Sutherland alone
was already home to 100,000 Cheviots.

The wealth generated by this sort of success was available to landlords,
recent or more established, for the pursuit of romance. Under the
inspiration of MacDonnell of Glengarry, a number of gentlemen
convened at Inverlochy to band themselves into a 'pure Highland Society,
in support of the true Dress, Language, Music and Characteristics of our

illustrious and ancient race'. In Skye, a 'magnificent mansion' was being erected on the shore of the Sound of Sleat by Lord MacDonald and his kelp profits (though with the end of the French wars, the price of kelp would plummet – signalling a further round of hardship for the indigents who had gathered it). And the following summer Glengarry's Society of True Highlanders was dancing and feasting at Inverlochy, everyone attired in the 'globular silver buttons of their ancestry, with the highly finished pistols, dirks, powder horns and other paraphernalia giving an air of magnificence'. Glengarry himself had by now taken to wearing for his public appearances what he called 'the complete Highland garb, belted plaid, broadsword, pistols, and dirk'. Thus was the 'promised land of modern romance' launched on passage.

For the common people of the Highlands, of course, there was little on offer from this promised land, except patronage and oppression. But in the face of it, popular disaffection with the new order remained unabated throughout the first half of the nineteenth century.

Indeed, the Kildonan dispute was hardly over when a new one developed at Assynt. It was formally concerned with the installation of a new clergyman by the landlord, in whose gift such an appointment lay: but behind it ran a swift current of more general anti-landlordism. As one agent of the Sutherland family complained to Loch, he had gone to the district with the new minister but they had been driven home by these 'mountain savages', who had also plotted to kidnap him and send him bound by the wrists in an open boat to sea. According to Donald Sage's chronicle of the period, the new minister's appointment among these 'savages' was a personal arrangement between himself and the Sutherlands:

> The people of Assynt were not consulted in the matter but they took the liberty of thinking for themselves . . . The mob which now assembled told them, through their leaders, that the only way by which they could escape broken bones was that each should get on his nag with all convenient speed, nor slack bridle till they had crossed the boundaries of the parish, for they were determined that the presentee should not on that day nor on any other day be settled minister of Assynt.

As a result of this, a warship was ordered from Leith with 150 soldiers; and five leaders of the Assynt people were taken to Inverness, where one was sentenced to nine months in gaol. Once again, the authorities had triumphed. But by now, affairs in Sutherland were drawing attention far to the south. As one Lord Pitmilly wrote:

> It was the object of Lady Sutherland to turn the mountainous districts into sheep pasturage, to bring the inhabitants to the coast,

and set out portions of land for their convenience. At the same time, it was the intention of the Noble Proprietrix to introduce among the people regular habits of industry. This object, however advantageous, was extremely unpopular and the judicious attempts at improvement were thwarted in every possible way. So far, however, did these prejudices prevail, that in the years 1812 and 1813, open violence and riot ensued.

He added that even after these riots had been quelled, the 'unreasonable opposition' to 'improvement' was not at an end:

> A new mode of attack was reserved, and every attempt made to poison the public mind. Certain English journals, particularly a paper called the *Military Register*, teemed with the clamours of the disaffected. It contained attacks on the whole system of management and the most false and inflammatory statements of the mode in which this system was put in execution.

What Pitmilly meant by this was the popular attempt to thwart the Sutherland agent, and later tenant sheep farmer, Patrick Sellar. At the end of 1813 Sellar had leased land in Strathnaver for a sheep farm. This required the eviction of the glen's existing inhabitants – including the burning of homes and, allegedly, of at least one of their occupants. This time the people turned to the law courts and raised money for a prosecution of Sellar, who was promptly lodged in Dornoch gaol until release on the instructions of the Court of Justiciary in Edinburgh. In April 1816 Sellar nevertheless appeared before the Circuit Court in Inverness charged with murder, oppression and real injury.

His lawyers talked of 'the clamour which had been raised in the country, the prejudices of the people'; and added that, 'if truth and justice were to prevail over malice and conspiracy', Sellar 'would obtain an honourable and triumphant acquittal'. The contest in court, in short, was simply a 'trial of strength between the abettors of anarchy and misrule, and the magistracy, as well as the laws of the country'. The jury (massively weighted in favour of the defendant, if its social composition was any guide) found Sellar not guilty. The judge (none other than Lord Pitmilly) observed that he hoped the result would 'have due effect on the minds of the country, which have been so much and so improperly agitated'.

In short Sellar had won, and though twenty of his sheep had their throats cut, there was to be no further opposition recorded until 1820.

By the spring of that year Patrick Sellar had already retired as an agent for the Sutherland estates, but was keeping on his sheep-farming interests, from which he had already made a fortune. (Some years later he would buy himself an estate in Morvern for £30,000, suitably distant from the teeming clamours of Sutherland.) In the Highlands generally the profitability of sheep-farming was pushing to new heights the price of estates, and accelerating the ownership of the Highlands by non-residents. In five years, for instance, the price of the Castlehill estate rose from £8,000 to £80,000; Redcastle, worth £25,000 in 1790, would soon go for £135,000; and Fairburn, with a rental of £700 at the turn of the century, by 1820 was worth, £80,000.

Driven by the lure of these spectacular profits the landlord of Novar, Hugh Munro, announced his intention in the spring of 1820 to clear the natives away from his estate at Culrain and put the land under sheep. Over five hundred people were to be evicted from the west bank of the Kyle of Sutherland and from Strathoykel. At the beginning of February Novar's agents therefore arrived to serve the writs of removal, warning those who received them to be gone by Whitsun.

Strathoykel, however, was the place where the people had gathered for the great sheep drive of 1792; and when Novar's agents went to the glen they were met by a hostile crowd which drove them away. The sheriff-depute wrote in alarm to the *Inverness Courier* that not only had the party been driven out by force, but it had been 'threatened that if they returned their lives would be taken and themselves thrown into the Kyle . . . One of the witnesses who had run away from the terror was pursued and struck with stones to the danger of his life'.

The local gentry urged Novar to enforce his writs. Meanwhile the sheriff-depute asked the Lord Advocate for five hundred soldiers and three cannon, as if seriously anticipating another 'year of the sheep'. In the event forty policemen and twenty-five militiamen, along with a party of local gentlemen, marched on the recalcitrant natives to enforce the writs. A riot ensued, in which one woman was shot dead. The *Inverness Courier* reported, 'A body of three or four hundred people, chiefly women, posted behind a stone dyke, rushed out upon the soldiers with a hideous yell and attacked them with sticks, stones and other missiles . . . Two or three of the women were severely wounded.' And the new factor for the Sutherland estate wrote that the sheriff-depute's force had been:

> opposed by an overwhelming number of men and women organised and armed to give battle. Hardly a gentleman present or soldier came back without being hurt, and several severely. One woman was shot and it is supposed mortally, another was badly wounded in the mouth and eye by a bayonet and a young lad was shot in the legs. Their principal force of reserve, it was said, were armed and reported to be about five hundred.

The sheriff-depute, his carriage overturned and his writs scattered, fled, to be pursued for four miles to the inn at Ardgay and much abused. But the local minister went among the rebels, counselling 'the madness and inutility of violence', and their short-lived rising came to an end.

However the rising served as a caution to the landlords that they proceed warily, and take care to avoid publicity. James Loch wrote to his agent in Sutherland that 'every motion is watched and if you do anything at all which will occasion public observation it will be brought before the House of Commons'. Loch also instructed his agents that the burning of houses should no longer be associated with clearing operations – but clearing, nevertheless, was still to proceed on both Sutherland and other estates.

Shortly after the events at Culrain, further evictions were planned for Gruids. It was reported that the Gruids people were 'mustering and preparing all sorts of weapons' and making ready 'to oppose whatever species of force may be brought against them'. Sheriff-officers arrived with writs of removal; but they were 'literally stripped of their clothes, deprived of their Papers, and switched off the bounds of the Property'.

There were soon further disturbances at Achness; and again at Gruids, where the previous attempt to evict the people had clearly failed. For Achness, one hundred soldiers were made ready, as it was feared that the people there were to be reinforced by supporters from Caithness and Ross-shire; while at Gruids the following year a sheriff-officer was again assaulted and deforced of his papers. One landlord's agent complained that the authorities were not strong enough to eject the Gruids people, and that the constables were untrustworthy as they 'supported the general feeling of the natives'. Loch himself believed that there existed 'a regular organised system of resistance' to the civil power in the north of Scotland, and feared something like a co-ordinated and general rising against the landlords.

Thus in the spring of 1821 soldiers were sent towards Achness and Gruids. Again, if understandably, opposition collapsed, with the local agent of the Sutherlands boasting that 'they are completely cowed and I am certain we shall have no more trouble'. Plots of land on the barren northern coast were made available. The local agents of the estate were instructed (in an uncanny echo of events at Knoydart 130 years later), 'Let the less guilty have lots on their signing that they are sorry for their conduct and that they acknowledge the kindness of Lord and Lady Stafford'; for as Loch himself observed, 'It would produce a great sensation if any set of people were wandering about without habitation'.

By then the clearances of Sutherland were all but completed; while for the Highland gentry life in general was better than ever.

In Edinburgh the newly-formed Celtic Society, whose principal object was to 'promote the use of the Highland garb in the Highlands', hosted a dinner under the patronage of Glengarry. Walter Scott was a guest and happy to sing for his supper; he remembered 'with delight' how he used to 'cling round the knees of some aged Highlanders' and listen to the tales and traditions of 'that romantic country'. A year later, Glengarry was to appear in London at the coronation of George IV, dressed in what he called the 'full costume of a Highland chief' – complete with a brace of pistols. When the same monarch appeared in Edinburgh shortly afterwards in a justly famous development of the 'traditional Highland costume' sixty-five synthetically 'traditional' Highlanders were there to meet him (the expense of the trip, and costumes, being borne by the Sutherlands). Within weeks Glengarry was hosting his Highland Games where three cows were torn limb from limb at a rate to the competitors of five guineas per limb: a pastime transmuted to our own gentler times as the doubtless equally-traditional entertainment of haggis-hurling.

Not for the last time in Highland history, the gentry assumed for their romantic antics a popular consent and acclaim that encompassed, as appropriate, joy or grief at the usual rites of passage. They ensured it, too, by paying handsomely for it. When Lady Vere presented Lochiel with an heir, for instance, the gentry dined in private while 2,000 lesser 'clansmen' were supplied 'plentifully but not improperly' with whisky: great rejoicing was reported. When Thomas Alexander Fraser attained the high eminence of his coming-of-age, no less than one hundred gentlemen dined in his honour, while for the lesser 'clansmen' there was free beef, with ale and whisky 'liberally distributed'. The rejoicing, it was reported, was tumultuous: though we may be sure that it was in no way improper. When the Sutherland's eldest son married Lady Howard at London's Devonshire House the union too was reportedly celebrated 'with great rejoicings in the county of Sutherland'.

And in 1828, when Glengarry (who by now was never seen in public without a retinue of kilted 'clansmen') killed himself in Loch Linnhe, 150 gentlemen dined at his funeral; 1,500 others, 'plentifully supplied with bread, cheese and whisky', were said to have 'grieved greatly'. A few years later when the Duke of Sutherland was laid out in Dornoch Cathedral, 'heartfelt grief' was reported of the thousands who came along for the vast quantities of bread, meat and liquor that had thoughtfully been laid on in expectation of their loyal and tumultuous mourning.

Underlying these events, of course, was a brisk trade in Highland property, which would continue from the year of the disturbances at Gruids and Achness right through for another twenty years. In 1829, for instance, the Sutherland family acquired the Reay estates for £300,000. These included the parishes of Tongue, Durness and Eddrachilis; the land ran to 400,000 acres. Some years later, the Duke of Gordon's lands in Badenoch were also transferred; while after Glengarry's death in 1828, his estates, heavily in debt, changed hands too. In 1840 Edward Ellice bought Glenquoich for £32,000 and Lord Ward got the lands of Glengarry for £91,000. (Twenty years later, Ellice bought Glengarry for £120,000.)

MacDonald of Clanranald, in the quarter century from 1813, sold land to the value of over £200,000. In 1840 Colonel Gordon of Cluny got the island of Barra for £38,000, and Lord Abinger purchased Inverlochy for £75,000. By 1825, Edinburgh lawyers had acquired four estates in Ross-shire; and in March of the same year Sir William Fettes paid £135,000 for Redcastle and Ferry – which had, forty years earlier, changed hands for just £26,000.

That year too, MacKenzie of Seaforth bought Lewis for £160,000; while in 1831 Waternish in Skye went to Major Allan MacDonald for around £13,000. A Mr Baillie, who sailed under the dignifying pennant 'of Dochfour', took Dochgarroch for £10,000, while Corriemony went to a Colonel Pearce for £13,000. In 1834 Glendale in Skye was sold for £8,600. A fortnight later Torbreck went for £23,000 and Aberlour for £15,000, respectively to the trustees of Colonel Baillie of Leys and Mr Grant, 'late of Jamaica'.

In July of 1835 Mr Baillie (this time merely 'of Bristol') took land in Badenoch for £7,000; then in October, at the sale of Cromartie lands in Ross, Fannich made £6,500 and Lochbroom made over £9,000. A few years earlier, such prices would have been considered ruinous, and the editor of the *Inverness Courier* attributed the rise in estate prices to the prosperity of sheep farming 'and the passion entertained by English gentlemen for field sports'.

By now, intensive sheep farming was indeed facing competition from the growing rage for deer-forests, as these entirely treeless stretches of mountain were – and are – known.

Thus in 1836 the Earl of Aboyne was reported to have acquired the Glengarry estate for sport. In the spring of that same year the sporting rights over huge areas of Sutherland were on offer, including the rights over the districts of Armadale and Strathnaver (their natural fertility having been brought to the edge of ruin by intensive over-grazing by sheep). The following year twenty-five square miles around Achnasheen and Loch Fannich were advertised for sporting purposes. In April 1837, Glenelg went for nearly £80,000; and Geanies in Ross went in June to Murray the banker for £60,000. A year later the new owner of Glenelg bought Glenshiel for £25,000; the late Sir Fettes Redcastle's lands changed hands for £120,000; and in 1839, Achany in Sutherland went to James Matheson. And a year after that 20,000 acres in Argyll-shire were advertised as being suitable for use as a deer forest; while estates that were not selling or not for sale were nevertheless enjoying a vast increase in rental income as the scramble for profit from sheep, sport from deer, and status from mere association gathered sway.

To the Highlands in these years the rich and romantic poured in a fashionably kilted stream. By 1826 alone 'the number of fashionable personages' who had visited the Highlands was 'beyond all precedent', with every shooting lodge filled. Soon the Lord Chancellor, on his way north for a holiday at Dunrobin, would be calling on the Duchess of Bedford at her autumn sporting quarters; a month later, he would progress south again, having collected at Bedford's lodge the company of 'Mr Edwin Landseer, the distinguished artist'. (A handful of her bastards, it has since been acknowledged, had been sired by the bold artiste himself. Not for nothing did her duke record that he'd bought her the place to 'gratify her passion for the heather'.) At the same time, Lord Southampton took the hunting, shooting and fishing of Lochbroom; Lords Loftus and Jocelyn were hunting at Flowerdale while the Duke of Bedford was entertaining Badenoch; and the Duke of St Albans and Lord Frederick Beauclerk were pleased to appear at the Inverness Northern Meeting 'in full Highland dress'.

Meanwhile, times were less easy for the common people of the Highlands. By now, the kelp industry was in ruins and in the outer Hebrides alone some four to five thousand people were on the edge of starvation. By 1828, as a result, hundreds were leaving the west-coast ports for the Americas. On 4 July that year two vessels sailed from Lochmaddy, bound towards Canada, with 600 souls aboard. A brig had earlier left Harris for the same destination and another was 'daily expected to sail from Canna'. Arrangements were also in hand for the departure of several hundred people from the MacDonald estates in Skye, bound towards Cape Breton. The emigrants were to provide their own food; but 'Highlanders, it is well known, can exist on very little when necessity requires them to do so . . . thus for somewhat less than £4 [they] will reach the promised land'.

By April of the following year, the 'fever of emigration' was 'raging' in Sutherland. Vessels had been organised to sail at about the end of May, and 300 people had already secured a passage. In early June, a shipload of emigrants sailed; and a fortnight later two brigs tacked away from Cromarty towards Quebec, carrying another 300 people. And in the summer of 1836, while the gentry of Lochaber met at Fort William with a view to encouraging the departure of their small tenants to the colonies, the *Brilliant* sailed from Tobermory towards New South Wales with 100 passengers from the area of Strontian, 100 from Coll and Tiree, and yet another 100 from Iona, Morvern and Argyll.

For those that remained conditions worsened. That winter two-thirds of the people in the southern Hebrides were without food. In Inverness, four prominent and wealthy townsmen reportedly received threatening letters signed 'Swing'; and a seditious placard, signed 'Meal Mob', calling on the common people to assemble the following night, was fixed to a church wall. The authorities, alarmed, 'took precautionary measures,' and offered the fortune – to a hungry man – of twenty guineas for the identity of the organisers. By summer, conditions in the Hebrides were desperate, 'a more deep and universal distress prevails than was ever remembered'. And by 1836 the people of Lewis were in a 'lamentable state of dearth and destitution'; while the following spring destitution was raging across Skye: 'We know not that the history of the British people ever presented such a picture of severe, unmitigated, want and misery as is exemplified by the case of the poor Highlanders.'

Unsurprisingly, the oppressions of the period inspired further episodes of overt direct action against the landlords. In the summer of 1839 there was trouble on Harris. A sheriff and soldiers marched to Borve on the west coast, and arrested five tenants. Thereafter open resistance crumbled. No legal action was taken against the people – it was scarcely required, though one member of the gentry observed that its absence did encourage 'resistance to the law' – and within just two seasons, Lord Dunmore and his guests were shooting 'ten excellent stags, some of them twenty stones in weight'.

A year later there was again trouble from the turbulent indigents of Culrain. The landlords claimed that a strong body of eviction agents was deforced and put to flight, with the buildings of the chief agent fired and twenty head of stock lost in the blaze. And in the autumn of 1841 there was serious conflict at Durness centred on the activities of one James Anderson. Anderson, in line with the long-established policy of the Sutherland estate, had encouraged the remaining natives to settle on tiny patches of land close to the shores, by which means he could engage them in his fishing activities at the lowest cost to himself; while ensuring that they slowly fell into a condition of debt-slavery.

Without warning he had cleared Shegra the previous year; and in August, 1841, he announced that it was his intention to evict 163 people in Durness at two days' notice. In September, therefore, a party composed of sheriff-substitute, procurator-fiscal, sheriff-officers and special constables met with 'stout resistance', in which the women took a 'leading part'. The authorities were put to flight and took refuge in Durine Inn, but the inn came under attack that same night and they were swiftly driven away. The sheriff, Lumsden, recorded that his party had been 'deforced, assaulted, threatened with instant death, and expelled at midnight', by what he called a 'ferocious mob', and reported that 'no consideration' would induce any of his men to return to Durness 'without the aid of military force'.

Lumsden said that he feared a connection with the previous year's trouble at Culrain, and he reported rumours of a general uprising in the whole district of Tongue. The sheriff wrote to the Lord Advocate demanding infantry to help in the capture of the leaders of the people; and the rumour of the request was enough to invite a popular surrender, with the women involved dispersing to Eddrachillis. Their minister arbitrated, in a manner appropriate (some said) to the nineteenth-century Church of Scotland: he apologised and repented on behalf of his parishioners, and in exchange for their penance and apology Anderson was pleased to delay their eviction proceedings for six months.

No criminal prosecution followed. Again, the landlords had won – though the failure to pursue in the courts those who had stood against them, albeit briefly, may well have been a measure of awareness of their unpopularity. The previous Christmas, after all, there had been a Chartist speaker in Inverness; even the *Inverness Courier*, 'the organ of the oppressors of Sutherlandshire', had been moved to report his presence. (The *Courier* had also thought it of relevant interest to its Highland – and overwhelmingly landlowning – readership to report the killing, earlier, of twenty Chartists in Wales during their attempt to seize Newport).

The landlords continued to demand that their redundant indigents, once barbarous, so recently profitable, but now rather worthless following the collapse of kelp and the demand for sheep farms and deer forests, be briskly emigrated. Therefore in early 1841 Henry Baillie, MP for Inverness-shire, brought before parliament the need for 'a general and extensive' system of emigration 'to relieve the destitute poor in the Highlands'. He wanted the Treasury to find £3 a head to ship 40,000 Highlanders to Canada, thus liberating farms and forests together from the threat to progress which the continuing presence of these indigents was perceived to present.

And by that summer, the official committee on Highland emigration was claiming for the western Highlands and islands alone what it called an excess of population of between 45,000 and 80,000 people. A 'well-arranged system of emigration' was 'of primary importance', for destitution (the committee added), had been so severe in the 1830s that many thousands would have starved had it not been for relief handouts.

Worse was to come. Five years later, with the failure of that year's potato crop, destitution was 'practically universal' in the Highlands. In June 1846, the people of Harris found their potatoes – by now the staple foodstuff – to be uneatable, and they were beginning to exist on scavenged shell-fish and sand-eels. Within two months, the total failure of the crop was 'everywhere realised' and 'distressing reports' were 'pouring in from every quarter'. Still on Harris, the poor went to the seashore and gathered limpets, cockles and other shellfish; and 'by digging in the sands of Scarista, they get a species of small fish called sand-eels. On these and these only do they subsist'.

By August, it was reported from Inverness that the blight was 'fast spreading its ravages over this and neighbouring counties'. Black and withered shaws appeared in days; the blight seemed to touch potatoes of any seed, in any land, without warning. In Inverness the Town Provost called emergency meetings; in Portree Lord MacDonald also chaired meetings which decided to ask for aid from the government; while in Glenmoriston the blight had created 'havoc in the entire glen'. In Knoydart, Skye, Lochalsh and Kintail every field was infected; and in Easter Ross, too, where the crop was turning into a rotten pulp.

The famine in the Highlands accelerated the process of emigration throughout the following years. From Gairloch and Torridon, for instance, 200 made their way to Canada. In early 1847, the Duke of Sutherland sent 400 people from the Reay country to Montreal – while proposing to make 'the same liberal arrangements' the next year as well.

The following year, the barque *Liscard* hauled away from Loch Hourn with 300 people from Glenelg, Scotland, bound towards the community of Glenelg, Canada: their landlord had generously 'provided the means for emigration'. A month later, large-scale emigration was reported from Gordon of Cluny's estates in the southern Hebrides. The *Tusker* took 500 men from Loch Boisdale for Quebec, and another 250 were ready to follow them; the colonel was reported as having 'willingly supported' the emigration.

In the three years from 1847 some 1,000 people left from the Scourie district of Sutherland alone, in which transportation the Duke was pleased to invest no less that £7,000 of his money. Sir James Matheson paid 1,000 people to leave Lewis in 1852. In the same year, the Highland Emigration Society despatched 2,500 Highlanders to Australia. In the summer of 1851 emigrants sailed from Scrabster for Quebec. In July, a ship set sail from Loch Roag in Lewis; by then, 1,000 people had already left the island. The following month Colonel Gordon was 'supporting' the departure of 1,000 people from South Uist, and of another 500 from Barra.

A year later the *Georgina* stood away from Greenock with 500 emigrants, bound for Australia. The Revd Dr MacLeod, on the day of sailing before they put to sea, addressed them in Gaelic, this being 'the only language they understood'. Two months after that 400 people, mostly from Skye, departed from Birkenhead, also for the Antipodes. That winter the *Captain Baynton* sailed from Argyll for Australia, carrying 730 people from Skye, Harris and the Uists. In 1853 the 255-ton brig *Countess of Cawdor* cleared Inverness with a walking cargo of emigrants on the first day of August; she arrived at Geelong two days after Christmas.

Some of these emigrants were to return abruptly whence they had come. In September 1853 an emigrant ship from Liverpool, bound towards Quebec, was driven ashore on the western coast of Vatersay and 360 people were lost; but the process went on unhindered. Just a month later 100 people of Lochaber left for Australia: their landlord, Lochiel, paid one third of their expenses and promised not to pursue his erstwhile Lochaber tenants for any arrears of rent they might have left behind them. Soon afterwards the *David MacIver* was sailing from Birkenhead with 400 emigrants, a 'considerable number' of whom were 'natives of the Highlands'.

Popular hunger did not disrupt unduly the lives of the Highland élite, most of whom in any case increasingly spent their time far from their northern and western estates. Already the landowning class in the Highlands was showing a taste for breeding within its own gentle ranks. In the years following the famine the 2nd Duke of Sutherland's eldest son, the Marquis of Stafford, married at Cliveden Miss Hay MacKenzie of Cromartie. Later Sutherland's daughter, Lady Constance, would marry the Earl Grosvenor, heir of the Marquis of Westminster; while two years before the famine, Lady Elizabeth Georgina, Sutherland's eldest daughter, had married the Marquis of Lorne, only son of the Duke of Argyll. We may suppose with no undue confidence that, throughout the Highlands, popular celebration of these great unions, if tumultuous, was in no way beyond the borders of strict propriety.

Nor did famine interrupt the prerogatives and responsibilities of commerce. In 1844, James Matheson bought Lewis for £200,000 of the profits he had made from drug-dealing on a giant scale in China. In the next thirty years he was to spend another £400,000 on his insular property – some of it on a plan to extract oil from peat, but much of it on the construction of a mock castle at Stornoway. A year later, in 1845, the Marquis of Salisbury bought the island of Rhum, recently cleared, 'in order to form a shooting ground or deer-forest'; and in 1855 Sir John Orde bought North Uist. Thus 'the whole of the Hebrides has changed hands within the last quarter of a century'. That same year, Kilmuir in north Skye went to Captain Fraser for £80,000; his name was one of which much would be heard, and even more said, in the years to come.

Distant echoes of the outside world began to reach the Highlands with a degree of frequency. In the winter of 1847, for instance, the cobblers of Inverness formed what the authorities identified as an illegal combination and declared a closed shop. Four of their leaders were promptly arrested. They were judged at the spring Circuit Court by none other than Lord Cockburn, who had in his younger days been advocate for Patrick Sellar.

In April 1846 the centenary of Culloden went largely unremembered (at least in public) though part of the dyke behind which the Jacobite line had taken position for a time was still in place. By that summer hunger-riots were spreading across the eastern Highlands, as the failure of the potato crop grew imminent, and as corn-merchants stock-piled and exported meal too expensive for the people to buy. Already a series of riots, extending over several days, had shaken Inverness, concerning the export of potatoes. Several waggons were turned back; the provost's windows were broken; one cart-load was overturned on the pier and the cart thrown into the harbour. At one point 5,000 people were involved in the disturbance, including navvies working on the Caledonian Canal. Two hundred special constables were sworn in, a detachment of the 87th summoned from Fort George, and a number of leaders arrested. The riot 'arose from a fear of scarcity and high prices', it was reported; and as another, smaller, disturbance occurred at Tain, twenty rioters were remanded in custody, of whom three would later be gaoled.

At the same time (ominously, for it was still the spring), 'potato pits opened in Lochcarron were found to be mostly rotten'. By the winter there was a riot in Grantown-on-Spey, where special constables were sworn-in to defend the dealers from the meal-mob – the dealers had refused to sell in small quantities to the villagers. Soon, hunger-disturbances were reported from many parts of the Highlands. Speculation in the south had increased the price of grain 'to a very grievous extent', and – added to the daily shipment of grain away from the Highland ports – had 'very generally alarmed the least informed classes on the shores of the whole northern counties'.

In Ross-shire, there had been 'riotous demonstration' to keep the dealers at home. In Inverness carts of meal had been turned back at the Waterloo Bridge, and attempts had been made to raid meal-stores. At Evanton a large crowd prevented the shipment of grain – and the *Inverness Courier* printed a long list of disturbances, or threatened disturbances, across the Highlands. There were further meal-mob riots in many places, including Beauly, Rosemarkie and Balintraid; and in Avoch soldiers were called from Fort George to put down a riot in the village. At the beginning of March 1847, riots occurred in Ross-shire, many of them in Invergordon and the surrounding area: 100 soldiers were summoned to guard strings of waggons coming to the port with shipments of grain after country people had broken into the granaries, to mix various corns and render them unfit for sale (though still edible). In Castleton and Wick there were riots too, and that spring and summer the courts were busy as a result.

Meanwhile, from 1843, the Disruption had overrun the Church of Scotland and torn it apart in the Highlands. Lay patronage, the power of a landlord to appoint as minister a man politically suitable to the landlord cause, was not popular, as the events of previous years had shown. There were precendents from Clyne, Creich, Assynt, Croy and Kinlochbervie; and in the year of the Disruption, the people of Rosskeen too resisted the induction of a new minister. At Tongue the church bell-rope was cut, the keyholes in the doors blocked; and at Farr the hammer of the bell was removed and 'the church otherwise opprobriously treated. The Duke of Sutherland had refused sites for Free Churches'. That autumn, at Invergordon, a force of soldiers was landed to repress the 'Church rioters'; however, 'apprehensions were made without resistance'.

At Logie and Resolis in the Black Isle, crowds armed with sticks and stones prevented entrance to the churches, incensed at the introduction of new ministers. At Resolis a woman was arrested and gaoled at Cromarty, but she was freed by the mob from her underground cell; her gaoler, on the arrival of the mob, locked himself in another cell. In many places throughout the Highlands, indeed, the landlords were to resist the new Free Church. That resistance can only have encouraged the growing opposition to landlordism in the four decades after 1840. And from that year, certainly, there was a continuing trickle of landlord-centred direct action across the Highlands.

In 1842, trouble flared at Glencalvie, on the Kindeace estate in Ross-shire. A sheriff-officer was sent to warn away 100 people but his papers were taken from him, by a party of men and women, and burnt before his eyes. Three days later, the sheriff-substitute and the procurator-fiscal visited the place, but the natives were not intimidated and again they deforced their visitors. The same month there was a great demonstration at Fort William by small tenants and cottars against an attempt to squeeze money from them to pay for roads primarily used by the carriages of the gentry; 500 of the Lochaber poor marched to the town led by pipers; while that summer the women of the 300-strong community of Lochshell, in the parish of Lochs, drove away an eviction party of officials.

The following year, a party of sheriff-officers was deforced at Balcladdich in Assynt while attempting to evict one John MacLeod, and were driven away by perhaps fifty people. The sheriff gathered a force of thirty special constables, marched to Assynt, and arrested the leaders of the action. In 1845, notices of eviction were served on between two and four thousand people in Ross and Cromarty alone. The matter was raised in the House of Commons and the Home Secretary, Sir James Graham, went so far as to condemn the proceedings, though he was sure that they had been what he called exaggerated. The editor of the *Inverness Courier* replied that, on the contrary, the numbers were an underestimation of those involved.

The following month the case of Glencalvie was also raised in the Commons. The Lord Advocate announced to the House that, though the landlord was absent in Australia, the facts of the case had been greatly exaggerated and the people had been offered money to help them emigrate. The dispute was reported in the newspapers of the day, not just in the *Courier*: one John Robertson covered the story for the *Glasgow National* and *The Times* sent a special correspondent to the north. Their presence and reports underlay, at least partly, the mildly apologetic and certainly defensive excuses given to parliament by the government's spokesmen.

The estate's factor, however, pressed ahead with the plan to evict people from the land for which they paid £55 in rent, though the *Times* correspondent reported incredulously that 'for the same land no farmer in England would give [more than] £15 at the utmost'. Of the people themselves, Robertson wrote, 'They are exceedingly attached to the glen. Their associations are all within it . . . their hearts are rooted to the heather'.

Temporarily, the authorities retreated. But within a year the people had been cleared, all 'removed peaceably' by Whitsunday – having left scrawled on the windows of the church in which they briefly took refuge some names, and the legends: 'Glencalvie people was in the churchyard here, May 24, 1845; Glencalvie tenants resided here May 24 1845; Glencalvie tenants resided in the Kirkyard here, May 24, 1845; Glencalvie people the wicked generation.'

(The gable in which the inscribed window is set faces down the glen. Opposite the other gable is the graveyard, the inscriptions on its headstones themselves constituting a poignant if potted history of Highland affairs: Robert MacKay, shepherd, Glasgow, accidentally shot 13

August 1880, aged 47; Private C.A. MacLean, Seaforth Highlanders, 26 January 1915, aged 17; William Smeaton or Ross, died of wounds, 24 April 1916, and his mother Isabella Ross died 1935, aged 76; and George Munro Ross, born Glencalvie 1845, for thirty-four years keeper in Glencalvie Forest, and his son Thomas, died 1910, aged 19, of typhoid fever, Stoneyplain, Alberta.)

Yet another defeat lay on the far side of the Highlands, at Sollas in North Uist. In 1849, Lord MacDonald decided to evict 600 or more people who were starving in the aftermath of the potato famine, with some families living for weeks on nothing but shellfish scavenged from the seashore. The government had made meal available for famine relief, though the people had to work 96 hours a week for their pittance. Some of the men worked on draining the landlord's land; and though the government made money available to the proprietors, to be handed over to these men, many factors withheld the cash in lieu, they said, of outstanding rent arrears. In Sollas, as elsewhere, 'the people were permitted generally to starve'.

Lord MacDonald was nephew to the man who had built the castle at Armadale from which the Knoydart clearances could be watched in comfort; and though he was said to have been one of the less-bad landlords during the famine, he did have debts of £200,000, and he did wish that the natives would remove themselves to Canada. (Indeed, at that moment the *Tusker* was loading a walking freight of indigents at Lochboisdale, just a few miles to the south.)

Thomas Muloch of the *Inverness Advertiser* wrote that the rents of Sollas had been paid regularly until 1848, and quoted a MacDonald factor as evidence; but Sollas was foredoomed, he added, for it had caught the eye of two or three prospective sheep farmers. Thus in July 1849 the factor, Patrick Cooper, and the sheriff-substitute, one Shaw, went to Sollas with a party of officers to warn the people not to resist their forthcoming eviction. Cooper and his party were deforced, however, and anyone attempting henceforth to evict any tenant was 'threatened with instant death'. A few days later a party of officials trying to serve writs was stoned and driven away from the place, and when these officials returned with twenty constables they were again driven back.

The next day they tried again. As they approached Sollas, they came upon a party 300-strong, with warning flags flying (as they would in Skye thirty-five years later). Again the authorities retreated across Uist to their base in Lochmaddy, and his lordship wrote from the castle at Armadale to the Home Secretary asking for 'an armed force'. The *Inverness Courier* spoke for the Highland gentry when it suggested of the Sollas tenants, 'Their conduct was very unlike what Highlanders might be expected to exhibit, and some mischievous demagogue must have been among them.' (Again, almost exactly what would be said of the Skye crofters three and a half decades later.)

By 30 July the *Cygnet* had arrived at Oban to collect the procurator-fiscal, the sheriff-substitute, thirty-three constables and one minister, MacRae, before proceeding to Armadale to consult with his lordship. The following evening they arrived in Lochmaddy, and on the morning of 1 August they marched in rain across the island to Sollas, where they found warning flags flying again, and a great crowd gathered. The factor appealed to the people to respect the law and their laird, and get away to Canada; and the minister MacRae, did his best in Gaelic to pacify the people. By way of reinforcement the police also seized two men and took them in handcuffs to Lochmaddy.

They returned the following day and simply moved into the houses of the people, emptying them of goods and possessions, and tearing away the roofs. At that point the people of neighbouring townships, the women in the lead, charged the police, and a running battle ensued. The police finally made prisoners of the leaders, or those they called the leaders; and the people finally agreed to leave for Canada the following year. In September four men appeared at the Inverness Circuit Court, charged with mobbing, rioting, obstruction, deforcement and police assault. The judge, Lord Cockburn, cautioned the jury that the case involved moral and political considerations 'with which you and I have no concern . . . Your duty and mine is simply to uphold the majesty of the law'.

The jury found the accused guilty, but recommended the utmost leniency in 'consideration of the cruel, though it may be legal, proceeding adopted in ejecting the people of Sollas' – at which there was applause from the public gallery, not for the last time in a Highland court with regard to landlord-centred conflict. But Cockburn gaoled the men anyway, and committed to his journal the observation, 'The popular feeling is so strong against these (as I think necessary but odious) operations, that I was afraid of an acquittal.'

The following year, therefore, the district was 'completely and mercilessly cleared of all its remaining inhabitants'. Just before Christmas 1852, the Sollas people journeyed to Campbeltown to join the Harris and Skye emigrants already aboard the *Hercules*. On Boxing Day, she stood away to the open sea.

FOUR

THE ROAD TO GLENDALE

'They would geld a louse if it would rise in value by a farthing . . .'

From the 1850s, driven by the popular experience of the best part of the previous century, landlord-centred conflict in the Highlands approached the threshold – albeit still somewhat distant – of a qualitatively new stage.

By then the people had fought, and almost always lost, at a striking number of known locations (and may well also have fought, and lost, at an un-counted and unknown number of others). The people had, by the 1850s, encountered and contested landlord might at Balnagowan, Rosskeen, Strathoykel (in the great 'year of the sheep'), Kildonan, Culrain, Gruids, Achness, Borve, Durness, Glencalvie, Lochshell, Assynt and Sollas; as well as in the course of sundry hunger-riots and religious disturbances at other locations.

Most of these encounters and contests, so far as the record indicates, were in the eastern Highlands (while in later years, the engine of opposition would find itself along the western seaboard and in the Hebrides). But anti-landlordism was no prerogative of the men and women of Ross and Sutherland, as the record of direct-action conflict in Harris and Lewis indicates. And thus, on a general, if yet uneven scale, the common people of the Highlands had, as the second half of the century opened, smelt something of the sweetness of success, touched the wheel of united popular action and glimpsed the hot torch of publicity – albeit in a language that was not their own.

A long history of oppression had been matched, though not yet overcome, by a long history of resistance. In the course of this oppression and resistance, the makings of a tactical and strategic awareness had been laid, along with a consciousness of the power of united action and co-ordinated leadership.

Centrally, such vision as the common people of the Highlands claimed with regard to the land was hardly more sophisticated (or fundamental) than the concept that they continued to occupy it in peace and with some sort of prosperity appropriate to their times. However this was not a vision that the landlord class was prepared to concede in any way whatsover. From the 1850s, therefore, the stage was set for an escalation of land-centred conflict in the Highlands. But there were still many defeats to come.

The first of these defeats occurred when Lord MacDonald determined to evict 600 impoverished tenants from Strathaird (lying to the west of Loch Slapin in Skye) so that their departure might make room for sheep. An officer sent with writs was deforced and ejected, however, and he reported subsequently that 'the people will do all in their power to resist any number or force that may be brought against them'. The sheriff demanded police and soldiers, but subtler suasion was readily to hand in the form of the Destitution Board. The Board informed the people that they would get no more relief should they persist in their turbulent attitudes. Thus encouraged by the prospect of state-sanctioned starvation, the people came to their senses and cleared themselves forth from the island.

But signs of discontent were to be observed in other parts of the Highlands. The previous year, for instance, James Loch had contested (and failed to win) the parliamentary seat of Wick. In the course of the campaign he had been subject to loud and public abuse, while his agent considered the town 'a den of radicalism under the rule of demagogues'.

At much the same time there was further trouble on the mainland, at Coigeach on the western coast of Ross-shire. Writs of removal were issued against the people involved, tenants of the Marquis of Stafford: 'They made a stout resistance, the women disarming about twenty policemen and sheriff-officers, burning the summonses in a heap, throwing their batons into the sea, and ducking the representatives of the law in a neighbouring pool.' The party of officials was then forced to return whence it had come without serving a single summons or evicting a single crofter.

Scott, the factor, had been warned not to approach Coigeach by road, 'so hostile are the inhabitants of Ullapool and surrounding country'. Instead, therefore, he went by boat across Loch Broom, from which loch the *Hector* had sailed for Canada in the previous century. 'Some scores of women dragged the boat up the face of the hill for about 200 yards from the water, one man sitting in it, the whole cheering them on, and placed it high and dry in front of the inn.' Scott wrote to the marquis that the whole thing was 'a distinguished triumph of brute force over law and order' and added that while 'such mob-rule' continued in the ascendant, 'the rights of proprietors must remain in abeyance'. Or, to express the matter in another way, the rights of the indigents had at last overcome the brute force of factor and proprietor to which they had so long been subject.

More significantly, however, no further attempts were made to evict the people; and thus Coigeach must be counted as one of the first, unequivocal victories in the long record of landlord-centred conflict in the Highlands.

In Skye, meanwhile, the following year witnessed evictions in Suisnish and Boreraig, with Lord MacDonald's trustees removing 120 families to make way for a sheep farm and explaining that the people had been 'steadily retrograding', and that the landlord had been 'over-indulgent'. According to Donald Ross, an eye-witness of the evictions, MacDonald's debts by this time were such that his creditors had appointed trustees over his lands. The lands were entailed and could not therefore be sold, and the purpose of these trustees was to 'intercept certain portions of the rent' in payment of the debt: 'The tenants of Suisnish and Boreraig were the descendants of a long line of peasantry on the MacDonald estates, and were remarkable for their patience, loyalty, and general good conduct.'

That spring they were nevertheless warned to get out of their holdings. They petitioned for a reversal of the demand. The reply came in due course that they could have other land, on another part of the estate – part of a barren moor, unfit for cultivation. And so:

> In the middle of September following, Lord MacDonald's ground-officer, with a body of constables, arrived, and at once proceeded to eject, in the most heartless manner, the whole population, numbering thirty two families, and that at a period when the able-bodied male members of the families were away from home trying to earn something by which to pay their rents, and help to carry their families through the coming winter.

The people were thrown out of their houses, their meagre belongings tumbled after them, and the doors of their huts nailed up. According to the *Inverness Advertiser*'s long report of the proceedings, the eviction had been:

> One of a fearful series of ejectments now being carried through in the Highlands. Here were thirty-two families, averaging four members each, or from 130 to 150 in all, driven out from their houses. But it was the will of Lord MacDonald – he has driven the miserable inhabitants out to the barren heaths and wet mosses. He has come with the force of the civil power to dispossess them, and make way for sheep and cattle.

But the eviction had not gone entirely uncontested. Three men later appeared before the Justiciary Court in Inverness charged with deforcement, having first been imprisoned at Portree. The accused, however, enjoyed a sympathetic jury which found them not guilty. They returned home. Still, at the end of December the factor came again and threw them out, to live in the open or under such shelter as they could find for themselves. Eighteen of them were still there the following spring; but by the summer, they had all gone, and MacDonald's trustees had the place to themselves and their sheep.

And worse was to follow in Knoydart. At the same time as the events at Suisnish and Boreraig, Knoydart was being cleared in a savage manner. A year earlier Aeneas MacDonnell, owner of Glengarry, had died and the administration of the estate had passed to his widow and his young son's trustees – along with a mountain of debt. As usual, the tenants were to be made to pay for it, and though they were themselves in debt to the estate, due to the effects of the potato famine of the previous decade, it amounted to a small sum by their standards and an extremely tiny one by the standards of the trustees.

Their indebtedness, however, served as an excuse to remove them and replace them with sheep. A petition that they be allowed to remain was rejected out of hand. That summer, a government transport ship, the *Sillery*, was summoned to Isle Ornsay, across the sound of Sleat and just a mile or two to the north of MacDonald's castle at Armadale. Her boats were sent across the sound to take the people away. 'From house to house, from hut to hut, and from barn to barn, the factor and his menials proceeded carrying on the work of demolition, until there was scarcely a habitation left standing in the district. No voice could be heard. Those who refused to go aboard the *Sillery* were in hiding among the rocks and caves.'

For a while some natives did manage to remain in Knoydart. But two years later, when the estate was sold to a southern iron magnate by the name of Baird, almost all of Knoydart was under sheep, and only a dozen or so impoverished 'clansmen' and their families held off starvation with the shellfish to be scavenged along the shores of the sound of Sleat. But the meaning of the events at Knoydart may not have been lost on the wider Highland community; and just one year later, there was serious trouble at Greenyards, on the other side of the country. Fierce violence accompanied a riot (and two survivors of the violence were alive and passing on their story in the early years of the twentieth century, to a man who was still alive to relate their tale as late as 1981).

For some weeks the rumour had circulated in the district that four tenants of Robertson of Kindeace were to be evicted. The people, many of whom would of course have recalled the Culrain riot of 1820, decided on united resistance. In March, when the sheriff-officer came, he and his assistants were stopped and deforced. The *Inverness Courier* had already warned that 'considerable obstruction was anticipated in the execution of the summonses of removal' upon the tenants, and the affair indeed turned out to be 'of a very formidable character'.

The sheriff, several sheriff-officers, and thirty policemen from the forces of Ross and Inverness had marched from Tain:

> On arriving at Greenyards, which is nearly four miles from Bonar Bridge, it was found that about three hundred persons, fully two-thirds of whom were women, had assembled from the country

round about, all apparently prepared to resist the execution of the law. The women stood in front, armed with stones, and the men occupied the background, all, or nearly all, furnished with sticks.

By seven in the morning, each party confronted the other. A riot then ensued, with twenty women seriously injured by the batons and boots of the police. One woman later died; two at least bore thereafter on their bodies, until very old age, the marks and crippling effects of the violence inflicted on them that day. According to the *Courier*, 'The feeling of indignation is so strong against the manner in which the constables have acted, that I fully believe the life of any stranger, if he were supposed to be an officer of the law, would not be worth twopence in the district'.

The courts therefore took a severe view of the affair. That September, an Ann Ross and a Peter Ross appeared in Inverness before Lord Justice Hope, who had just spent the shooting season in Sutherland. The Greenyards accused got twelve and eighteen months respectively and a lecture from the bench on the wickedness of rebellion, along with a warning of the need to suppress it. And the law was called on shortly afterwards too, when in 1856 Lord Saltoun of Ness Castle attempted to evict thirty-two people from what they saw as their land in the cause of establishing a pheasant-preserve. Trouble followed.

By now, however, developments in the wider world had served to strengthen the crofters' cause; or were, at least, beginning to do so. Patrick Sellar – 'Sellar of Ardtornish' by now – was already dead; and if his passing was mourned, there were few tenants left in Morvern to be part of it, tumultuous quantities of free whisky or not. Within a couple of years, James Loch was also finally gone (it being reported years later by one traveller in Sutherland at the time that on every hand he heard the urgent and exultant whisper, over and again: 'Did you hear the news? Loch is dead, Loch is dead!').

The landlords nevertheless continued to conduct their affairs in the established manner of whimsical tyranny at the expense of the tenantry. On Skye, for instance, the standard method of maintaining a proper degree of discipline between the classes was a summons for eviction for rent arrears, rather than a civil-action small-debt claim. And again, when a tenant was removed for non-payment of rent, the estate required that any new tenant take the crippling responsibility for the previous tenant's debt-burden.

The collection of seaweed for use as fertiliser was also reserved as an estate-right, infringement of which could lead to court action; while the rights of deer-stalking sportsmen were superior to those of crofters, who in some places across the Highlands were forbidden even to keep dogs for fear that they might disturb the deer.

Meanwhile, in Lewis, crofting tenants would be fined for failing to remove their caps in the presence of the factor.

But by the 1850s, new pressures were ready to come to the fore in Highland affairs. The 1843 split in the ranks of the Church of Scotland had already helped alienate tenants from gentry in many parts of the Highlands, the latter remaining largely faithful to the old church, the former deserting it for the Free Church. The effects of this Disruption were to give organisational expression to the alienation, and serve as a focus for it – not least on account of the landlords' response to it. In Strontian, for instance, when the people were denied a site for their new church by the landlord, they built one on a raft floating in Loch Sunart; while on Skye Lord MacDonald would not make any land available to the Snizort, Kilmuir and Portree congregations, who for years were required to hold their services in the open air.

A religious revival in the late 1850s also offered the community its own recognised and independent leaders, albeit in a form that was neither overtly secular nor political; while the development of railways and steamship services (and in due course the telegraph) served to facilitate seasonal migration to the south for employment, and can only have had the effect of widening the horizons of the crofting villages of the Highlands. (Fishing also brought Highlanders to Ireland, where much was to be learnt about the brisk style of the Irish in their own opposition to landlordism.)

These years also witnessed the development of a Gaelic movement in the south of Scotland, allied to the development of interest in Gaelic culture at both a popular and academic level. There was also a marked growth in city-based societies composed of Highlanders, particularly during the 1860s and 1870s. Glasgow alone was host to regular meetings of the Sutherlandshire Association, founded in 1860; the Skye Association, founded in 1865; the Tiree Association, founded in 1870; the Lewis Association, founded in 1876; the Mull and Iona Association; the Ross-shire Association; the Islay Association; the Lochaber Society; the Appin Society; the Coll Society; and the Ardnamurchan, Morvern and Sunart Association.

And the formation of the Gaelic Society of Inverness in 1871 was followed by the establishment of similar groups in Glasgow, Greenock, Aberdeen and Dundee, between them pushing for the teaching of Gaelic in the schools, and for the foundation of a chair of Celtic at Edinburgh University. Indeed it was, in 1877, the Gaelic Society of Inverness which first petitioned parliament for a royal commission into the Highland land question; and the next year, the Federation of Celtic Societies was formed. Very quickly indeed, it became a powerful clearing-house for land-agitation matters.

These societies, or their activists, brought the question of the Highlands before a wider audience too. For instance, a Society of Highlanders was formed in Liverpool in November, 1880, following a discussion on the land question; *The Highlander* reported that 'the meeting was one of the most enthusiastic ever held in Liverpool, the prevailing tone being "no compromise with feudalism or eviction"'. The same edition of the paper announced, 'Mr Murdoch, editor of *The Highlander*, reports great interest in the Highland land question in Bolton and Manchester, which he has just visited.' And later that month, the paper was reporting, 'The *Liverpool Argus* has been giving forcible support to the land claims of the Highlanders'.

Indeed, the printed press was to be an important factor in the coming years of landlord-centred conflict. As the turn-of-the-century press had publicised events in Sutherland, so by the middle of the century was the *Inverness Courier* recording the wider world of Highland affairs. In 1856 it was joined by the *Invergordon Times*, which in due course proved to be perhaps the most outspoken of all regional papers in promoting the popular cause, along with the *Ross-shire Journal*, dating from 1875. The *Oban Times* would also be a strong advocate of the crofters, while the *North British Daily Mail* would chronicle on a daily basis the agitation of the 1880s and later; as did *The Scotsman*, though from an anti-tenant point of view. Alexander MacKenzie's *Celtic Magazine* and later *Scottish Highlander* seldom failed to keep the landlord question in the public eye, either. And throughout the 1870s, John Murdoch's *Highlander* campaigned strongly on the land and related questions. As Murdoch later recorded in his autobiography: 'From the first my aim was to have a high-toned journal and to let Highlanders feel as much as possible that [it] was an espousement of their views, feelings, and hopes'.

The scrutiny of a pro-crofter press doubtless served as something of a disincentive to the earlier style of full-blooded clearing on the part of the landlords; but a trickle of conflict continued to flow through the 1860s and 1870s. On the last day of September, 1873, for instance, a Tiree widow by name of MacFarlane was found guilty at a court in Tobermory. The previous month she had defended her house with fire-tongs against eviction, 'in the process injuring one of her evictors', as Murdoch's *Highlander* reported with scarcely-concealed glee. There were doubtless many similar incidents, unnoticed in the wider world, and never reported.

But the spirit of anti-landlordism was soon to surface publicly and spectacularly on the island of Bernera off the west coast of Lewis, as a 'significant and expressive overture' to the even greater battles to come.

The island was part of the estate of Sir James Matheson, a drug-dealer and self-made billionaire in the Victorian mould. He had acquired Lewis in 1844, for around £200,000, from the representatives of the last Earl of Seaforth. Under his ownership the rental had almost doubled in thirty years, to £24,000.

The dispute on Bernera centred on the conduct of the landlord's factor. As one witness would recall in June 1883, 'My firm conviction is that his policy from the first day of his factorship to the last was to extirpate the

Lewis people so far as he could.' The factor, Donald Munro, was also the senior legal officer on Lewis, not to mention the occupier of at least sixteen other posts in public administration. He was, in other words, an extremely powerful man, given to threatening eviction for any tenant who might be incautious enough to leave his hands in his pockets, or cap on head, when Munro was about; and also given to fining tenants on account of an (alleged) unwashed face.

The factor of any estate was seldom a popular figure, of course. At the funeral of one Lewis factor, who had choked to death on a lump of meat, one of the crofters hired to work the burial spade was heard to comment: 'Heap it on him, heap it on him; it's him that would have heaped it upon us; and if he but rise again he will heap the more on us.' And a few years later, following Cameron of Lochiel's winning of a parliamentary seat, it was noted that during the losing candidate's speech there were cries from the crowd that the landlord's victory had been engineered by the factors.

But on Lewis in 1874, Munro – and his master, Matheson – walked into full-out resistance. The dispute arose with regard to a summer grazing on the mainland of Lewis used by the Bernera people, which the estate now proposed to deny them. Protests followed; and the factor threatened to mobilise the volunteer militia in Stornoway (of which he was commanding officer), warning that the people would all be evicted from their homes for the temerity of protesting (though none of them was in arrears of rent).

In March a sheriff-officer, along with a sub-factor and one other assistant, arrived on Bernera and began to serve fifty-eight notices to quit. That evening, the sheriff-officer was verbally assaulted by children; and the following morning, he and his party were somewhat more robustly accosted by a crowd of about fourteen men. In the scuffle that followed the coat of the sheriff-officer was torn – certainly an act of dangerous sedition given the social conditions of Lewis at the time. Three men were charged and given notice of their forthcoming appearance in court. But prior to this, one of the three was spotted in Stornoway, the island capital, and arrested just a hundred yards from the police station. The intervention of a crowd of local sympathisers, however, meant that it took the police four hours to make the journey to their station; while the sheriff was meantime sent for, to read the Riot Act.

One hundred and thirty men then marched from Bernera (no mean march in a Lewis spring) to effect the release of the arrested man, armed with such implements as were available to them, and headed by a piper. The prisoner was, however, released before any violence could take place. The procession sent instead a deputation to Sir James at the castle (where he simply claimed that he knew nothing about the eviction schemes on Bernera).

In July the three accused appeared in court in Stornoway, charged that they, in March, had 'wickedly and feloniously attacked and assaulted' one of the factor's agents – and the stage might well have been thought ready for yet another popular defeat at the hands of the law. From the viewpoint of the authorities, the likelihood of conviction was strong. The common people had never won a land-centred dispute in a Highland court, and there was little to suggest that they would win this one either. For the authorities, therefore, the outcome of the trial must have been thought certain: conviction, exemplary sentence, some further police work, collapse of opposition, and implementation of estate policy.

The trial of the Bernera people, however, did not run to plan – and its result can only have had an extraordinary effect on popular anti-landlord consciousness across the Highlands when the result became known (as it would have, no doubt, with very great rapidity).

The Bernera men pleaded not guilty. The factor, Munro, was the first witness. To the delight of a packed public gallery, he was cleverly examined, by the lawyer for the accused, Charles Innes of Inverness. Munro was not a good witness. He had difficulty in remembering all of the many posts he held in the administration of Lewis. Nor did he know how many people he was attempting to evict from Bernera: such things, he said, he left to his subordinates, as he was a busy man. He had not consulted Sir James Matheson about the proposed removals, either: he was 'not in the habit of consulting Sir James about every little detail connected with the management of the estate'.

As Innes told the court, 'Had he been in either Connaught or Munster [Munro] would long ago have licked the dust he had for many years made the poor people of Lewis to swallow' – a reference, or implication, that a full century later would be considered daring indeed in a Scottish court. The men were acquitted; while soon afterwards, the sheriff-officer himself was charged with assault on one of the Bernera men, found guilty, and fined.

This, in effect, was the end of Munro (he progressively lost all his posts, finally being dismissed as factor). It was also a tremendously significant victory for the cause of the common people of the Highlands, and was widely reported as such. The notices of eviction were allowed to lapse. In other words, the estate surrendered – as it would soon afterwards with the people of Ness, from whose widows Munro had for years withheld publicly-raised monies deriving from a fishing-tragedy fund established during the 1860s, in lieu of alleged rent-arrears.

Munro's departure, of course, did not solve the land question in the island. As *The Highlander* noted: 'The central problem still remains that the land is badly distributed. In Uig, for example, one half of the parish has only eight families, while in the other half one hundred families are so pinched for land that they have to toil on sea as well as on the land to eke out a poor existence'.

Nevertheless his leaving signalled a major setback for landlord power, and one all the more significant in that it was the first of such popular successes.

More were quickly to follow. On the mainland, for instance, trouble was soon brewing on the estate of Leckmelm on Lochbroom, which had been bought for £19,000 by an Aberdeen paper-maker, Pirie, from Colonel Davidson of Tulloch. Pirie had at once demanded that all the tenants on the estate surrender their stock to him at valuation prices and become his employees; or face eviction. A storm of publicity followed, with little of it favourable to Pirie. The local Free Church minister circulated letters to every newspaper in the north of Scotland about the threatened evictions. Charles Fraser-MacIntosh, MP for Inverness, raised the issue of Leckmelm in the Commons, and the Home Secretary was drawn into the matter. Every newspaper, with the exception of the pro-landlord *Scotsman*, was unremittingly hostile to Pirie's demands.

Murdoch's *Highlander* reported events at Leckmelm across three of its columns and editorialised that the name of Leckmelm was becoming a by-word for 'iniquitous evictions'. In an expression that must surely have had an ominous ring for such of the landlord class as read the paper, it added, 'Our Irish cousins are using a way of their own to rid their part of the earth of oppressors. Who can blame them?'

As a result of the Leckmelm controversy, Murdoch felt able to assert that 'the land question is now felt to be the leading question of the day'. Many landowners, the paper thought, must be cursing Pirie for creating so much discussion and helping so much to 'ripen' the question. It was a question given extra piquancy by a report in that same issue that Gordon of Cluny, owner of the southern Hebrides, had been recently suggesting his tenants there should 'have the opportunity of improving their position by emigrating to America' – the landlord offering to provide financial assistance to get them there.

That November too, *The Highlander* gave almost seven columns to a speech in Inverness by the Revd John MacMillan of Ullapool, on the subject of the Leckmelm evictions. The paper thanked him 'for setting the clergy a-going on the land question'.

In Skye there was trouble, almost at once, at Valtos on the Kilmuir estate. The estate was owned by William Fraser, from Nairnshire, who had bought its 46,000 acres from Lord MacDonald in 1855, and who had since set out to rack-rent his tenantry along the Irish model. Under his ownership, rental income from most tenants had almost doubled, though there had been a substantial lessening in the quantity of land available for their use. Some rents had increased by almost three times.

In 1877, *The Scotsman* had reported widespread dissatisfaction with Fraser's regime in Kilmuir. In the same year a storm of wind and rain had swept the estate, flooding the Conan and Hinnisdale rivers, 'carrying away bridges, obliterating crops, sweeping flocks of sheep into the sea, and entirely changing the face of the country'. More to the point, the floods also wrecked Fraser's lodge at Uig. While his estate manager was drowned, the nearby graveyard was washed-out and bodies carried into the gardens of the lodge.

With its usual editorial genius, *The Highlander* reported:

> The belief is common throughout the parish that the disaster is a judgement upon Captain Fraser's property. It is very remarkable, it is said, that all the destruction in Skye should be on his estate. What looks so singular is that two rivers should break through every barrier and aim at Captain Fraser's house. Again, it is strange that nearly all the dead buried in Uig in the last five hundred years should be brought up as it were against his house, as if the dead in their graves rose to perform the work of vengeance which the living had not the spirit to execute. But though the living would not put forth a hand against the laird, they do not hesitate to express their regret that the proprietor was not in the place of the manager when he was swept away.

In 1881 some of Fraser's tenants at Valtos defiantly refused to pay the rents, as they had been increased since his arrival at Kilmuir. This rent-strike followed a petition asking for a rent reduction; which petition was promptly refused, and those who had put their names to it threatened with eviction. The strike followed. Without explanation, the estate suddenly reduced rents by twenty-five per cent in Valtos and Elishader. As Alexander MacDonald later reported, 'that was the beginning of it' – by which he meant a generalised agitation on the land question across the island, and soon the Highlands, as a whole.

Taken together, the events and their results at Bernera, Leckmelm and Valtos did indeed suggest the start of a qualitatively new and generalised stage of land-centred conflict in the Highlands; not least in the degree to which events in the Highlands were attracting attention on an increasingly wide scale. For instance a mass meeting in Glasgow's City Hall, called to condemn landlord action at Valtos, was publicised by Murdoch's *Highlander* in that spirit; while among the speakers was the Irish nationalist Charles Stewart Parnell. But the first major shot fired in this generalised agitation was to be at Glendale, on the west of Skye, towards the end of 1881 and continuing into the following year.

For the first time in the record of Highland resistance, anti-landlordism at Glendale combined fundamental tactics – rent-strike, land-occupation, deforcement and refusal to recognise court orders – with wide publicity, a keen and informed idea of the protestors' own case, and above all a sense of organisation that would serve to carry their cause from the end of 1881 right through the following year.

Glendale towards the end of 1881 comprised two estates: the 5,000-acre Husabost estate in the ownership of the eighty-year old Dr Nicol Martin; and the 35,000-acre estate of Glendale proper, in the ownership of the trustees of Sir John MacPherson MacLeod. Sir John had acquired the land in the early 1850s from the impoverished MacLeod of Dunvegan. Since that time, conditions had been harsh for the tenants of the district in a number of ways. When the Napier Commission came to the glen two years later, the assurance was required on a number of occasions that no tenant would be victimised for speaking before it.

This may not have been surprising, given the views of Dr Martin before the same commission on what he identified as the 'extravagance' of the tenants, for whose impoverished condition he saw no remedy but emigration: 'I don't see how the land can be improved. The only remedy, I think, for them is to go where they can get land – that is, America. Go to Manitoba and various parts of America.' A mass departure he thought best for Skye, and it was one for which the landlords would pay.

From the tenants themselves, of course, there was a different interpretation on offer, with a whole series of witnesses relating their conditions and grievances. John MacPherson, for instance, by 1883 nationally known as the 'Glendale Martyr', spoke to the Commission at some length on housing conditions: 'Of the twenty crofters' houses, there are only two in which the cattle are not under the same roof with the family.' What MacPherson wanted was 'the land, as there is plenty of it'. And as to payment for it: 'My father, my grandfather and my great grandfather have already paid in money far more than the value of the land.' When they had asked the landlords of Glendale for more land, MacPherson said, they had been told to be patient: 'We told them that our forefathers had died in good patience, and that we ourselves had been waiting in patience till now, and that we could wait no longer – that they never got anything by their patience, but constantly getting worse.'

One of the commissioners, in a question that reveals the extent to which the authorities expected a deferent tenantry in Skye, wanted to know whether MacPherson's manners on this occasion had been 'civil, such as Highlanders are accustomed to use in talking to those of superior social station'. MacPherson said they were, but noted objection to the suitability of the factor, on the grounds that 'he does not speak our language, and many of us cannot speak English'. As to subsidised emigration, MacPherson thought that it would be 'more satisfactory to the people if the money . . . should be spent at home, and, when the land at home would be peopled, than to send us away to other countries'.

MacPherson added that it would be 'a capital thing' for the island's population of large, incomer-farmers – 'those who have the £1,800 tacks' – to emigrate. But as for the emigration of his own people, 'at present we see no reason for it, as there is plenty of land in our country and I don't know how we do not get it; this is not our kingdom, we have nothing where we are'.

According to MacPherson:

We are not home scarcely a week with our earnings when we pay it
over to the proprietors, and they are off to London and elsewhere
abroad to spend it, and not a penny of it is spent on the place for
which the rent is paid . . . [There is] better justice in the south than
in the north. There are two sides of the law; but we never saw the
just side, always the worst side . . . I know that many of our
landlords never purchased the properties which they have – that it
was our forefathers who purchased the properties with their own
blood and that, therefore, we have as much right as anyone else to
have it by purchase.

The points made by MacPherson were not, of course, new. They had been
made in one form or another for the previous century. But their
significance was the extent to which they can be seen to represent a typical
version of what the Napier Commission heard across the Highlands –
and the extent to which they won unprecedented publicity.

In a long statement from the tenants of Boreraig, Alexander MacKenzie
presented similar grievances, encapsulating the poverty, overcrowding
and tyranny of conditions in Glendale:

We complain generally of the smallness of our crofts, the want of
hill pasture, that we are too highly rented. Forty-five years ago our
proprietor subdivided and cut up our twelve crofts into twenty-four
different small lots and raised the rent. When the former crofts
were cut up into small lots tenants were brought from Waternish
and Bracadale for them, and all were crowded together in this little
township. The land, having been in perpetual cultivation for
hundreds of years, is become so poor and so much reduced that it
is incapable of yielding any crop except of the very poorest. The
result is that we are for ever sunk in debt, and have to spend the
greater part of the year away from home to earn money to buy food
for our families, and to pay the rent for the landlord . . . if [the
people] did not work as hard as he wished, or were absent for a day,
he would threaten them with eviction . . . there is plenty of land in
Skye for all the people in it, and that land which originally
belonged to our own forefathers.

Not only were the delegates from the people of Glendale before the
Napier Commission articulate and clear in their opinions. They also
presented a list of demands, which indicates a significant degree of prior
discussion of their grievances. These grievances included more land,
security of tenure and compensation for improvement.

As a result of such conditions and demands, the people of Glendale
were ready to go on the offensive by the closing months of 1881. And
almost at once they were goaded into action by a warning notice

displayed by the landlords at the local post office, with regard to the former right of the people to collect timber on the seashore for their own purposes. This warning was reported in the *Aberdeen Free Press*, later printed in Alexander MacKenzie's history of the clearances, and noted at Glendale by the Napier commission; but by the time that it was posted, Glendale was clearly on the brink of open rebellion.

There was talk of a formal and openly-organised District Alliance against the landlords, a clear consciousness of the rent-strike weapon and the possibility of land-raiding; MacPherson would shortly be gaoled for his anti-landlord activities; and the people were increasingly restive about estate regulations of whatever nature. As Alexander Ross would tell the commission, 'I cannot judge a factor's heart by the heart of any man.' The factor had earlier shot his sheep-dog: 'He shot him with his gun in the well, and the well is dry since then. It was one of the best wells in the country, but since then it has denied water. I do not know what he did to the well, but likely if he could kill the well, he would do it.' Such, in one striking image, were social relations in the west of Skye at the beginning of the 1880s.

By then, there may already have been knowledge in the glen of the Irish land league and its forms of popular persuasion; certainly, an Irishman would be in the district soon enough. Tenants inclined to pay rent would shortly be threatened; and certainly too, John Murdoch of *The Highlander* was on his way to Glendale, where his host in the glen would be threatened by the factor for giving room to 'Irishmen and blackguards'.

In any case, a direct result of the edict displayed at the post office was the calling of a general meeting of the tenants. In time-honoured fashion, petitions were sent to the landlords – and in precisely the same fashion, rejected. The tenants at once declared a rent-strike. For good measure they also announced that they would shortly occupy the Waterstein sheep farm, with or without permission.

Now, in a gesture of unprecedented moderation, the landlords asked for time to consider the position. They were told, however, that the people had run out of patience. By the end of May, their sheep were on the farm; Court of Session orders were ignored; warrants of arrest could not be executed; and at the Martinmas rent collection in Glendale, only five of the estate's one hundred crofters came forward to pay.

Nor did events in the glen go unnoticed elsewhere. Apart from lengthy reports in the pro-crofter weeklies, journalists were sent by train, steamer and dog-cart from the *Aberdeen Free Press*, the *Dundee Advertiser* and the *Glasgow Citizen*; while papers like the *North British Daily Mail* covered events in Glendale with a keen eye and helped to keep affairs there before a wider public.

In short, Glendale was now the scene of open rebellion on the land question, the locus of head-on conflict between two clear positions on the ownership and use of land in the Highlands. The view of the common people had been given voice by John MacPherson, quoted above, with an eloquence that any paraphrase must fail to match: the land belonged to the people whose country it was and whose ancestors had lived in it and worked on it.

The view of the landlord class was equally simple: that the land, its use and occupancy, was in the gift of those who owned it in law, along with the associated right to do with it (and such as scraped a living from it) precisely as they chose.

Between these positions on the land, its use and ownership, there was little room for compromise. Nor, in any case, was there any taste for compromise on either side. Two radically different, and irreconcilable, viewpoints thus stood opposed: in one corner, the landlords, of whom a Hebridean poet had observed over a century earlier that they were men so mean 'they would geld a louse if it would rise in value by a farthing'; and in the other, the common people in, if not arms, then certainly unarmed rebellion.

FIVE

BRAES AND THE NAPIER COMMISSION

'I cannot bear evidence to the distress of my people without
bearing evidence to the oppression and high-handedness of the
landlord and his factor.'

From 1882 the people of the Highlands embarked on a qualitatively new
stage of agitation. It was one that would run right through to the passage
four years later of legislation designed to ameliorate, if not solve, the
land-problem; and on again at as high a pitch for at least another two
years, with a view to distributing the land in the cause of the crofter and
at the expense of the landlord. The experience of these years showed, or
at least most powerfully suggested, that, in the words of the slogan of the
Land League – the Highland Land Law Reform Association – the people
were indeed mightier than any landlord.

In 1882, as a prelude to the gathering storm, agitation was centred on
Skye. It arose first at Glendale and then at Braes, on the other side of the
island. Towards the end of the year there were surges of trouble in Lewis,
Barra, Tiree, Wester Ross and Sutherland as well. But it was the events at
Braes that really caught the imagination of a wider public. It was the
events at Braes that – at least for that wider public – signalled the opening
shot in the land war on which the Highlands appeared to have embarked.

The events at Braes also caught the attention of the authorities: estate,
legal, and governmental. Their confidential resport, notably those of
Sheriff Ivory of Inverness-shire, repose to this day in the archives and
demonstrate the extent to which popular agitation in the Highlands had
started to seriously alarm those same authorities.

Braes, too, illustrates the role of the press in publicising and promoting
(which was often the same thing) the crofter cause; and demonstrates the
'hot torch of publicity' in concerted action for the first time in the crofters'
war of the coming years. According to one report, for instance, the
newspapers represented in Skye during the month of the Battle of the
Braes included the *Dundee Advertiser*, *People's Journal* (which would be
giving strong coverage to crofting issues a full forty years later), *Glasgow*

Citizen, Scotsman, Glasgow Herald, Glasgow News, North British Daily Mail, Inverness Courier, Northern Chronicle, London Standard (reportedly sending its war correspondent) and the *Freeman's Journal.*

The matter was also raised in Parliament, with Charles Fraser-MacIntosh asking the Lord Advocate in the Commons on 20 April, 'if he can explain the circumstances under which fifty of the Glasgow Police Force have been sent to the Island of Skye?'; here was a further indication of how serious matters in the Highlands were now being regarded.

The background to the events of the spring of that year stretched back almost two decades. Until 1865, the people of Braes had had the use of the nearby hill of Ben Lee, when they were ejected by the MacDonald estate in favour of a sheep farm. In 1881, when the lease of this farm was about to end, they petitioned the estate for the return of the grazing of the hill. This petition was at once rejected. The people announced a rent-strike and marched into Portree to proclaim it.

The estate considered arrests on the grounds of 'intimidation', but did not think the claim would stand in court. So it resorted to attempting to evict a few tenants, on the grounds that the rent-strike had driven them into rent-arrears. Orders to quit were taken out against a dozen of the strikers; but the sheriff-officer attempting to serve these orders was accosted, and his papers burnt. This was deforcement – a criminal offence rather than a civil matter – and warrants for arrest were issued. At this point, Ivory, the sheriff of Inverness-shire, arrived with his force of fifty police. The celebrated riot then took place on the narrow track into the township, on the steep side of the hill, above the shore. Five men were arrested despite ferocious opposition from the Braes people.

Given the history of landlord–tenant relations in Braes, as the people themselves told it then and later, the ferocity of their opposition may scarcely have been remarkable. The very first meeting of the Napier Commission was held in Braes. Its very first witness was Angus Stewart, a crofter of Braes, who was questioned in Gaelic. Stewart was author of the much-quoted line, characteristic of everything Napier's commission would hear as it toured the Highland that summer, and one that well serves as epitaph to the commission's endeavours: 'I cannot bear evidence to the distress of my people without bearing evidence to the oppression and high-handedness of the landlord and his factor.'

Stewart set the tone for the proceedings by asking for a guarantee that he would not be victimised by the estate for giving evidence; and then proceeded to offer it anyway. His words to this day encapsulate to perfection the popular vision of what was wrong with the system of land-ownership in the Highlands:

> The smallness of our holdings and the inferior quality of the land
> is what has caused our poverty; and the way in which the poor

crofters are huddled together, and the best part of the land devoted
to deer forests and big farms.

His remedy was equally simple:

> What would remedy the people's grievances throughout the island
> of Skye is to give them plenty of land, as there is plenty of it, and
> they are willing to work it. Give us land out of the plenty of land
> that is about for cultivation. That is the principal remedy that I see.
> Give us the land.

A procession of other witnesses followed. Their stories offered evidence of
land-use and misuse over the previous century, evidence of the clear view
of the people that they had a natural right to the land on which they lived.
Evidence, too, of the strength of popular memory on the land question.
The simple and powerful eloquence of scores – hundreds – of other
crofting witnesses before the Napier Commission renders paraphrase
less than appropriate. The simple and powerful clarity (and certainty) of
this eloquence, and its unanimity, itself constitutes a searing indictment
of class relations and associated issues in the nineteenth-century
Highlands.

For instance, deportation (and the word is clearly merited) of the
common people – for long the only response of the landlord class to
popular land-hunger – was in Braes, as throughout the Highlands, briskly
rejected. According to one crofter, 'I would like very well if those who are
wallowing in wealth would go away where no crofters would obstruct
their wishes in land'. For another, in a typically memorable phrase, 'The
places I knew in my young days where the grass could be cut with the
scythe are now as bare as possible with deer and big sheep.'

The response of this single crofter was replicated time and again during
the course of the Napier hearings. And such a sustained and collective
view is not a thing of the past either. In very recent years, there have been
inhabitants of Braes who could lay claim to an informed and accurate
version of the events a century and more ago. John Nicolson, for example,
had both his great-grandfather and grandfather gaoled for their part in
the Battle of the Braes:

> The hill-land was being taken from the crofters. To do this the rents
> were increased to such an extent that the poor crofters couldn't
> afford to pay, so then they were threatened with eviction. This led
> to a lot of unrest and they refused to pay the rent and the story I
> have heard is that the sheriff-officer was sent to Braes with eviction
> notices. He was met by a deputation of crofters, when he was
> handed a glowing peat and made to burn the eviction notices. He
> then returned to Portree and reported to his superiors and as a

result it was decided that the crofters were in revolt. It was then decided to send a force of police to quell this revolt in Braes.

In the words of another Braes resident, Willie MacDonald (these words delivered with a cadence, wit and attention to detail that would not have shamed a witness before the Napier hearings):

> Well, it happened in 1882, the Battle of the Braes. They lost the grazing of Ben Lee, three townships, Peinchorran, Balmeanach and Gedintailor. And they were left with what they called the township common grazing. And this grazing that they lost, it was 3,440 acres, divided between 29 individual shares. They were only left with in Peinchorran, approximately 299 acres, in Balmeanach 214, and in Gedintailor, I amn't sure, about 230 or something. They started a rent-strike and the rent-strike took place and then they were going to be evicted by sheriff-officers, and these sheriff-officers came as far as Gedintailor, and the people resisted, taking the summonses and they went after them, and they took a burning peat, the matches wasn't so plentiful then, or the lighters, they took a burning peat from a man called Donald MacPherson in Ollach, upper Ollach, and they made the man blow the flames on the summons, and burned them.

In the words of Nicolson: 'The chief constable of Glasgow decided to send a force of policemen and they arrived in Braes on a wet and stormy morning in April 1882, and there the battle took place.' According to Kate MacPherson:

> My father was born in Braes and my grandparents lived there of course, my grandfather was a crofter. I can remember my father talking very much about the battle, he must have been five or six at the time, and what he remembered, what I remember about him telling the story so much, was how frightened he was when he saw his mother being attacked by the policemen and he was terrified because they were manhandling my grandfather, and of course my grandmother went to his rescue. She was a very tall, strapping, strong young woman, and three policemen she knocked out, and she was batoned, and what he remembered being so afraid of was his mother lying on the ground with blood pouring over her face. My grandmother wasn't the only woman in that situation but I know she was one in particular that was badly hurt. It was a black day, for the crofters of Braes, that day.

Yet another recollection goes thus:

My grandmother was Marion MacMillan, she was in the battle, we were told the policemen made for her, she was a very strong woman, and they made for her, she put one of them on his back. There are ruins there now, which Colin MacDonald uses for his sheep and things. There were two women staying there at the time, and when the police came and the battle started, they came out with a bucket of ashes and they threw the ashes to blind the police, it gave them a good advantage.

To this day, Ivory is recalled locally. In the words of one Braes resident, 'The police came to Portree and they marched down to Braes with the sheriff of the county, Sheriff Ivory, and it seems his height was about five feet four, and I read in a book all dictators were about that height, Mussolini and Hitler, yes; and Sheriff Ivory!'

According to John Nicolson: 'My great-grandfather and my grandfather were among those apprehended. They were taken to gaol in Inverness, but their fines were paid by well-wishers and they were released. They were met at Portree pier by people from all over Skye and carried shoulder-high to the local hostelry and well-fêted there.' And, in the words of Alasdair Beaton:

> Another thing I was told, that day the Balmeanach and Gedintailor people were there and they were saying, where are the Peinchorran people? So word was sent and they were on the shore, cutting seaweed, at that time they used to take boats and fill the boats, so they left the boats and made for the battle, probably they didn't care if they would lose the boats or not with the tide coming in, but anyway when they came back the boats were still high and dry, and they were saying afterwards, they never saw a tide in their lives that stayed out so long as it did that day.

The aftermath of the events at Braes, given the state of agitation by then sweeping over Skye, was predictable. Of the five men taken to Inverness, three were fined £1, and the others the equivalent of £2.50. When they returned home to their welcome, the crofters of Braes simply drove their stock on to Ben Lee; while MacDonald's agents applied for, and got, a Court of Session order demanding that they be removed, as they were there illegally. Fifty-three people were to be served with these orders. But in September, the messenger-at-arms carrying these orders was put to flight by the women of the district. Ivory asked for 100 soldiers to subdue Braes. But the request was denied – an interesting enough denial, in terms of what it suggests with regard to government perceptions of events in the Highlands – but the county's police force was increased by fifty men. In October, however, when the messenger-at-arms returned in the company of eleven policemen to serve his notices, they were all prevented even from entering the district by a crowd of crofters; and two months later, thwarted, the MacDonald estate retreated and agreed to lease the grazing of Ben Lee to the crofters of Braes.

In short, the crofters of Braes had won a tremendous victory.

By then, of course, the balance of forces had tilted against the landowners of Skye – both as landowners and, at least by implication, as bearers of a culture clearly viewed (by those who gave evidence to Napier), as alien: whether Fraser of Kilmuir and his 46,000 acres; Norman (Harrow and Athenaeum) MacLeod of Dunvegan, 'Isle of Skye, N.B.', and his 141,000; or Lord (Eton and Carlton) MacDonald of Armadale, 'Isle of Skye, N.B.', and his 130,000 acres. For, by the time of the battle at Braes, the anti-landlord movement had developed a momentum – encouraged not only by direct events, but also by the agitation of the Highland press.

In this, Alexander MacKenzie's *Celtic Magazine*, published out of Inverness, played more or less every month its own significant role. Indeed, the view is persuasive that the overall role of MacKenzie during the land agitation was at least as impressive as that of John Murdoch. A glance at the appropriate files of the *Celtic Magazine* quickly shows MacKenzie's sense of what was significant in the Highlands. In January 1882, for instance, it published as a special supplement a very long report on the annual meeting at Perth of the Federation of Celtic Societies. One issue later, it carried a long letter from 'A Canadian Highlander'. In it the refrain, inseparable from the land agitation of the time and later, of radicalism on one hand and nationalism on the other, is clearly heard:

> Give Scotland liberal Land Laws, for which we are glad to see they
> are now agitating, and hope they will soon obtain – surely there is
> enough spirit of independence in the descendants of the followers
> of Wallace and Bruce to assure and secure their civil rights and
> liberties, whether usurped by Scottish lairds or English
> millionaires.

The same issue carried a full-page report on the last meeting of the Edinburgh Sutherland Association. John MacKay of Hereford referred to the land question in Sutherlandshire, and warned, 'In the immediate future large tracts of their beloved country might be turned into huge deer-forests'. Professor Blackie added that the principle of the Irish Land Act 'applied to the Highlands as well as to Ireland', that the people had 'a right to the soil'. This was their 'favourable moment', the moment when they must speak out, and if they did not speak out they were 'lost for ever'.

Two issues later the magazine was carrying a piece by John MacKay on the Sutherland evictions. The following month, as well as covering the results of the Gaelic census, it was reporting events at Glendale:

The tenants paid their rents at Martinmas last, but they have given notice that unless their demands are conceded they will not pay the rent due at Martinmas next. They are in great hope that the friends of the Gael in the large towns of the south will manfully aid them in their battle with landlordism.

June's edition carried a short piece on the battle at Braes, and a much longer article on Lord MacDonald, the Highland destitution and the 'clearances of 1849–51–2'. The July edition gave space to a ten-page piece by Lachlan MacDonald of Skeabost on the land agitation in the Highlands, and Skye in particular. It also included a follow-up to the Lord MacDonald-and-destitution article of the previous issue; and three pages on particularly severe evictions then under way at Lochcarron.

The following month's *Celtic Magazine* carried a full-page report on the formation of a 'Highland Land Law Reform Association' at Inverness. It was intended by its founders to:

> . . . effect such changes in the Land Laws as shall prevent the waste of large tracts of productive land in the North, provide security of tenure, increase protection to the tillers of the soil, and promote the general welfare of the people. A special object of the Association shall be the encouragement and fostering of small holdings in the Highlands, and the collection and publication of the facts and circumstances connected with evictions in the North.

The same issue of the *Celtic Magazine* carried a report on the treatment of events in Skye by local and national newspapers; and an article on the 'Skye crofters and their claims'.

This was an early reference to the growing demand, brilliantly orchestrated by MacKenzie and his magazine, for an official enquiry into the condition of the crofters (as small tenants were increasingly called). A deputation from the Highland Land Law Reform Association had met with Fraser-MacIntosh, in Inverness, 'with reference to the necessity of energetic action in parliament in favour of special enquiry into the crofter question by Royal Commission'. MacKenzie himself announced that a majority of the members of the town council of Inverness were already members of the Land Law Reform Association. And he added, 'The time has passed for any half-hearted action', for unless something were done, he 'feared the people would themselves take to the settling of the question, and no one could predict the consequences'. At all events, there was 'looming in the near future a general movement throughout the Highlands on behalf of more equitable relations between landlord and tenant'. To this, Fraser-MacIntosh had agreed and promised to raise the matter in the next session of parliament, because 'events now occurring render inquiry imperative'.

Meanwhile, MacKenzie and the land-law association kept up the pressure for a commission right through the following winter. In November, his *Celtic Magazine* carried yet another piece on the Sutherland evictions; and a report on a trial following events at Rogart. Quoting the *Oban Times* of 7 October, the magazine reported, 'The crofter, Andrew MacKenzie, who was reinstated by his neighbours recently, was tried before the Sheriff at Dornoch on Saturday, and received the heavy sentence of one month's imprisonment, without the option of a fine'.

Professor Blackie had already been agitating on the matter. And now MacKenzie added:

> People who know the case thoroughly wonder why it was tried before the Sheriff-Principal, and not before the Sheriff-Substitute. Here we find Sheriff MacIntosh, himself a laird, and, in his capacity as advocate in Edinburgh, senior counsel in the case of Lord MacDonald against the crofters of Ben Lee, sitting to judge a case which arose out of an attempt to evict MacKenzie from his croft. It is probable that this will be brought before the notice of Parliament by the Federation of Celtic Societies.

In other words, even by this early point, publicists and agitators and parliamentarians were working in close collaboration; although on a scale that could not begin to match what was to come.

In the *Celtic Magazine*'s December issue, MacKenzie carried an article on land nationalisation, and another piece on the Braes crofters. In January he printed a piece on the depopulation of Argyll; and a four-page article on the first Highland emigration ship to Nova Scotia – the *Hector*. The following month he carried long quotes on the crofters' agitation from the *Greenock Telegraph* and the *Christian Leader*. By then, 'a number of gentlemen, summoned by Lord Archibald Campbell', had met in London and passed resolutions 'requesting the Government to grant the offending Skye crofters "sufficient time" to submit to the law before force is used, and urging the appointment of a Royal Commission'. And just days later in Edinburgh, some 2,500 people met to demand a commission that would enquire, among other things, into the 'extensive depopulation of fertile districts for the purposes of sport'.

With MacKenzie in attendance, as well as Blackie, and D.H. MacFarlane MP (these three were central to the city-based land-reform leadership of the coming years), the meeting also demanded the 'utilisation for productive purposes of the vast tracts of the country at present under deer'. And Blackie moved a motion – carried unanimously – that the meeting, 'recognising the necessity at this juncture for united action on the part of all friends of the Highlands, heartily endorses the objects of the Edinburgh Land Law Reform Association to provide a basis for combined action in favour of such changes in the land laws as may be necessary – and recommends the formation of similar Associations throughout the country'.

As a direct response to this publicity, organisation and agitation, the government did indeed grant the formation of a commission into crofters' grievances shortly afterwards. It was now six years since MacKenzie had first called for one, almost as long since the Gaelic Society of Inverness had asked for it; and since then it had been demanded by an 1880 public meeting in Inverness, by the Federation of Celtic Societies, the Gaelic Society of Perth, and the Highland Land Law Reform Associations of Inverness and Edinburgh. Fraser-MacIntosh had also written to the Home Secretary in February: 'I could not have believed that so soon after the meeting at Inverness in December 1880 the agitation should have gone to such a pitch. It will be imprudent to delay.'

MacKenzie promptly urged that steps be taken to counter the landlord influence that would, if allowed, be brought to bear on the commission: otherwise, 'It will only prove the commencement of an agitation on the Land Question, the end of which no one can predict.' A little later he warned, 'If it fails to give satisfaction, the people, by a more powerful, legitimate, and persistent agitation, will still have the remedy in their own hands.'

The commission, however, had the effect of unleashing on the public the history of class-relations in the Highlands over the best part of the previous century; and of serving as a focus for the anti-landlord movement in general. From the very first meeting at Braes this was the pattern that was set whether on the mainland or in the islands.

On Mull, for instance, the commission met at Tobermory. It heard that in 1841 there had been over 10,000 people residing on Mull, and yet within only ten years this number had fallen to no more than 6,500; and by the census of 1881, it was shown that the population had fallen even further, to just over half of the numbers of forty years earlier.

John MacCallum noted how he had witnessed great changes in Mull even in his own time. With every new landlord, he said, and with every so-called 'improvement', the crofters were left worse off than before. John MacKinnon, aged 93, told of a spot where there had once been 129 crofts, and now only two remained. Lachlan Kennedy reported repeated raisings of rent; successive reductions of land; and one occasion when the factor had compulsorily taken land from the crofters, leaving them without grazing for their cattle, and then bought those cattle at a price far below their real value. And Lachlan M'Guerrie (as the minutes of the commission style the name) described his eviction from his croft at Ormaic at the hands of the proprietor, a policeman and a sheriff-officer; and his experience of having to take refuge with his family in a hut on the shore six yards above the high-water mark.

This evidence was given against a wider background, the significance of which could not escape the attention of those giving it. By now, after all, it was August – the start of the 'sporting' season in the Highlands. According to the correspondent of *The Times*, for instance, prospects were excellent for 'Scotch' grouse: 'Daily and nightly the trains from the south come into Edinburgh and Glasgow heavily laden with passengers and baggage. They are sent on to Stirling and Perth, to Aberdeen and Inverness and Oban. Oban becomes a little Euston, and Inverness a miniature King's Cross.' Of all the moors in the island of Mull, those in the Bunessan district gave promise of the best sport. The birds there were said to be very numerous and unusually forward and strong, while in Inverness-shire the season was expected to be the best for at least six years. In the forests, the deer were in unusually good condition too: 'Good reports come from North Knapdale, Easdale, Ballachulish, Morvern, and from Tobermory, Salen and Bunessan in Mull'.

Meanwhile, it was to Bunessan that the Napier Commission moved after Tobermory. The district was for the most part in the ownership of the Duke of Argyll. Of his 54,000 acres, 49,000 were let for sheep farming, while the remaining 3,700 acres were let to 74 crofters. The crofters paid double in rents per acre what the sheep farmers paid; though as one of the commissioners noted, the best land was in the large farms, and the crofters had the worst.

The first crofters' delegate, Allan MacInnes, told of the repeated raising of crofting rents between 1850 and 1876; of how fifteen years earlier half of their hill-land had been taken away by the factor who then added it to his own land; of how they got no compensation for improving their crofts; and of how they had no security of tenure – so that, should they improve their land, they could be evicted and get nothing for their work, which was of course a positive discouragement to crofters trying to improve their position. (These were, of course, precisely the sort of grievances that the commission would attempt to remedy when it came to deliver its report on its findings.)

And in a joint statement from Alexander MacPherson and Malcolm MacLean, the commission heard:

> There is excellent land lying nearby in the hands of the proprietor, that is ready for the plough; and if he does not allow the men who are willing to work it to take a living out of it, and add to the wealth of the nation, it is a good enough reason why we should add our voice to that of the others who have suggested that the government should take it into their own hands, and make sure that it is applied to the purposes for which God created it.

Then the commission moved to the island of Lismore. There, the first crofter delegate to appear asked for immunity from victimisation by the estate on account of the evidence he intended to give. The factor refused such an undertaking – but the people of the island went on to tell their story anyway. Donald MacDonald was one such witness, who described what had happened when some of the island fell into the hands of a southern lawyer by the name of Cheyne:

> When he got the whole place under grass, instead of under crops, then he stocked it all, and the people were all away by that time. Those who had the means to take them to America went there, and some went to the largest towns. The poorest became labourers to him at one shilling a day for the men and sixpence for the women, and they were paid each Saturday by a kind of meal. If they would not go to work for him on these terms he threatened to pull down the houses of the poor people about their ears.

And on Lismore the commission also heard the factor for one of the owners of the island report on his employer's response to a petition for a rent-reduction:

> It seems to me that they have combined to put pressure on me, being apparently encouraged by the sympathy shown to the Skye crofters. I shall distinctly resist any attempt to coerce me. I think the crofter system a bad one. A crofter living on his croft has no right to expect anything but the most abject penury. His condition is one of idleness and, of necessity, poverty.

These three quotations demonstrate, with incomparable simplicity, crofter perception of what had happened in the previous half century or so to the Highland rural economy. They indicate what the crofters' view of landownership was, and what the landlord's position was. A marked undercurrent of class and cultural antipathy might, with justice, also be easily attributed to each side.

Throughout the rest of their tour, the Napier commissioners were to hear much more of the same. In Morvern, for instance, on the shores of Loch Sunart and the sound of Mull, 'where the land is good', the people were removed – down to narrow and small places by the shore. Some of them have a cow's grass, and some of them are simply cottars'. At the meeting in Acharacle, the commissioners heard:

> We cannot get any land to cultivate, although abundance of good land, formerly under cultivation, is going to waste at our very doors. The first evictions which took place in this district happened between fifty and sixty years ago. The second eviction happened between forty and fifty years ago, when the tenants of several townships on the estates of Acharn and Ardtornish received summonses of removal from the proprietors before they sold the estate to Mr Patrick Sellar of Sutherlandshire. There was another

cruel and very harsh eviction which took place in this district about seventeen years ago. There was yet another eviction on the estate of the late Lady Gordon of Drimnin.

The same story – of eviction, of no security of tenure, of marginalisation on the worst of the land, of uncompensated improvement – was to be told across the Highlands to Napier and his commissioners. In Arisaig, for instance, the common people of the district had suffered as the district passed from hand to hand, from Clanranald to Lady Ashburton to Lord Cranstoun to Mr MacKay and finally into the ownership of the Astley-Nicholson family.

The principal speaker at the meeting of the commission in Arisaig was the local minister, Donald MacCallum, who had been born at Craignish within a generation of the clearances and evictions there. His first parish, after Glasgow University, had been in Morvern. The following year, 1884, he would succeed in forming a Morvern branch of the Land Law Reform Association. His story was also one of eviction, overcrowding, rent increases and no security of tenure at all.

MacCallum also spoke of the so-called 'Seventeen Commandments', or estate regulations. He told of how, under these regulations, sons were not allowed to stay on their parents' crofts after the age of 21, and also of how they could not be given any house or land in the district in which to live. He described how crofters had to get estate permission even to dig a drain, and how they were forbidden even to improve a house or croft. 'One does not like to say that these English and other folk have a positive hatred to the native Highlander; but there is something at the bottom of it . . .'

In the islands, too, the commissioners were to hear the same sort of story. In South Uist, one witness reported:

> There is twice or thrice as much waste arable land in South Uist as there is under cultivation. As there is plenty of arable land in the country not used or cultivated, we want as much of it as will support our families comfortably, and that at a reasonable rent, with security that we shall not be removed from our holdings.

In Barra the crofters had the same complaints, and the same demands. Barra (and South Uist) had suffered from some of the worst clearing-landlords in the past – beginning with Colonel Gordon of Cluny buying the bankrupt property from the MacNeils, in 1839, and ending with the death of the inveterate Lady Gordon Cathcart in 1932. (Her will instructed that the island be sold and that the proceeds of the sale be used so that 'an emigration fund could be set up to encourage the tenants to emigrate from the estate to the Dominions, Colonies, and Dependencies'. In 1977 the fund, by then worth £194,000, was wound-up. The proceeds went to Putney's hospital for the incurables and the London leprosy mission.)

Ten years after Lady Cathcart's death, Donald Buchanan of Barra recalled in print his conversations with two of the crofters who gave evidence to the Napier Commission in May 1883. But as Buchanan observed, the tyrannies of the Gordon regime 'carried within their very nature the seeds of revolt'. And as the minutes of the Napier Commission demonstrate, their progress around the Highlands in the summer of 1883 served only to increase the anti-landlord agitation of the previous years. The report volume recorded: 'The land agitation of the Highlands is not likely to pass away without some adjustment of the claims of the occupiers acceptable to the greater number who are not yet possessed with extravagant expectations'.

Hence, agitation was going from strength to strength. From Kilmuir, the Free Church minister, MacPhail, was worried about 'disorder and lawlessness' and added that: 'There have been combinations among the people against payment of rent, and there have been threats posted up at the road side to deter men from settling with the factor on rent day. In the present circumstances of our island population, I feel sure that a little more strain and a little more agitation would soon fan them into a state of wild confusion'.

The farmers on Kilmuir, 'wished to point out' to the committee:

> An organised agitation was got up and prepared for the advent of the commission. Previous to the arrival of the commission, certain parties organised meetings of the tenantry, with a view to agitation and the allegation of grievances. It was almost hopeless at the time for proprietors or loyal tenants to express themselves, popular feeling, under the prevailing influences, being apparently all for revolutionary ideas.

As to the cause of the agitation: 'We believe that it was, in the first instance, due to the course of events in Ireland. It is well known that an Irish agitator was in Skye for the most of last season, as well as various others of similar type'.

From Waternish, Captain Allan MacDonald had the same complaint: 'no doubt all this land cry has been got up by outside agitators and by paid agents'. And from MacLeod of MacLeod the commission heard, 'For some considerable time there have been agitators in every corner of the island, circulating the most communistic doctrines, and endeavouring to set tenants against their landlords'.

From Strath, the Revd Donald MacKinnon complained that, 'As a consequence of the agitation, and unreasonable expectations of a crofters' millennium raised by well-meaning but injudicious counsellors and by disloyal socialistic demagogues, a tendency to exaggeration and misrepresentation has seized the minds of the people'. He added:

> What is the reason of the agitation and discontent which has been
> prevalent? Not a few have been unwillingly concussed by threats of
> personal violence to join in the agitation on account of the
> Utopian and communistic ideas instilled into their minds by
> professional and unprincipled agitators and further, by the way in
> which the disaffected and turbulent were permitted so long with
> impunity to go on setting the law at defiance.

MacKinnon also sent to the commission 'foolish and criminal pamphlets
and cartoons', and referred to 'others, more objectionable still, which I
have not been able to get, freely circulated by an agent of the Land
League'.

Captain Fraser himself made reference to his tenants as the 'tools of
agitators and the victims of political enthusiasts', and said he was 'quite
aware that there are parties who have been endeavouring to promote
discontent on my property. In my opinion the present disturbed state of
things in Skye is very much due to agitation in consequence of late events
in Ireland'.

From Stornoway the Church of Scotland minister, MacIver, thought
that 'it is evident [to] those who know the real state of the Highland
crofters that the commission has not been appointed a day too soon. In
many places matters have been getting into a dangerous state . . .' From
Knock the Free Church minister feared a 'future far more troublesome
than it has yet been, unless some remedy is applied'. The tenants of
Calbost, meanwhile, wrote to Lady Matheson, enclosing a copy of a
petition they had already sent, reminding her that it had not been replied
to, and 'trusting we may not be led to resort reluctantly to such steps as
many of our unfortunate countrymen are forced to adopt'.

Also from Stornoway, the solicitor wrote to the commission noting,
that 'the policy of the estate must be characterised as a tortuous, subtle,
and aggressive one in pursuit of territorial aggrandisement and despotic
power'. And he warned:

> The island most undoutedly is, and has long been, seething in a
> chronic state of discontent. Any vagrant spark might kindle a
> dangerous conflagration. What precise shape this unhealthy feeling
> might ultimately assume no one can predict. The crofters have long
> been, and still are, insulted, trampled on, and terrorised over.

In Orkney, too, the agitation had been having an effect. Lieutenant-
General Traill Burroughs complained, 'They are endeavouring to establish
a reign of lawlessness and terror here.' He referred to attacks made on him
in the *Orkney Herald*, and of a letter, received some days after the

commission had left Kirkwall, 'threatening me with death should I ever remove a tenant from my estate'. Threats of vengeance and destruction to stock, crop and property were being dealt out by 'agitators', he claimed. '[The] more I have inquired into this agitation, the more convinced I am that it is an exotic product which has been fostered into growth by the unscrupulous agency of outside agitators'. And his lady wife, 'whose one idea has always been to do good and make happy all around her', was so hurt at the 'wicked and untruthful statements made by the so-called "delegates" before the Royal Commission in Kirkwall, on behalf, as they said, of all my tenants', that she 'has resolved not to take any trouble on their account any more, and declined to give the childrens' party . . .'

In short, the ruling class in the Highlands was under threat, and something had to be done. According to one Gilchrist, an Alness farmer: 'It is a fact that good men and true, throughout the country, are feeling that something is far wrong, and that something must be done by and for the public safety.'

News of the commission was spreading far beyond the Scottish Highlands. Its doings were watched closely, and without great patience, as the letters of emigrants indicate. In the abrupt words of one, writing from Benbecula Settlement, North-West Territory, 'Tell me if the commissioners did any good.'

It should be evident, then, that the tour of the Napier Commission fuelled the flames of an agitation that was in any case growing apace across the Highlands. Indeed, the commission was a product of popular unrest and combined pressure from two groups: those who were outwith the community and yet of it, like Alexander MacKenzie, along with simple allies from the south of Scotland, like Blackie.

But the powerhouse of agitation was the direct action of the crofters themselves, albeit a direct action that lay within strictly reformist limits. The crofters spurned, for instance, the sort of agrarian terror and clandestine organisation characteristic of Russia at various points throughout the century. And though they could not, perhaps, be expected to know of this history (despite Donald MacKinnon's reference to communistic agitators), it is at least arguable that their external leaders did.

Nor is there any substantial evidence to the effect that some of the brisker examples of Irish land agitation were considered. Although the leadership was not coy in referring to events in Ireland, the references seem to have been intended as no more than verbal provocation. There was no burning of lodges, mansions and castles, for instance – though this would hardly have been difficult in much of the Highlands. Nor was there any attempt at murder of landlords or their agents, either. Above all there was no attempt to form an armed organisation, any truly secret brotherhood, on an Irish, Russian or any other model. (Or at least, no one ever heard of it.)

Had these courses been followed, the stakes would have increased substantially in the Highland land agitation. And they might have led to a conflagration on a Scottish scale. Whether the forces to sustain it existed in the south in sufficient depth is open to question, of course – as is the likely response of the authorities.

In any case, the tactics developed up until Braes and the tour of the Napier Commission had served well enough, certainly to that point. But though there was always a marked current of antipathy to a landlordism that was in essence English, the crofters' struggle was not in any immediate sense an integral part of some wider struggle for national independence. In the absence, on any significant scale, of such a wider controlling ideological vision, the tactics developed by the time of Braes were strictly reformist. But they had served well enough; and as the agitation continued to grow, they would continue to serve the movement well enough too.

SIX

THE LAND LEAGUE GROWS

'The movement is carried on with almost incredible enthusiasm and determination. Meetings are being held at regular intervals and speeches delivered by crofters that would do credit to a Member of Parliament.'

⌇⌇⌇

The 1880s opened, on a European scale, with a magnificent flourish in the direction of posterity: peace had been declared in the Balkans. An orgy of self-congratulation followed the Congress of Berlin which systematised this great Peace with Honour, as the great powers were pleased to chorus. In 1875 the province of Herzegovina had risen in rebellion against its Turkish (and Muslim) masters. Some of its Slavonic (and Christian) neighbours in the Turkish empire also rose, along with the people of independent Serbia. The Turks set out to crush the rebellion; the British prepared to expel the Turks 'bag and baggage' from their Bulgarian territories; and the Russians declared war and invaded Turkey. Britain sent a fleet of battleships to the Dardanelles and prepared to invade too. Bismarck, however, summoned the powers to Berlin in 1878. At that congress it was decided that Macedonia would remain Turkish; Serbia and Montenegro would be independent states; and Bosnia and Herzegovina would be administered by Austria, though remaining nominally Turkish possessions. The Balkans, in short, had been sliced up and handed out. A European war, sparked by conflict in the region, had been avoided, at least for the time being. And the great powers were able to continue the unfettered indulgence of their taste for imperial expansion. Nobody mentioned a place called Kosovo.

In Britain, public affairs were characterised by the alternation of Liberal and Conservative governments, agricultural (and industrial) depression, social change, continuing agitation in Ireland, and the slow but sure development of a labour movement independent of the two great parties. Gladstone had led a Liberal administration from 1868 till 1874; Disraeli a Conservative, from then until 1880 (he died a year later); and Gladstone again, from 1880 to 1885. In these years, competition from the products of colonial farmers – wheat, meat and wool – drove domestic agriculture into a depression from which it was never to recover. In consequence the landed classes began to be displaced from the pre-eminence which they had for so long enjoyed in the realms of national affairs.

With a shorter-term depression in manufacturing industry also under way, these years saw the growth of state intervention in the economic and social life of Britain. The Climbing Boys' Act of 1875 modified somewhat the atrocious conditions endured by the soot-encrusted apprentices of master chimney-sweeps. The Artisans' Dwelling Act of the same year gave local authorities the power to demolish urban slums and build new workers' houses in their place. (Urban artisans had had the vote since the second Reform Act of eight years earlier.) In 1875, too, Samuel Plimsoll's famous outburst in the House of Commons finally inclined the government to move against murderous shipowners (though no one yet thought it proper to concern themselves with the fearsome conditions of workhouse lads effectively traded as slaves to the deep-sea fishing industry).

In Ireland, which had been governed directly from Westminster since the abolition of its Dublin parliament two years after the great rebellion of 1798, agitation for independence was endless. Much of it centred on the land question. In 1870 Gladstone's first Land Act made some provision in the direction of tenants' interests. Among other things, it allowed the government to lend money to a tenant to buy his holding if the landlord was prepared to sell it. But the landlords were not so willing, and the tenants were therefore unable to buy. A second Land Act followed in 1881, two years after Michael Davitt had formed his Land League and introduced the concept of boycotting. The legislation was characterised by the famous 'Three Fs': fair rent set by a land court; fixity of tenure for any tenant who paid his fair rent; and free sale of land, rather than obligatory sale to the existing landlord. None of this affected in the slightest the Irish demand for independence, but its significance can scarcely have escaped the agitators for land-reform in the Highlands.

Nor can they have overlooked developments relating to the united organisation of workers and to the lawful rights of combination in trades unions of these workers. From early in the century, combined organisation had been strictly illegal. The Gag Act criminalised the sort of oath of allegiance characteristic of membership of such an organisation. And legislation also disallowed the combination of workers with a view to collectively forcing employers to increase wages or shorten hours of work.

But in 1871, Gladstone – following the report of a Royal Commission – gave some legal recognition to trades unions. He forbade any sort of picketing, however. Four years later Disraeli made picketing, as long as it was non-violent, lawful; and in 1876 he effectively legalised mass strike action, opening the way to a growth of trades unions that had never before been possible. This also led to a great growth in the early stages of a labour movement independent of the established parties. As *Reynold's Newspaper* declared in 1875:

> The working classes did very much for Mr Gladstone in the election of 1868, and what had been their reward? Mr Gladstone made use of his great majority to rule for the benefit of the middle class and to conserve the interests of the higher classes. What the order of labour should do is to get their own candidates ready – their own men, men of their own order – who will keep clear of the intrigues of both parties.

Central to this developing movement was the land question. Debate relating to land-reform, whether in the shape of the taxation of land values or even public ownership of the land, had been common currency among working- and middle-class radicals since the days of the Chartists in the 1840s. The Land and Labour League had been formed in 1869. A year later, the Land Tenure Reform Association had been established, to urge that the 'unearned increase of the land' should properly be the possession of society as a whole. Nine years after that, the publication of the American Henry George's *Progress and Poverty* further stimulated the debate. The book sold in huge numbers – around 100,000 copies – and George was arrested when he subsequently toured Ireland to promote its central thesis that all taxation should be abolished except a tax on the rental income of land. A year later the Democratic Federation was formed, advocating land nationalisation. Four years later still, with the affiliation of the Scottish Land and Labour League and the Labour Emancipation League, the federation took the name by which it was henceforth known: the Social Democratic Federation. And then, of course, there was the Highland Land Law Reform Association.

The Highlands, meantime, had witnessed the development of an extensive steamer service, linking the western mainland coast and the inner and outer Hebrides to each other and to Glasgow. The railway, too, connected many parts of the mainland by the end of the century. The line from London via Edinburgh and Perth had made its way by Inverness to Invergordon in 1863. By 1870 Dingwall was linked to Strome Ferry, with its steamer connections onward to Skye. Four years later, there was a link north to Wick and Thurso. And shortly after the turn of the century, the line from Glasgow to Fort William had been extended to Mallaig. Links with the wider world were also serviced on a seasonal basis, whether in the form of migration in the wake of the herring fisheries, or in the form of agricultural and domestic service in the southern counties and towns of Scotland.

By the early 1880s, therefore, the common people of the Highlands could draw on an extensive tradition of land agitation; a shorter tradition of victory in this agitation; a national audience in the form of Lord Napier's commission into their grievances; an extensive network of supporters in the developing labour movement in the southern cities; and a leadership that united agitators on the ground (MacPherson of Glendale) with the intelligentsia (Blackie of Edinburgh University) and parliamentarians (Fraser-MacIntosh). They could also draw on the support of much, if not all, of the general press in the south.

The importance of this support was not overlooked. Later in the decade, for instance, a protestor 'threatened to baptise' a reporter with a basin of slops. 'Someone else restrained her saying they would be glad to see reporters among them at any time.' Nor should the close links between some of the local agitators and the sympathetic press be overlooked either. In one trial later in the decade, it became apparent that a key witness worked as a stringer for *The Scotsman*, the *Glasgow Herald*, the *Inverness Courier* and the *Press Association*. (In the spring of the following year this same witness launched the short-lived *Lewisman* – the first-ever paper in the Western Isles.) During the same trial, it became clear that the Land League leader Donald MacRae also reported on a regular basis for the *Scottish Leader* and the *North British Daily Mail*.

Important above all, however, was the agitational and organisational role of John Murdoch's *Highlander* and Alexander Mackenzie's *Celtic Magazine*.

From the very first issue, Murdoch's paper had demonstrated a clear vision of the Highlands and the proper place of the Highlands in a progressive Scotland. The themes covered by *The Highlander* included the importance of Gaelic (to which it gave a considerable amount of space), affairs in parliament and the game laws; but above all, the land laws and the relations between crofter and landlord. The second edition carried a long and strong editorial on evictions. Within weeks every issue was carrying articles on the game laws, letters against deer-forests and editorials on the land question. The paper covered the Clearances at length, and from the beginning gave room to Blackie on the land question; while throughout its first year a torrent of articles, editorials and letters found space on these same central themes. One typical issue, for example, carried substantial pieces on resistance to evictions on Tiree and on conditions for crofters inside a deer-forest, along with scrutiny of the machinations of titled Highland landlords in the House of Lords.

Further pieces reported on the Gaelic bards and the Clearances, evictions on Mull and Iona, and – of course – the victorious dispute on Bernera, off the west side of Lewis. Events on Skye were also covered, between long and combative editorials on the pressing need for land-reform, and trenchant criticism of the prevailing legal relations between landlords and their crofting tenants. The mid-1870s also saw the first of many highly critical articles on the state of affairs on the Gordon estates in South Uist. The conduct of Charles Fraser-MacIntosh in parliament and elsewhere was carefully and approvingly reported, as were the doings of Blackie and any others who chose to involve themselves in, or comment on, the land question.

Through the course of 1876, a full decade before the passage of any legislation in favour of the crofters, Murdoch kept up his agitation on the land question, and published detailed reports of Blackie's efforts to establish a chair of Celtic at Edinburgh University. Polemic, meantime, was engaged in every quarter. And no quarter was shown: in one issue the pro-landlord *Scotsman* was briskly dismissed as a paper characterised by its 'notorious, crawling and unscrupulous' nature. (Oddly enough, the marriage of Charles Fraser-MacIntosh was also covered: which may – or may not – have occasioned some editorial anguish over priorities and principles.)

There were 'local notes' too, to this day the staple of many a local newspaper; and detailed reports of the doings of the numerous Highland societies at home and abroad. These included the likes of the Glasgow Gaelic Association, the San Francisco Caledonian Club, Manchester Camanachd Club, the Sons of Scotland in Toronto, the Greenock Highland Society, and of course the Gaelic Society of Inverness.

(The original members of the Federation of Celtic Societies included: the Gaelic Society of London; the Gaelic Society of Inverness; Birmingham Highland Society; Aberdeen Gaelic Society; Edinburgh University Celtic Society; Edinburgh Sutherland Society; Greenock Highland Society; Greenock Ossianic Club; Tobermory Gaelic Society; and a number of Glasgow-based district societies, including those of Skye, Islay, Sutherland, Cowal, Lewis, Mull and Ardnamurchan. The Liverpool Highland Association was also a member.)

Murdoch's energy appears never to have slackened, nor his firmness of purpose. *The Highlander*, he editorialised, was an 'irresistible power for good in the land'. And though the simultaneous possession of talent and ambition is not, in the newspaper editor, as common as is sometimes supposed, Murdoch had talent and selfless ambition in abundance. For instance, a month after increasing the number of pages by a third and moving from tabloid to broadsheet format, he announced with an authority that rings strangely down the years: 'There is no good reason why *The Highlander* should not have the largest circulation of any newspaper in Scotland.'

Above all, perhaps, Murdoch had an instinctive understanding of the dynamics of political campaigning. As early as January, 1878, *The Highlander* could report with a prophetic resonance that the Greenock Highland Society was calling for a Royal Commission into the condition of crofters in the Highlands: a demand that, at the time, must have seemed absurd.

But the same stray call would of course harden over time into the central demand of the crofters' movement, taken up and promoted strongly by MacKenzie in his *Celtic Magazine* into the 1880s.

In early 1882, for instance, he published, as a special broadsheet-format supplement, a report on the Federation of Celtic Societies' annual meeting, which was held at Perth. Coverage of the Edinburgh Sutherland Association followed, as well as a short piece by John MacKay on the Sutherland evictions; a mention of the Gaelic census in Scotland; a comment on the Skye crofters and the press; and a long piece on social unrest in that island.

Just a month later the magazine was covering the Battle of the Braes, and the agitation for which both papers had so long campaigned was under way – with an energy, perhaps, that neither Murdoch nor MacKenzie could have hoped for just a few years earlier. And within another year Napier's commission had arrived in Braes to open its work, precisely as the Greenock Highland Society had demanded five years earlier.

Throughout the course of the commission's tour, MacKenzie kept up a relentless barrage of propaganda. In May, the *Celtic Magazine* covered the gaoling in Edinburgh of three Glendale crofters. It quoted the *Greenock Telegraph*:

> The Judges are obliged to act upon statutes framed by a class in their own interests. Nobody thinks any the worse of the poor men who are now in prison. They were loudly cheered as they left the dock. Their families will be well seen to – in spite of *The Scotsman*'s sneers at their friends – while they remain in custody; and they will be certain to get a warm welcome from the public when the day of liberation arrives.

MacKenzie himself had visited the three men in the city's Calton Gaol and found them in good spirits. He reported that 'they were much delighted at the enlivenment of their evenings by frequently hearing the bagpipes in the neighbourhood playing familiar airs'. This was, added MacKenzie with admirable panache, 'an arrangement by their Edinburgh friends of a remarkably considerate and delicate nature'. It was against this background, then, and with this sort of encouragement, that the land agitation flourished across the Highlands in the early 1880s.

When the Glendale men gaoled in Edinburgh for breach of interdict were freed, they were met by a crowd of 1,000 supporters along with two pipers. That same evening John MacPherson travelled, via Glasgow, north by train for Strome Ferry and thence by steamer to Portree, in the cause of getting to Glendale in time to give evidence before the Napier Commission. Off Braes, on the way into Portree, he could see bonfires blazing and flags flying. At the pier the steamer carrying him was met by a large crowd of supporters. MacPherson later told them that he believed 'the imprisonment of the Glendale crofters had done more to remove landlord tyranny and oppression from Skye than anything which had happened during the present century'.

Later that month the Highland Land Law Reform Association (HLLRA) branch in Inverness thanked the General Assembly of the Free Church for its (progressive) views on the crofters' cause. And in London a Land Law Reform Association meeting, with Blackie and D.H. MacFarlane on the platform, passed resolutions 'regretting that no representative of the crofters had been placed on the commission, and declaring that no alteration of the Land Laws would give permanent satisfaction which did not give the Highlanders a permanent footing on the soil'.

Meanwhile *The Scotsman* was claiming manipulation of the commission by outside agitators. It was a claim strongly denied by MacKenzie, who nevertheless turned it to advantage in terms of publicity, for which he clearly had a significant talent. Murdoch, too, was accused by *The Scotsman* of complicity in Irish politics and of having taken Irish money to buy dynamite. Though he denied it the paper, as he later confided to his diary, 'never withdrew its accusations, nor in any way made amends for its foul attack on me'.

None of this, however, appeared to dissuade crofters from giving such evidence as they chose before the commission – though in at least one case the landlord in question formally and publicly refused to undertake not to victimise witnesses for what they might say. MacKenzie noted: 'Whatever may be the outcome of its labours the commission has already done unspeakable good, by exposing the evils of Highland estate management to the world.' And a few months later he would add, in a notice carried by the hundredth edition of the *Celtic Magazine* (to the effect that he would shortly begin publication of the *Scottish Highlander*): 'The real work of those who demand and will insist upon a change in the present Land Laws will only begin in earnest when the nature of the report is known.'

Meanwhile, fired in part by the energising effect on communal consciousness of the evidence to the commission, the agitation was going from strength to strength – as the landlords and authorities had feared. There was trouble in Lewis, with the Melbost crofters taking over Lady Matheson's links and driving away her tenant-farmer's sheep. When the factor returned the creatures, they were again driven off; and her ladyship turned to the Court of Session for action against thirty-three of the men said to have been involved.

In the Uists there was trouble too. From Lochboisdale it was reported that meetings were being widely held and widely attended, that flags were flying in nearly every township, and that at Stoneybridge the people were threatening to seize land for cultivation. In Skye, also, the attitude of 'the crofters in their opposition to all constituted authority' was 'as determined and defiant as during the last outbreak', according to one report.

At Leckmelm, in defiance of a Court of Session order, crofters invaded the property by boats and sailed them away loaded with seaweed. Legal proceedings were at once initiated. From Tiree came this report:

> The land question forms the chief topic of discussion on the island at the present time. While opinions differ as to the ultimate results of the agitation, it is generally entertained that the crofters now mean business. On Saturday night a considerable number marched in a body to Island House to ascertain of the factor whether a certain one of their number had paid his rent lately. Our sheriff-officer stands in actual danger of bodily harm should he attempt the performance of his duty. The crofters threaten to take forcible possession of Ben Hynish and Ben Hough as grazing grounds.

Police reports from across the Highlands indicated the same depth of popular feeling.

On Skye, according to the chief constable, meetings had been held at Broadford, Waternish and Fairy Bridge in one week alone. In Broadford, John MacPherson addressed sixty crofters and announced that 'the time had now arrived' when the crofters 'should unite together and agitate their cause for freedom and more land, and by doing so they would be sure to succeed'. At that meeting alone, fifty crofters joined the Land League. And three days later the police constable in Waternish was reporting that:

> A meeting of the HLLRA was held by the Revd Donald MacCallum, Waternish, within the Established Church, Waternish, on Friday. The meeting was attended by about thirty of the crofters of Waternish; but none was admitted to the meeting except those who became members of the association. There is a report current here today that a mass meeting of the crofters of the parishes of Duirinish, Bracadale, and Snizort is to be held at Fairy Bridge on Tuesday.

Four days later John MacPherson addressed a Land League meeting at Flashadder. That same afternoon he and MacCallum had spoken to 800 men who had gathered at Fairy Bridge, from the districts of Edinbane, Waternish, Dunvegan, Glendale and Bracadale.

By then League membership was growing rapidly on Skye. MacPherson returned via Glasgow – where he addressed, in Queen Street Station from his carriage window, a crowd of well-wishers, in Gaelic – and at once plunged into agitation. In August he spoke to 2,000 Highlanders at Fraserburgh for the summer fishing. By that December, as president of what the authorities saw as a 'Fenian fraternity', the Glendale branch of the League, he was opening its first meeting in the local school-house. In the new year, fifty men of Dunvegan met to form their own branch. The *Oban Times* reported in February that 'branch societies of this new mode of agitating crofters' grievances are now in full swing'.

That same month the Land Law Reform Association of London issued, in English and Gaelic, an appeal to the public and the crofters. It urged the support of the former for land-reform. To the latter, its advice was:

> Your first duty now is to form, as soon as possible, Associations, through which you could speak and act and make your grievances known. In forming a district association, you might first convene a public meeting to discuss your affairs, resolve that an Association be formed, and appoint a provisional secretary and small committee. Then, the townships included in the district might each, under the direction of the committee choose representatives, and these representatives, at a convenient time and place, might meet to frame a constitution and elect officer-bearers. An organisation embracing the whole Highlands should be aimed at.

The *Oban Times* reported a Glasgow meeting of the Scottish Land Restoration League, at which 'thousands were unable to obtain admission', and covered the formation of branches of the League throughout Mull. It also reported the London 'headquarters' demanding 'such changes in the Land Laws as will secure fair rents, durability of tenure, and compensation for improvements, with such an apportionment of the land as will promote the welfare of the people'.

In April, the Stenscholl branch of the League met at a township in the possession of a farmer described as being 'a land shark of no small voracity'. According to Norman Stewart of Valtos it was necessary to agitate more loudly and more unitedly still. At this meeting, 'all the speeches were enthusiastically cheered throughout', while there were 'interruptions of a very uncomplimentary nature about the lairds, factors, and tacksmen. This is a fair specimen of what is going on in almost every township in the West'.

A month later a speaker from the Scottish Land Restoration League was in Skye, with arrangements made for him to speak at Dunvegan, Waternish, Glendale, Valtos, Uig, Portree and Braes. As the *Oban Times* reported, 'The movement is carried on with almost incredible enthusiasm and determination. Meetings are being held at regular intervals, and speeches delivered by crofters that would do credit to a Member of Parliament.' There were further reports of agitation across the Highlands, from Barra, Strath in Skye, Loch Eport, Loch Alsh, from Lewis, and across the mainland. In June the HLLRA of London heard its secretary report that it now had 29 branches with 5,000 members; while a month later the Edinburgh association was preparing to amalgamate its branches with London.

By then, police reports in Inverness-shire were recording a Land League meeting at Fort William – 'which meeting was addressed by a man named John MacDonald, native of Uig, Isle of Skye, the property of Fraser of Kilmuir . . . [who] spoke in strong terms against the existing land laws'. A month later they were noting Professor Blackie's presence on Skye, in the company of Donald MacFarlane. That evening they both spoke at a meeting in Portree. Blackie strongly advised the people 'to keep up the agitation as hot as possible, and not to fear landlord or factor, and that he himself would not die until he would see the right of the poor established and the landlords done away with'.

And a month later, John MacPherson, MacCallum and the secretary of the London HLLRA were touring Skye, along with delegates from Uist. At Skeabost they addressed a meeting of 150 crofters (and one police agent suitably disguised as per the Procurator Fiscal's suggestion). MacCallum offered, as usual, a benedicition on the gathering, after which the speakers addressed the crofters in Gaelic. MacCallum thereafter retired to an 'unknown place' (in the words of, and to the chagrin, or relief, of the police spy) for a private meeting with local crofters' leaders.

In Argyll too, the agitation grew throughout the spring and summer of 1884. John MacPherson spent a month there, helping to form branches of the League at Easdale, Salen, Tobermory, Bunessan, Creich, Iona, Tiree, Lismore, Lochaline, Strontian, Ardnamurchan, Taynuilt and Oban. At the Easdale meeting 400 people turned out to hear him. At Lochaline, 100 were present, 'which may be considered a large turnout for such a sparsely populated district'. On Luing 'the whole audience showed their readiness to join the association'. In Salen 'almost every man present agreed to become a member'. And on Lismore, 'on a motion being put to the meeting for a show of hands on the side of the HLLRA, all hands were up in an instant'.

From Barra it was reported that 'the advent of Mr MacFarlane and Professor Blackie is held in high esteem', while in Shetland hundreds of fishermen met to demand land-reform, 'many of whom are crofters from Skye, Lewis, Caithness, Sutherland, and Argyll, presently engaged in the herring fishing here'. On Iona 'most of the householders' were members; 'and those who had not previously joined intimated their intentions of doing so at once, so that these districts may be considered as rapidly ripening for the great struggle'. At Strontian 'a large proportion of those present enrolled'. At Lochaline the motion to form a branch was accepted unanimously. And in Kilchoan, while a large meeting heard MacPherson, there were repeated requests that he return to the district in the near future.

In the spring of 1884, the Napier Commission reported. In essence, it proposed to institutionalise larger-scale crofting townships operated on a communal basis, and to abolish smaller-scale crofts under half a dozen acres. Whatever the merits of the details of the report, it implicitly conceded the case for a thoroughgoing reform of the land system in the Highlands. Thus the government, willingly or otherwise, confronted the prospect of having to legislate, in some way or another, on the crofters' grievances; while at the beginning of September, the HLLRA met at Dingwall in national conference.

By any standards it was an impressive enough gathering. But by the standards of hitherto-existing class relations in the Highlands, until so recently unchallenged on anything other than a local scale, it was surely an extraordinary gathering. Branches and associations came together on a national basis: from the county associations of Ross-shire, Inverness-shire, Argyll and Sutherland, as well as from Edinburgh and London. Along with representatives from the Scottish Farmers' Alliance and the Scottish Land Restoration League, there were crofters' delegates from Lewis, Halladale, Strathy, Forres, Grantown, Lochalsh, Skye (of the island's thirteen delegates, three came from Kilmuir), Culbokie, Resolis, Evanton, Inverness, Strathpeffer, Gairloch, Kintail, both Uists, and Caithness.

Individuals in attendance read like a roll-call of those who had been active in the agitation on a national scale – Blackie, Fraser-MacIntosh, Donald MacCallum, Alexander MacKenzie, John MacPherson, Donald MacFarlane, Michael Buchanan of Barra. And there were others who had also played a role outwith the Highlands, or who shortly would do so in parliament – Charles Cameron MP, Dr Clark, next constituency candidate for Caithness, Dr MacDonald, who had recently stood for the crofters' cause in a Ross-shire by-election, Donald Murray of the London HLLRA, John MacKay of Hereford, Dugald Cowan of the Edinburgh HLLRA, and Angus Sutherland of Glasgow.

The conference rejected the proposals of the Napier Commission, demanded the compulsory enlargement of crofters' holdings, and called for the law to be changed in the favour of crofters with regard to deer-forests and the game laws. It was agreed to establish a newspaper for the movement; and above all, it was decided to run candidates for parliament.

Ten years on from the Bernera riot, the crofters' movement had made extraordinary advances – to the hostility of the pro-landlord press. *The Times*, for instance, 'could only characterise the whole proceeding as a piece of pernicious nonsense', and 'could anticipate nothing but mischief from a policy of public agitation'.

Despite the strictures of *The Times*, however, the Highlands were on the brink of a period of agitation fiercer than anything that had gone before. As MacKenzie himself had written just two years earlier, in the circular of the Inverness branch of the HLLRA: 'All that is wanted to make it a real power for good in the land is that those who believe in its object should at once enrol themselves among its members.' And by the autumn of 1884 membership was widespread in the crofting counties, while in Skye the rent-strike weapon was increasingly popular.

The report of a government agent, McNeill, sent north to report later in the decade, is eloquent witness to the state of agitation in the Highlands in these years. From Skye, for instance, he would record that:

> The teachings of the Land League seem to have penetrated to every district. It is probable that every man of the crofter and cottar classes, with many merchants and artisans besides, is an enrolled member. Open dissentients are now rare, and even those who still profess independence are secretly anticipating a future when the landlords and tacksmen shall have disappeared from the island.

The story was the same on Harris, in the Uists and Barra:

> The individuals occupied in arousing agitation are the same whose names occur so frequently on the other side of the Minch. The doctrines preached by these persons are all but universally accepted in Barra. As to the other islands the mass of the population continue fully in sympathy with the movement. The truth I believe to be is that Land Leagueing is as popular in Harris and North Uist as in Barra, but that the latter island enjoys the services of a specially active local secretary. Thus the population of South Uist are probably prepared for mischief when opportunity occurs, as also those of Benbecula.

From Lewis, McNeill's secret report was particularly alarming. He had conferred, he reported, with the factor for Lady Matheson, but had otherwise concealed from everyone the purpose of his visit to the island, on the factor's advice. The facts disclosed by the factor were so important that he could not delay in forwarding them:

> All the cottars, squatters, and young men in Lewis, especially those belonging to the Naval Reserve, are members of the League. The first emissaries who visited the district seem to have been Messrs Murdoch (late of *The Highlander*) and MacKenzie (of the *Celtic Magazine*). The next public meeting was held in October 1884, when Messrs MacIver, MacCallum (Waternish), MacPherson (Glendale) and several local agitators were present. Outrages have been numerous. I am led to the conclusion that it is the deliberate intention of the people to deprive Lady Matheson of the whole revenue hitherto derived from sporting rents.

On the mainland and in the inner islands McNeill thought the movement less numerous than in the Hebrides. But still it 'appears to have attained a firm hold of the people in Sutherlandshire, Ardnamurchan, Tiree and some parts of Mull'. There seemed, he said, to have been 'hardly a parish on the coast which was not visited by the same active emissaries whose names so frequently occur in the islands, viz, Messrs MacCallum, MacKenzie and Murdoch, and John MacPherson'.

On Mull, and in the general area, the movement was especially active on Tiree, the Ross of Mull, and Iona, with influential branches at Salen and Dervaig. In Ardnamurchan, 'the whole population belongs and forms one of the centres of its greatest activity'. In McNeill's view, this was because Donald MacCallum's brother was minister at Strontian.

And in Arisaig, where the bulk of the crofters' evidence to the Napier Commission had largely been given by Donald MacCallum, the head stalker explained that the numbers of members probably did not exceed fifty in Arisaig and Morar. 'But the great bulk of the population were in sympathy. The first agitators here were the Revd Donald MacCallum (now of Waternish) and Mr Aeneas MacDonnell of Morar. Mr Murdoch was also here, and Mr Alexander MacKenzie of Inverness'. According to the Arisaig doctor, too, 'it may be said that every man of the crofter and cottar class is a Land Leaguer, either actually a member, or in sympathy with the league. The Revd Donald MacCallum (now of Waternish, then a minister here) was the first agent of the League. Mr Murdoch was also here.' But, with the exception of the *Oban Times*, no incendiary literature was circulated: 'There was no need of coercion, as the sympathy was general.'

Northwards too, along the western seaboard, McNeill found the same conditions prevailing. In Lochbroom the sub-factor at Ullapool for the Duchess of Sutherland reported that, the people 'are thoroughly imbued' with the principles of the League and 'believe that the land should (and will) be distributed among them. In short they think that the land is justly theirs and that rent is an unjust action. Extreme newspapers are also circulated in the district'.

From Ullapool, the local police sergeant claimed that 'the whole population is in sympathy' with the Land League. And from Inverewe, strong support for the agitation was reported in the district of Gairloch and Gruinard Bay. In Gairloch:

> The League has a strong hold on the people here, especially of the younger people, and numbers probably 150 enrolled members, with a regular organisation, a chairman, and a secretary. Mr Alexander MacKenzie was the first to bring Land League teaching here, and being a native of the parish, he was listened to. John MacPherson (Glendale) also addressed a meeting, and advised no rent.

From Applecross, the minister told McNeill: 'There is a regular Land League organisation, with president and secretary. There was, and is, a good deal of sympathy with Land League doctrines.' From Loch Carron it was reported that 'practically the whole crofter and cottar population are Land Leaguers. The active members are mostly the young men.' At Lochinver McNeill spoke to the wife of the local Free Church minister. 'The League has complete hold of the people in Sutherlandshire, and she knows hardly any exception among her neighbours.' Her husband believed that 'the League has great hold of the people', while extreme views were increasingly being expressed at its meetings. The police constable from Lochinver also reported: 'The Land League is universally favoured by crofters and cottars throughout the country. There is a considerable circulation of Land League literature, both newspapers and leaflets, which impress on the people they have a right to the land.'

And in the closing months of 1884, the people of the Highlands thus showed signs of simply taking possession of the land they believed to be their land, by right. Scarcely had the Dingwall conference of the League ended, but the crofters in South Uist were in open conflict with Lady Gordon Cathcart. At Grogary one of her ladyship's fields was seized forcibly by the crofters. Gordon's cattle were driven away, and crofters' stock replaced them. Furthermore, 'on Saturday an attempt was made to waylay Mr MacLennan, the factor on the estate, and he only escaped injury by friendly warning'; while just a week later, the local press was reporting a 'most malicious outrage' in South Uist.

Within a week of the Dingwall conference, Donald MacFarlane had arrived on Tiree, and at Baugh he convened a 'monster meeting' of crofters. He was welcomed ashore by Neil MacNeill, delegate of the crofters from the east of the island, who would also welcome John MacPherson, touring with MacFarlane. And a week later feeling was running high in the outer islands, with MacCallum and John MacPherson touring Benbecula, South Uist and Barra; at Stoneybridge they were met by pipers and flag-waving supporters. A growing number of minor cases of arson, under cover of darkness, was reported as well.

By the end of the month, the *Oban Telegraph* could report that:

> In Skye, the centres of agitation are at Glendale, in the parish of Duirinish, and Eastside in Kilmuir. To all appearances the agitation is becoming intensified, and extending; and deeds have been done with impunity for some time back which would not be tolerated for a day in other parts of the country, deeds of malice and lawlessness. Since so many officers of the law have been thrashed and beaten in these districts with impunity, no hope of enforcing legal action can be seriously entertained and it is becoming proverbial that 'there is no law in Skye'.

And from South Uist the same report noted, 'Many acts of shameful mischief have recently been committed. The outlook now is most discouraging.'

From Mull, by the end of September, the League was reported to be operating with vigour at Salen and other centres of population. It had created 'an amount of interest and excitement on the land question' which was unknown before. 'Fuel has undoubtedly been heaped upon a smouldering fire, and if proper remedies are not forthcoming, it will burst forth with volcanic fierceness over the length and breadth of the Highlands.'

In October, men in South Uist expropriated yet another of Lady Gordon's fields. In Kilmuir the crofters resolved to withhold payment of rent, and to subscribe to a legal fund for their defence in the event of proceedings being taken against them. Unanimously, it was also agreed to boycott the factor; and it was made known that any crofter who chose not to support the League in the matter could expect the destruction of his property.

From Lewis, meanwhile, came the news that 'the land agitation has reached a very acute and critical stage'. In the parish of Uig the crofters of practically every township were on rent-strike, and though the factor had toured for a week attempting to collect rent, he had returned home without a penny. By mid-October land-seizure was well advanced in Uig, with the crofters having possession of the holdings of large farmers, and refusing even to meet the authorities and discuss the seizures. As the *Oban Telegraph* reported, 'Respect for law and order has for some time past been at a discount in the island. But the open and avowed renunciation of all authority and government which now prevails is only of recent date.'

In South Uist too, the land question, was 'fast becoming the all-absorbing one here. The agitation seems to be spreading rapidly, and is taking shape in a very determined way.' And from Skye: 'In all probability the land agitation in this island may well soon reach its climax. In the two most disaffected districts, matters are surely coming to a crisis.'

In Glendale, by mid-October, some of the men interdicted two years earlier had again taken over landlords' land. All crofters, it was reported, had been instructed to put their stock on the field. Those who did not were subject to the attentions of a League delegation. So too were any who did not attend League meetings. The miller of Kilmuir, having defaulted on a League meeting, found his corn stacks scattered to the wind; while from throughout the island, reports indicated that the land-seizing phase of the agitation was only just getting into its stride.

By the end of October, the sixty-strong Glenelg branch of the League was 'prospering greatly' and meeting weekly. In Barra the people were 'extremely interested' in the question of land-reform: 'Wherever two or three are gathered together, one may safely wager that the land is the subject of conversation.' At the beginning of November, the new style of agitation was spreading like wildfire on Skye:

> Deeds of lawlessness such as seizing proprietors' land, placing stock on the same, intimidating shepherds from interfering with

such stock, scattering the corn-stacks, and burning peat-stacks of crofters who do not join the land association, and assault upon such, are becoming altogether too frequent to be put up with much longer. In Glendale, crofters have placed stock on the farms of Waterstein and Scor, and propose ploughing old arable lands in the proprietors' hands, all of them to sow a given quantity of seed in the same, first spring, and divide the produce in the following autumn. Wilder schemes are discussed, and deeds that would shock the people some ten years ago are now coolly proposed.

And in Lewis, by November, 400 crofters in Uig were more firmly than ever on rent-strike; and lands had been seized from the estate and from the large farmers. On one occasion the farmer attempted to put stock on some of the occupied land. Over a hundred men removed him and his stock, with threats of violence should he persist. In Lochs there was also a rent-strike in progress, and so well-organised was the agitation that those who privately claimed a willingness to pay did not dare do so, for fear of retribution.

By the middle of that same month, all non-croft grazing land in Uig had been occupied. In Lochs, no-rent proclamations had been issued from the townships of Crossbost, Raernish, Luerbost, Calbost, Marvig, Limervaig and Gravir. In Gravir one man was declared outcast and boycotted, for having paid his rent. During the second week of the month the boundary dyke between the farm of Orinsay and the townships of Gravir and Limervaig was destroyed by bands of men.

At least on the face of it, therefore, by the autumn of 1884 the Highlands were on the brink of something approaching open insurrection. For the government and authorities in general, some sort of action was a matter of increasing urgency. And as they delayed, so the agitation continued to grow.

SEVEΠ

CROFTERS' PARTY, CROFTERS' ACT

'We must not rest satisfied until every inch of productive land in the Highlands is placed at the disposal of those who are able and willing to till it. Until this is assured, the people must resolve to maintain the most persistent and determined agitation.'

From 1884 the efforts of the crofters themselves on the one hand, and their external allies on the other, began to produce results that could scarcely have been dreamt of a matter of years earlier. The press continued to play the role pioneered by Murdoch's *Highlander* and Mackenzie's *Celtic Magazine*. The churches, at least, offered no consolation to the social forces urging a return to the economic relations that had hitherto pertained. The agitation on the ground was more determined than ever. And in the southern towns the Gaelic societies with their progressive allies retained their place as an urban focus of publicity for the cause of the Highland crofters.

Thus the two years from the autumn of 1884 to the passage of the Crofters' Act in the summer of 1886 were the high point of the Crofters' War – as it has justly been called – when agitation and organisation came together in an unprecedented way to win for the crofter cause very considerable attention in the press, parliament and public life in general.

At the beginning of November, Fraser-MacIntosh was challenging the Home Secretary in the House of Commons as to whether he would make available police–government communications with regard to the situation in Skye. Harcourt stalled, saying that such communications were not complete, but that when they were he would 'have no objection to lay them on the Table of the House'. And five days later MPs again clashed with Harcourt over developments in the Highlands. One asked about Kilmuir and the interests of its proprietor, Fraser, adding that the demands of the crofters, 'are nothing more than a fair-rent, and the restoration of the sheep land of which they were deprived many years ago'. Had the government, he asked, considered the 'expediency of creating a public tribunal to fix the rents to be paid by tenants in the exceptional conditions of crofters in the Highlands and Islands'? Was the government considering the report of the Napier Commission with a view to acting on it? And, finally, would the government therefore be bringing legislation on the crofter question at the opening of the next session of parliament?

Harcourt thought that there was no justification for the defiance of the law and the breach of the peace which had 'unhappily occurred at Skye'. But he added, 'The government will feel it to be their duty to take action at the earliest possible time, so far as they can, upon the report of the Royal Commission.' Harcourt also clashed with MacFarlane in the same sitting over 'petty outrages in Skye'.

The matter of the crofters also came up later that same month in the House of Lords. The attack there on their cause was led by the Duke of Argyll, a leading apologist for the landlords. His views on the matter were simple. Emigration (though not for the landlord class) was the answer:

> I am in favour of emigration, and I hope the day will come when the overcrowded districts will be relieved of their surplus population. I do not say that the Highlands are over-populated as a whole; far from it. But in the Long Island [Lewis] and other places they are undoubtedly over-populated. Before I sit down I wish to say a few words with regard to the lawlessness which has prevailed in some districts of the Western Highlands. I believe, and I know, that this lawlessness has not been born among the people of the country. It is the work and active propaganda of Socialistic agitators. In the Island of Skye, when I was there last year, I heard details which left no doubt whatsoever that the minds of the people have been poisoned by active emissaries altogether outside the people. Naturally, they are the most tractable, the most loyal, and the most law-abiding people in the world. The whole thing has been got up by one of the societies in London. I wish to explain to the House the extent to which the lawlessness has gone. So far as I know the fact, it is not a question of resisting rents. It is not a question of resisting evictions or removals. It is a question of seizing other people's land. A great many of the crofting townships there have issued and executed a threat of entering on the ground of the larger tenants and seizing it by main force. If such a state of things is allowed to go on all capital will be driven from the country.

It was a clear expression of the Highland landlord case: of its urge to deport the common people (allied to a concession that they suffered a shortage of land), its fear of united popular action, its enduring loyalty to the tradition of recreational patronage, and of its attribution of popular discontent to the effect of 'outside agitators'.

By way of reply, Lord Napier himself noted – somewhat drily it might be thought – that the Duke of Argyll was 'usually ranked among those who, in theory at least, would rather apply a strict economical principle to the management of land than those practices of benevolence and mutual accommodation which are advocated by others'.

That same month the Commons debated the question of the crofters, on the motion of Donald MacFarlane, with Fraser-MacIntosh seconding. The motion asked government to give effect to the proposals of the Napier Commission, 'or to apply such other remedies as they deem advisable'. In a markedly favourable speech from the crofters' point of view, Harcourt noted that he had spent his leisure-time on Skye for the best part of twenty years and claimed that two years earlier he had refused appeals to send a force of soldiers to the island. He added, 'Some people say, Oh, the remedy for this is emigration. Well, sir, in my opinion emigration is a very poor remedy indeed. (Irish cheers.) I have myself no sympathy with a policy which improves a country by getting rid of its people. To my mind this is the policy of despair. I, at all events, do not accept the policy of making a solitude and calling it political economy.'

Then, speaking more generally of land-ownership in the Highlands, Harcourt added:

> The number of proprietors in these districts is very small. I think in the outer islands, in the Long Island, I doubt whether there are six separate proprietors altogether. When you come to Skye the number is very few of proprietors of any magnitude at all. When you come even to the mainland the number is not considerable. Certainly there are no people who have more reason to desire to see this question settled than the proprietors of the West Highlands. It is certainly not in their interest to raise a great land question in Scotland.

The motion, to give effect to the proposals of the Napier Commission, was accepted by the government and passed unanimously. By this point, however, a force of soldiers and police was already on Skye.

The intervention stemmed from reports that some crofters in the west of Skye were preparing forcibly to bring before their mass-meetings such of those as did not agree with them – and in particular some farmers, 'for statements reported to have been made by them' in connection with the evidence taken by the Napier Commission. Though Harcourt repeated these claims in the Commons, according to MacKenzie they were manufactured. But they do serve to highlight the confidence of a movement that had as yet won in law nothing of its demands. To paraphrase Argyll, the people clearly were ready to take by this point what they demanded, whatever the law and its agencies might rule or attempt to enforce.

Whatever the truth of the matter, a small party of police was sent to 'protect persons threatened with outrage by the crofters'. But it was turned back forcibly. As a result the demands of the landlords and authorities in Inverness-shire for the military were at last met.

As the county chief constable, MacHardy, reported at the end of October, 'the state of the land agitation has been gradually increasing', over the previous four months. At Glendale, there had been land-raiding by the Hamara and Ferrinvicquarrie crofters, while in August Blackie and MacFarlane had visited the glen. It was also rumoured, MacHardy reported, that 'secret societies' existed in the district 'for the purpose of committing outrages on proprietors, and their property, and also for the injury of persons unfavourable to the crofters' agitation'. However, beyond the declaration of secrecy exacted from persons who became members of the Land League, and 'kindred' associations, 'no direct evidence has been got of the formation of secret societies of the serious nature referred to'.

Glendale, of course, and the west of Skye in general, was perhaps the area in the Highlands which had enjoyed closest contact with Ireland over the previous ten years. Such contact existed via the Kinsale fishings, the visits of trading vessels, and 'emissaries' of the Irish Land League (and the long tradition of secret and direct-action societies that lay behind it). Whether secret societies did really exist is now not known, far less their extent or proposed tactical and policy programmes; nor the precise nature of the 'outrages' they may have considered.

At the end of the previous August, one of the land-raiding crofters in the district had been ordered by the landlord to take his stock off the raided land. The crofter refused, and went to Uist to buy more stock – which he also put on the land in question. In September, a party of landlord's men removed some crofters' stock from raided land at Scor. They were interrupted in this by a body of crofters, and the stock returned. As Sheriff Ivory noted of the district and his agent there, 'The people of the district continue in an excited state over these matters, and it is with the utmost caution that Constable MacVicar performs his patrol duty among them.'

Affairs were similarly tense elsewhere in the island. In Kilmuir and Uig, the authorities were reporting a 'crisis' in landlord–tenant relations:

> Meetings of the local branch of the Land League have been frequently held throughout the district, and large gatherings of the people have taken place. At Land League meetings later held, those who attended the same are said to have made a declaration, and banded themselves together to carry out several resolutions passed at such meetings in regard to land. Each crofter agrees to pay ten shillings, and each cottar five shillings, agreeing not to do any work to any of the district farmers, and that under pain of injury to person or property, and it is stated that they have appointed persons to watch over the district to see that these directions are carried out. It has been arranged that all the crofters on the Kilmuir estate are to hold a mass meeting at Quiraing on 31st October. A no-rent

proclamation has been issued, and published in the *Oban Times* of 25th October, from the Kilmuir branch.

To this clearly high degree of community organisation, rent striking and land-seizing, the crofters were now adding the 'Irish' tactics of boycott and enforcement of it. They were also preparing, in a remarkable form of popular trial, to force the attendance at a mass-meeting of two local farmers and a factor, 'for the purpose of demanding some explanation from them'.

It was, in the chief-constable's phrase, 'in anticipation of these outrages' that Fraser of Kilmuir asked for additional police protection. And though MacHardy had sent more men, and a consignment of fifty revolvers from the War Office, he also reported, 'With special reference to the present serious outbreak of disorder and lawlessness in Skye, I beg respectfully, but candidly, to state that the available force of police under my command, is entirely inadequate to maintain order, and carry out the law'.

And indeed the force of police sent to Kilmuir, under the command of Superintendent Aitchison, was turned back by force, as his exchange of telegrams with MacHardy bears witness. While he awaited orders in Portree the sub-committee of Inverness police, with the strongly anti-crofter Lord Lovat in the chair, wrote to the Home Secretary noting the urgent need for more police to be made available for Skye. Over and above this, 'all the additional police sent to Skye as well as those located in the disturbed districts should be armed with revolvers. The men should be openly instructed in the use of these at Portree'. He added that as many as possible of the additional police – more especially those engaged in patrol duty – should be mounted, 'and an application should be made to Government to station a gunboat with marines at Portree'.

Sheriff Ivory also wrote to the Lord Advocate, in similar terms. He was strongly of the opinion 'that the immediate despatch of a gunboat and marines to Skye is absolutely necessary to protect the police and assist them in protecting the property and persons of the lieges in that island'.

Thus the Highland élite, at least, was keen for a trial of strength with the Skye crofters (though the authorities in the south were less keen, or more cautious). The outcome of such an all-out trial, both in the short and the longer term, is open to a degree of interesting speculation. Might a violent intervention by soldiers have ignited in the island a response on the Irish (to name but one) model, with shootings, lootings and burnings? Such a confrontation would not exactly have gone unnoticed in the rest of the Highlands, where absentee landlord property was peculiarly open to destruction at no cost and very little risk to the crofters' movement. If nothing else, it might well have led, on a generalised scale, to a downward trend in property values and even recreational occupancy. The publicity attendant on such a course of events would also have been enormous; and though its effects on the rest of Scotland might be incalculable, they were scarcely likely to be in favour of the landlord or industrial capitalist classes or government.

In the event, matters did not come to this stage. But popular morale in Skye against the police was certainly very high.

To accommodate the force of constables planned for the island, for instance, a steamer was to be chartered on the grounds that nowhere safe could be found ashore for such a purpose. This popular antipathy was known to the chief constable, MacHardy, who was clearly spoiling for some sort of fight at the bidding of his police committee under Lord Lovat. According to his reports, since the earlier rebuff of his men:

> The people of Kilmuir have turned out and held possession of the district, determined to resist the police entering or going among them. They have for the past week assembled in hundreds, day and night armed with sticks for the purpose of assaulting an expected body of police, and declare that they will attack any number of constables so long as soldiers are not sent. A force of fifty constables including those presently stationed in Skye, has been made available for the enforcement of law and restoring order to the island, under the Government protection.

MacHardy then went to London, while from Inverness Aitchison kept him informed of developments on Skye. His reports testify to the extent of popular solidarity in the island with regard to the land question. According to one such report, for instance, there was 'great excitement prevailing in Uig and East Side today. Watchers on all conspicuous places armed with long sticks. Crowds going about Uig.' Two days later there was 'great excitement prevailing in district. Still determined to resist any police force whatever. Groups constantly on watch.' And the following day, people were seen 'going about in great numbers about one in the morning, waiting for receiving police. Great meeting held at top of Rha yesterday evening, watchmen posted all over Kilmuir. The agitation throughout the whole island is in highest degree, and undoubtedly all would turn out.'

By then Harcourt had told the Commons that the conduct of the Skye crofters could no longer be tolerated and that it was the duty of the local authorities, 'with the entire support of the executive government, to take all such measures as may be necessary to the observance of the law'. By the second week of November, the *Lochiel* was ready at Stornoway, whence she was to steam south for Strome Ferry, and collect the force of police coming by train from Inverness. A violent gale over the weekend delayed a proposed mass-meeting of crofters at Kilmuir. Nevertheless, supporters from throughout Skye were expected to lend their weight, and it was anticipated that the crofters could perhaps field a demonstration of 2,000 people.

On Monday the crofters heard that the police had yet to leave Inverness, as Sheriff Ivory and chief constable MacHardy had still not returned from London. They also heard from Stornoway that the *Lochiel* was unable to sail, as her skipper and crew were refusing to 'serve in the ungrateful task of carrying armed men for the purpose of shooting down their helpless and unoffending brethren'. And on Tuesday, 12 November, supporters in Stornoway telegrammed: '*Lochiel*'s crew refuse to proceed to Skye. Thousands of Lewis men threatening to proceed to Skye to help crofters. Great excitement here.'

By this point a veritable fleet of vessels was heading for Skye, in the cause of restoring its crofters to the condition of traditional subservience and good temper attributed to them by the Duke of Argyll in the House of Lords.

On the Monday evening the gunboat *Forester* had sailed from Greenock. She called briefly at Tobermory (where her temporary presence must have caused something of a sensation among the Land Leaguers of Mull) and thereafter headed for Skye. On the Wednesday the *Lochiel* was coaling at Stornoway, her owners still trying to find a crew for her; MacHardy arrived back in Inverness; and the *Assistance* and the *Stormcock* were reported on their way north to join the *Forester*. That afternoon, the *Forester* herself came into Portree Bay (anchoring half a mile off, which suggests that her commanding officer feared some sort of assault on his vessel).

The following morning the *Lochiel* arrived at Strome where she was met by a relief skipper and crew, 'in room of Captain Cameron and the Highland crew who have refused duty'. And on Saturday afternoon she arrived in Portree with twenty-five police, Ivory, MacHardy, and the Inverness procurator-fiscal – who had all travelled down from the Highland capital by train that morning. On the Sunday the *Assistance* arrived, with 350 marines and 100 sailors; the following afternoon, the *Banterer* arrived at Portree with another sixty-five marines.

By then the *Forester*, *Assistance* and *Lochiel* had all steamed for Uig. The *Forester*, being the last to arrive, anchored in such a way that she could cover with her guns the landing of the marines and police: a comment on the seriousness with which the county authorities, at least, were prepared to confront the crofters' movement in the island. That afternoon seven police came ashore along with Ivory, MacHardy, Aitchison, the Fiscal, the captain of the *Assistance*, and the officer in command of the marines. At the inn, however, they were refused accommodation, by way of introduction to the opinion prevailing on the island. The police were therefore sent to the school and the sheriff's party retired to their ships. As darkness fell, seventy marines came ashore in full marching order, that they could protect the seven policemen in the school from the attentions of the crofters.

To all this, however, the response of the crofters was one of passive resistance. Such action may well suggest a very intelligent response on the part of the local Land League leadership – for, though the national leadership was publicly counselling just such a course, there can be no doubt that direction of the immediate course of events on Skye lay in the hands of the islands' crofter leaders themselves.

There was to be no violence, there were to be no outrages. Even as Ivory's fleet had steamed along the eastern coast of Skye, 'everywhere people were ostentatiously and conspicuously seen to be at work, along the coast, digging potatoes'. At Staffin, where opposition had been expected, 'the utmost quietude and decorum prevailed'. And at Uig 'the crofter population made big efforts to look busy. Not a single grown-up crofter came down to the shore, either to defy or welcome' the visitors. As the special correspondent of the *Glasgow Herald* observed, 'The long-threatened expedition to the country of the crofters is now an accomplished fact. The district was found in a state of the most perfect peace, with every crofter minding his own business.'

The morning following the arrival of the fleet at Uig, 250 marines were marched over to Staffin, the flanks of their force protected with marine artillery and scouting parties. But this four-hour procession, by any standards a provocation, was the occasion of no violence at all; and night fell, 'amid a scene of perfect tranquillity on the part of the villagers'.

The same sort of tactic was applied in the west of the island. At the end of that week, Ivory took three of his ships to Glendale and went ashore with twenty police and three companies of marines. Once ashore, and on the march for Hamara, they came on a Land League meeting with John MacPherson in command. Marine buglers failed to disrupt or provoke the meeting; and Ivory was left to station six police and seventy-five marines at Hamara Lodge. On the Sunday following more marines and police were stationed at Dunvegan and Ivory, who had already indicated his willingness to undertake 'pacification' of other 'disaffected' islands and areas, returned to Portree to organise it. By the Monday his fleet had completed coaling and provisioning for such an expedition to Uist; but the Home Secretary prohibited it 'for the time being'.

Under the spotlight of very considerable national publicity, and the watchful scrutiny of their friends in parliament, the crofters, it can be argued in retrospect, scarcely put a foot wrong in a situation fraught with the possibility of tactical errors. To Ivory's expedition, however, they paid scant attention. The men of Valtos and Staffin, for instance, met in public (with the press in attendance to record and report) and announced a new rent-strike, having first expelled four of Ivory's men from the meeting. And at Uig the people also met in an autumn gale of wind and rain, 'in order that the sheriff and armed men in the bay might see what was going on, and learn the fact that the men of Uig have not yet been frightened into forgetting their grievances'.

In Glendale too, the tenants of both estates agreed that they would not pay any rent until further notice; and when the factor called for his rents, no one was there to pay him. Indeed, the tenants of Fasach wrote to their landlord baldly informing him that they too were on rent-strike. The announcement formalised the *de facto* strikes of earlier and signalled a new confidence and organisation in the movement – as well as a consciousness of the publicity and support it enjoyed in the wider political world. They also added the explanation (itself mute testimony to the crofter viewpoint on the ownership and use of land and the origin of profit deriving from it) that they were in any case not morally bound to pay rent, because:

> Our poverty is not our fault. We have worked to pay you for what should be our houses. But we are now so poor that we must first obey the law of nature, to feed and clothe ourselves, and we therefore cannot pay you the rent which you wish to exact from us. Owing to thus being deprived, we consider that you are owing us £40, and in all seriousness we say that you should pay us this instead of asking us for rent.

And in the south and east of the island, on Lord MacDonald's estates, the rent-strike tactic was spreading too. In the words of John MacPherson at a meeting of MacDonald's striking tenants at Braes, 'it would be as easy to stop the Atlantic Ocean as to stop the present agitation until justice has been done to the people'.

The long record of conspicuous expenditure of what the people saw as their rents by the MacDonalds was not unknown, of course, to the tenantry of the estate. And while a rent-strike was promptly declared at Snizort, the people of Braes and Sconser also announced a suspension of all monies formerly payable to the estate – bringing the number of townships on strike to fourteen on the MacDonald estate alone.

By this point, in other words, social relations on Skye had tilted alarmingly (from the landlord point of view) in favour of the crofters, and the landlord fear of a generalised expropriation had been given eloquent expression. For instance in Kilmuir the landlord, Fraser, invited the crofters to send delegates to discuss matters with him – itself something of a concession. But the crofters, their expectations clearly expanding in precisely the way that pro-landlord observers so feared, refused. Instead they invited Fraser to come to the crofters and explain himself – before a mass meeting of his tenants, at that.

Similar conditions existed throughout the island; and while the rent-strikes and other strikes began to bite at the landlord purse, the marines could not be used in a military capacity for fear of what such an action might by then ignite across the Highlands. Nor could anything be done in effect about the thousands of crofters technically breaking the law whether by striking or land-raiding. In Westminster, their supporters, in a skilled demonstration of parliamentary tactics, agitated for emergency legislation to illegalise eviction for rent-arrears until such time as laws were enacted to meet the crofters' grievances.

As a result of this public scrutiny on the one hand, and the crofters' passive response to the marine invasion of their island on the other, the bulk of Ivory's force was shortly withdrawn from Skye, with just a token party left on the island. The Home Office told the Lord Advocate in January: 'You will make it quite clear to the police committee that Her Majesty's government regard the military force as acting in support of, and not in substitution of, the police, on whom properly devolves the duty of maintaining order and executing the law.'

The will of the Skye crofters was underpinned by other events occurring at the same time as Ivory's invasion. By that winter, for instance, poverty had become particularly severe in the island, with £2,000 needed for meal and clothes to meet the relief of distress, 'which is of an exceptional character and may be expected to be at its worst at the beginning of February'. Just a week after that report, Henry George was touring the island urging the people to take 'what was justly theirs' – an appeal, whatever the precise details of George's remedies, that can only have powerfully reinforced crofter opinion on the land question.

And by way of further reinforcement, there was widespread – and highly unfavourable – publicity on a civil action in the sheriff court at Dingwall, where the American millionaire Walter Winans was taking legal action against a Kintail crofter and shoemaker who had allowed his pet lamb to graze on land owned by the railway tycoon. (Winans was not the first or last eccentric to own land for deer-stalking in the Highlands. A superb shot and fanatical stalker, he once had a white pony camouflaged with make-up acquired from a hairdresser in the West End of London).

In Kilmuir, meanwhile, Fraser was continuing with action in the courts against some of his tenants (including the local minister, Davidson). The grounds for the action were that, 'if under Land League direction tenants, who until of late have paid their rents so well, will not now pay them at all, and if no processes are to be used against them, how can landlords so placed recover their rents, or defend their non-crofter farms from seizure'? And further: 'In such cases how can those whose incomes may be derivable from their estates pay their accounts if the crofters cannot be called upon to pay theirs?'

This hint referred to the forthcoming landlord version of the rent-strike, their short-lived 'rates-strike' on Skye. Meanwhile on a Highland-wide scale the landlords, recognising that the government could not be depended on for an all-out coercive move against the crofters, met in conference at Inverness to offer concessions to their crofters. These inclued 'an undertaking to increase the size of their holdings as suitable opportunities offer, and where the crofters are in a position, profitably to occupy and stock the same'. Such offers were more or less risible by this stage, given that the record of landlordism did not suggest a high frequency of 'suitability' with regard either to land availability, or to 'profitability' as far as their crofters were concerned. The landlords also offered long-term leases, such as Lord Lovat had introduced for some of his own tenants (though only to crofters who were not in arrears with rent). But as Lovat's conduct with regard to leases within three years would demonstrate, the offer was properly judged by the crofters as little more than a manoeuvre. The landlords also suggested compensation to outgoing tenants for improvements they had made to their holding; but did not forget their old refrain on the importance of 'granting assistance to those who may be anxious to emigrate'.

The outcome of the conference, in fact, served to demonstrate just how little the landlords could agree on any significant measure of concession. By the crofters, therefore, their offers were simply ignored – itself a powerful demonstration of the extent to which the agitation of the previous years had encouraged 'visions of a crofters' millennium'.

On the ground the agitation was unabated. By the end of January, the sheriff of Ross had been visiting Lewis aboard the *Seahorse*, for the purpose of arresting crofters charged with deforcement of a messenger-at-arms while he was attempting to serve interdicts from the Court of Session. By now the roads in the west of Lewis were blocked with boulders, to dissuade any other expedition of sheriff's messengers; while in Skye too, sheriff-officers were deforced at Valtos and Glendale, in the course of serving summonses for rent-arrears. Later that month, therefore, following widespread speculation fuelled by the crofters' contacts in the south, Ivory returned to Skye with another fleet carrying marines and police. At Glendale six men, including John MacPherson, were arrested and accused of rioting and deforcement. As they were led away, MacPherson assured his fellow-tenants that they had nothing to worry about, as he and the other arrested men would soon be back.

Ivory's force was also deployed at Valtos, landing from the *Assistance*. Immediately on landing, 'operations for arrests were commenced', but after a whole day's search the officers of the law were 'only successful in apprehending two out of the eight against whom warrants had been issued. The other six had betaken themselves with a number of others to the surrounding hills. The excitement throughout the island is intense.' In Valtos there had been a struggle with the police, requiring 100 marines to fix bayonets; and that evening when the party reached Portree with its prisoners, further trouble was feared. In the morning, when the prisoners were taken under very heavy guard to the County Buildings, they were 'greeted by the assembled crowd with ringing cheers, again and again repeated. The excitement in Portree on Saturday night continued most intense, and the policemen who patrolled the streets were hooted and hissed in the wildest manner.'

To this sort of intimidation, however, the crofters on Skye and elsewhere paid scant attention. At Strome (from which ten men had appeared in court eighteen months earlier on a church-riot charge), the crofters demanded the distribution of sheep farms and deer-forests among the people, 'and shall not permit these to be robbed by the landlords as they have notoriously been'. Similar demands came from Stornoway, at the inaugural meeting of the League's branch there; while on the Dalglish estate in Ardnamurchan, fears were being entertained that 'troublesome times are impending'. In the Ross of Mull, the League branch on the Duke of Argyll's estate was reported active, and of especial worry to the authorities on account of its decision (suggestive of the 'secret societies' reports from Skye), to conduct its proceedings in private; while nationally, the League announced that it would arrange the legal defence of the men lately taken prisoner at Valtos and Glendale.

In South Uist land-raiding was under way, the people of Boisdale taking possession of an island in the loch for potato ground. At Lochcarron Donald MacCallum and John MacPherson addressed the crofters, the latter assuring them that from the first he had 'discerned the hand of Providence in the agitation, and now rejoiced at the dimensions and importance it had assumed'. In Daliburgh, South Uist, three fields were seized and the factor's remonstrations simply ignored. In Lewis 400 men met at Barvas to demand land-reform; while on Tiree, 'a large number of rents due at Martinmas last are still unpaid, and as his grace has now expressed his resolution to enforce payment in the usual way, the outlook at the present time is very dark'.

Throughout the following months the agitation grew across the Highlands. It was also pursued without rest in the pro-crofter press and by the pro-crofter MPs. Prospective pro-crofter MPs were also playing a role, for the Third Reform Act gave crofters the chance to vote, and they were now preparing to run their own candidates in elections at the end of the year.

From the *Celtic Magazine*, a steady stream of articles poured in the crofters' favour. Fraser-MacIntosh wrote on where to get money for the stocking of 'new and enlarged crofts', and MacKenzie himself reported on the annual meeting of the Gaelic Society of Inverness where speeches were delivered by Cameron of Lochiel and Sir Kenneth MacKenzie – both ex-members of the Napier Commission. In March, MacKenzie found room for cartoon coverage of the Skye invasion from *The Graphic* and the *Pictorial World*; for John MacKay of Hereford on croft and farm rents in Sutherland; and for reports on affairs in Kilmuir; on the landlord conference at Inverness; and (as his lead story), 'terrorism in Skye; Sheriff Ivory's latest folly'.

In April, space was given to land courts and Highland sheriffs, the trial of the Lewis crofters, Lord Napier and the Duke of Argyll, and a review of Blackie's newly published *Scottish Highlanders and the Land Laws*. May's edition covered MacDonald of Skeabost on the landlord conference at Inverness (with a reply by MacKenzie), 'Sheriff Ivory's mountain and his mice' (the trial of the Glendale and Valtos men), and a general piece on the land-reform movement in Skye.

In June, MacKenzie covered American sympathy for Highland crofters, reprinted a biography of John MacKay of Hereford, and carried an analysis of the proposed crofting legislation introduced to parliament in May (which would fall with the government in due course). And in July, in the last edition of the *Celtic Magazine* to carry agitational material relating to crofting (due to the launch of the *Scottish Highlander*) MacKenzie again covered the proposed crofting legislation; he also carried a piece on the Scottish Land League of America.

By then preparations were in hand for the national League conference, held in Portree in September. This was covered by the national and English press as the major event that it had, by then, become. The *Glasgow Herald*, *Scotsman*, *North British Daily Mail* and *Times* covered at great length in their broadsheet pages both the conference and the demonstration through Portree that followed it. By any standards, certainly, it was an impressive exhibition of the extent to which the crofting movement was organised by the autumn of 1885.

Delegates from within Skye marched in from Braes, Glendale, Valtos, Snizort and Staffin, carrying banners and headed by pipers. There were delegates from Lewis and Harris and the Uists, and every corner of the mainland Highlands – nearly 200 in all, as well as visitors from a host of southern organisations, and also from the United States, Canada and Australia. The Glenelg delegate set the tone of the proceedings when he announced that 'the people walk about with a new freedom for they have almost entirely thrown off the nightmare of landlordism'. And from Lewis Alexander Morrison, anticipating developments there, said: 'The question of the hour is the destruction of the deer-forests. The people have been kept down in poverty and oppression for centuries through the unjust and cruel land laws.'

That evening a general meeting drew speakers from not only the Land League, but also the Scottish Land League of America, the Land Nationalisation League, and both the English and the Scottish Land Restoration Leagues. There were speakers from Skye, Chicago, London, Hull, Caithness, Glasgow, Edinburgh, Oban, Liverpool and Barra (Michael Buchanan was the crofters' delegate from there). The next day, thousands of people marched through Portree:

> It is not too much to say that an equally animated scene has never before been witnessed in that place. When all was in order, the procession, following its banners, and with its pipers playing, marched round about and through the village of Portree. As many of the inhabitants as were not in the procession turned out to see it, and during its progress cheered with the greatest enthusiasm.

A string of resolutions was announced. Of them *The Scotsman* observed, 'If we are not to break up our whole social system the demands of the conference at Portree must be set aside as monstrous and utterly inadmissible.' According to the paper, the 'incendiarism' of the Portree conference no more than 'held out a bribe to the lawless to encourage and practise lawlessness'.

Most critically, however, the conference agreed on candidates to stand in the crofters' cause at the coming general election.

Prior to the extension of the franchise, the electorates of the Highland counties were tiny compared to their populations: for Argyll 3,300; for Caithness 1,250; for Inverness-shire 1,860; for Ross and Cromarty 1,720; and in Sutherland no more than 325. And traditionally these seats had been in the hands of the landlords. In Argyll the sons of the Duke had held the seat non-stop since 1868. In Sutherland one of the Duke's family had been returned since 1852 (with the exception of six years, when it was held by Sir D. Dundas, who got it on the elevation to the peerage of the previous holder, the Marquess of Stafford, and resigned to let Lord Ronald Leveson-Gower back in during 1867). Caithness told the same story; while in Ross and Cromarty there had been but one election between 1847 and 1884, during which time the seat was held by Sir James Matheson and then by his nephew, Sir Alexander Matheson. Inverness-shire, meanwhile, was held from 1840 to 1865 by H.J. Baillie, and then mainly by Cameron of Lochiel.

But the extension of the franchise increased the electorate in Argyll by over 200 per cent, in Inverness-shire by over 400 per cent, in Ross and Cromarty by nearly 500 per cent, and in Sutherland by nearly 880 per cent. The campaign, therefore, was a fierce one, with the landlords attempting to defeat the crofters' own candidates of Fraser-MacIntosh for Inverness-shire; MacFarlane for Argyll; Roderick MacDonald for Ross-shire; G.B. Clark for Caithness (where his opponent's father, grandfather and great-grandfather had all been MPs for the county); and Angus Sutherland for his home county. In Ross-shire the opposing candidate was the young Munro-Ferguson of Novar, who had plotted with the Duke of Argyll an attempt to gerrymander the Highland constituencies in the landlords' favour, and who would go on to a successful career in British imperial affairs in later life.

From the beginning, however, it was clear that the crofters' candidates had massive popular support – not least in Inverness-shire, where Fraser-MacIntosh toured the western coasts and islands of the constituency by boat. At Kilmaluag, for instance, in Staffin, the League branch meeting (the first since the return of the menfolk from the east-coast fishing) agreed to complete support for Fraser-MacIntosh. Throughout the district the League was ensuring that every crofter was on the roll of voters. At Stein, men were set to watch from the highest hill in the district, that the people might have time to prepare a suitable welcome for the visit of their candidate.

In Lewis the Park branch of the League met at Gravir, to show support for Dr MacDonald, the Ross-shire candidate. The secretary of the branch assured the meeting that, 'Novar is a landlord, and that is a sufficient reason why we should do all in our power to oust him at the general election. Whatever landlords say, we cannot place any confidence in their promises, when we consider how they have acted towards us during the last eighty years.'

In Fort William, Cameron of Lochiel was shouted-down at an election meeting with demands that he reverse an eviction at Achintore. On the Dochfour estate, the factor reportedly went 'among the tenantry using such methods as factors know how to use for procuring support for the landlord candidate'. And in Argyll, mocked the new *Scottish Highlander*, 'the climax of daring wickedness was attained when the minister of Inveraray chose to oppose the electoral choice of the Duke of Argyll'.

In the event all the candidates won, with the exception of Angus Sutherland (who would take the seat the following year anyway), although in the *Scottish Highlander*, MacKenzie thought Sutherland's defeat a victory for the 'most disgraceful servility'. The results, nevertheless, led MacKenzie to believe overall that 'the crofters' cause is advancing at an extraordinary and unexpected pace'. As the pro-crofter *Oban Times* memorably proclaimed, 'From the Mull of Kintyre to the Butt of Lewis the land is before us'; while the pro-crofter *Invergordon Times* thought the result showed landlordism 'trampled in the dust', at last, 'an object of derision to even its former slaves'.

The Invergordon paper – if anything stronger in its language than even the *Oban Times* – reported:

> Dr MacDonald was everywhere received with loud demonstrations of welcome. His views, especially on the land question, were in entire harmony with the vast majority of the electors, who were sickened of landlord rule, and who were determined that they would have a member who thoroughly understood their wants and wishes to represent them. The victory was hailed with great delight throughout the counties by the crofters, and bonfires blazed and general rejoicings took place in honour of the victory. It was a terrible defeat to the holders of the soil, and we trust that it will have a good effect.

As a result of this electoral victory, the 'Crofters' Party' entered Parliament on a tide of expectation in the Highlands – where agitation, if anything, was encouraged by the prospects of parliamentary fireworks. From South Uist, for instance, even as the Crofter Members took their places, the landlords were alerting the authorities that 'influences have been at work which if allowed to remain unchecked must lead to a very alarming state of matters'. Land League associations had been formed throughout the Hebrides, forcible possession had been taken of the land with threats of violence, the fences had been destroyed, the telegraph wires cut, and 'dangerous obstructions made at night on the public road near Sir

Reginald and Lady Cathcart's residence'. The 'terrorism' prevailing was such that no culprit could be identified (by the authorities); and throughout the island, 'law is practically in abeyance'.

If anything, in fact, the early months of 1886 saw an escalation of agitation. During the first fortnight of the new year, the *Invergordon Times* covered anti-landlord meetings at Alness and Creich; there was another meeting at Melness (where ten new subscriptions to the paper were taken out) during which the League chairman – once again eloquently voicing the popular view of land ownership and use – hoped that the people would soon show the landlords 'that they had been robbed of their natural rights in their native soil, and that they would not be satisfied with less than a full restoration of the lands of which they had been deprived by fraud and usurpation'.

Further meetings were reported from Clyne, Loth and Kildonan, Rosehall and Laid, and at Golspie and Stoer, as well as Halladale, Strathpeffer, Garve and Dornoch. At Durness the people demanded 'a proper and final settlement of the land question'. At Lochinver the League branch demanded the restoration to the people of the deer-forest of Glen Canisp, 'where there is plenty of provision for ourselves and families. It extends twenty-one miles and is in the possession of an Englishman called Painter, while we are at home starving and the land of our fathers lying waste.'

Similar demands were reported from Strathy, Drumbeg, Achmelvich, Resolis, Ferrintosh and Culbokie; while at Tongue the chairman reminded a League meeting that they should stick more closely together than ever, for 'to the eye of the political seer', the future was 'pregnant with work'. This was as clear a warning as any that, to the League's local leaders at least, an item very much on the agenda was something akin to the 'restoration of the land to the people'.

The same feeling was evident across the Highlands. Sheriff Ivory, for instance, warned his superiors in Edinburgh that the Skye crofters were now two years in rent-arrears, to the value of something like £17,000. Meanwhile an Inverness law firm was calling urgent attention to the cottars on the estate of Kintail, 'who had pledged themselves to take the land'. At Resolis the tenantry refused to pay their rents for the previous six months unless it was reduced by one third. In Lewis some Uig people were in court following charges of assault. In Skye the landlords were by now on rates-strike, as Fraser of Kilmuir had earlier hinted, pleading poverty as a result of their tenants' rent-strike (and Lord MacDonald's factor thought it 'perfectly plain that a most serious crisis has arrived – the present state of matters cannot last').

Again, the Inverness solicitors wrote to Edinburgh reporting that 'the cottars on the estate of Kintail have carried out their resolution to take possession of the land'. They added, 'If the government do not look to the matter they may soon find themselves face to face with an insurrection of the labouring population of the Highlands.'

By this point, the government had indeed introduced a Bill to parliament on the subject of crofters. But time and again Sheriff Ivory wrote to Edinburgh warning that the Edinbane, Waternish and Kilmuir crofters were not satisfied with the provisions of the Bill. He reported that in April 'only one fisherman has left Staffin for the Irish fishing, instead of thirty as usual', and that 'the crofters are determined to agitate for more land than the Crofters' Bill proposes to give them'. That same month he warned that, at Waternish, 120 crofters had made an announcement: unless the Bill, with amendments to meet their objections to its shortcomings, was law within a month, they 'would begin to cultivate the land wherever they found it suitable'. In May Ivory reported that on Barra Michael Buchanan had conceded that the Bill was only a 'step in the right direction', and asserted that the agitation must be kept up.

Nor did the Bill please the crofters' members in parliament either. MacFarlane, for one, called it a 'miserable, deluded, rubbishy measure' – a phrase that in general matched crofter opinion. But the government was by now headed for a general election, and determined to enact something, at least, on the 'crofter problem'. As a result, on the last day of the parliamentary session, the Bill received its royal assent, and the 1886 Crofters' Act passed on to the statute book.

Its principal provisions were security of tenure and fair rents: concessions of outrageous character, in the view of landlord ideologists such as the Duke of Argyll, and testimony to the power of the crofters' agitation of the previous years. But if the Act was a response to agitation, it did not meet all of its demands. The agitation therefore went on. It was, in the memorable words of the *Oban Times*, no more than 'an instalment of justice'. It did nothing, for instance, about returning the land to the people. And it was left to Alexander MacKenzie to warn:

> We must not rest satisfied until every inch of productive land in the Highlands is placed at the disposal of those who are able and willing to till it. Until this is assured, the people must resolve to maintain the most persistent and determined agitation. And if this resolute and comprehensive movement should end in the total abolition of the Game Laws, the sporting element, in and out of parliament, who so stolidly opposed the demands of the people, will only have themselves to blame.

They were 'sowing the wind', concluded MacKenzie, 'and they will most assuredly reap the whirlwind.'

EIGHT
THE MASS MOVEMENT IN ACTION

'On the very day the expedition arrived at the island the lairds paid
their rates, leaving the expedition to be directed entirely against the
crofters. It is all very clever [but] one week of a local parliament in
Scotland would smash-up the rotten system.'

———⟨⟩———

Despite the passage of the Crofters' Act (or perhaps as a partial
consequence of it), the following two years were marked by an
intensification of popular agitation on the land question in the
Highlands. The autumn of 1886 saw, first, a combined police and marine
invasion of Tiree; second, a notably militant conference of the Land
League at Bonar Bridge; and third, yet another naval invasion of Skye. This
agitation continued right throughout the following year, and on into
1888, with large-scale anti-landlord direct-action and associated military
activity, in the outer Hebrides in particular.

Tiree, however, was the first location to draw the attention of the
authorities. As early as July 1886, the county sheriff was warning that the
Duke of Argyll feared a violent response to his forthcoming attempt to
serve interdicts 'in consequence of certain lawless acts by crofters'. The
authorities therefore sought 'the help of a detachment of military in aid
of the civil power'.

The background to this request was, as the *Oban Times* reported, a
Land League meeting of Tiree crofters some weeks earlier, which had
decided – in the spirit of crofters right across the Highlands during those
weeks – that 'some of the lands unjustly taken from themselves and their
fathers, and now lying waste, be taken possession of and planted with
potatoes'.

Within the month, therefore, planting was under way on the lands of
the farm of Greenhill, which had been occupied and distributed among
300 crofters and cottars. As a result, the duke had petitioned the
Edinburgh courts for more of the sort of intimidatory provocation that
was already well known on the island. When the Napier Commission had
arrived to take evidence on Tiree, for instance, it was only with
considerable reluctance that an undertaking was offered by the duke's

factor (and not by the duke himself) that no one would be victimised for what they might tell Napier's commissioners.

In any case, and as a direct result of the occupation of the farm, forty policemen were sent along with a sheriff-officer, to serve writs on the raiders at Greenhill. They were met, however, by a force of 300 men and boys armed with sticks and clubs, which promptly drove them to a refuge in the inn at Scarinish. And then, at the end of July, the inn itself was mobbed, with the police forced to leave the island that same day: a precipitate departure that serves to highlight the extent to which popular confidence had grown across the Highlands since the Battle of Braes.

Years later, the depute procurator-fiscal of the county recalled events on Tiree: 'Whether the authorities acted wisely in sending an escort at all has been open to doubt. The very nature of it was provocative.' It is arguable, indeed, that the sending of the police party was intended as a provocation; the notices, after all, could have been sent by post.

In any case the scene was now set for a test of will between the classes – a flavour of whose relationship with each other can be guessed from an ascerbic observation penned a full century later (by a university professor of island origin):

> Tiree was worth between four and five thousand pounds a year to the duke. His son was singled out as a suitable bridegroom for the daughter of Queen Victoria. To have a Royal Personage tweak one's whiskers and call one 'dear Papa' was something which only came the way of the well-lined. It was the fate of the citizens of Tiree to supply some of that lining.

In the 1840s, when the Destitution Committee of the Free Church raised money for the relief of poverty in the island, it found the duke trying to get some of the cash, which he intended to spend on the deportation of the island's crofters to Canada. And when some did leave, the duke had refused to give the land they vacated to those who remained – but made sheep farms out of it, as the local doctor told the Napier Commission.

James Cameron later recorded that the policy of the Argylls with regard to Tiree had rendered it keenly ready for the League. He observed, 'His Grace could not get over the damning fact that between himself and the potato disease of 1845 the population of Tiree was reduced in four years after his accession from 5,000 to a little over 3,000'; or, as the county's depute-procurator recalled afterwards, 'The frame of mind of the islanders saw only the application of the law for the benefit of the rich against the poor.'

And thus, on the last Friday of July, lookouts posted above Scarinish spotted off Coll the Royal Navy's guardship on the Clyde, the *Ajax*, a recently built 280-foot warship, armoured with 17-inch iron plates, and armed with four 15-ton guns, two quick-fire 14-ton guns, and fourteen smaller quick-fire guns. Along with the *Assistance* (lately of Skye) and a chartered steamer, the *Nigel*, the *Ajax* was proceeding for Tiree.

Having left Oban that morning, the ships made anchor while the day was still light. And as night fell the people of the island were left to the wonders of the *Ajax*, the depute-procurator being 'witness of the terror which the ship's searchlights aroused in the minds of these simple people'.

The next morning, 100 police and 250 marines were landed at Scarinish, pitching camp there; and within a week eight crofters' leaders had been arrested on charges of mobbing, rioting, and deforcement. (The nephew of Colin Henderson, one of those arrested, would become professor of theology at Glasgow University and author of the spiced observation on the well-lined duke, noted above.)

The eight were taken to Inveraray, where they lay in gaol for a week, until a lawyer came from Glasgow and bailed them. They were met at the gates of Inveraray gaol by a piper and a large crowd of supporters. Their departure for Tiree on the steamer, *Lord of the Isles*, was marked by sustained cheering – as the depute-procurator noted, there was 'no question as to where public sympathy lay'.

Throughout August, meanwhile, Tiree was garrisoned by 250 marines and 16 policemen; though this did not prevent a speaker from the English Land Restoration League addressing a crofters' meeting at Moss (from which the correspondent of the pro-duke *Scotsman* was ejected). Nor did it prevent D.H. MacFarlane arriving at the end of the month in the yacht *Hiawatha*, 'displaying a red flag', and coming ashore to be met by 150 cheering crofters.

In October the eight Land Leaguers, though entitled to be tried at Inveraray, were taken instead to the High Court in Edinburgh. After a trial lasting three days, they were found guilty and sentenced to six months in the Calton Gaol. The following January, however, they were freed, and returned home to a tumultuous – and entirely unrepentant – welcome.

Meanwhile, during the autumn of 1886, the Land League met for its annual conference at Bonar Bridge. The spirit of the delegates was heightened by the results of the general election which had closely followed the passing of the Crofters' Act. Once again, it had been a good election for the crofters' movement. J.M. Cameron, standing in Wick (with Land League support), took 57 per cent of the vote. In Caithness Dr Clark took 78 per cent. Fraser-MacIntosh had been unopposed in Inverness-shire. Dr MacDonald got nearly 80 per cent in Ross-shire. And Angus Sutherland had taken Sutherland with well over two-thirds of the vote. Only in Argyll had D.H. MacFarlane been beaten, by 613 votes (but he would win the seat back in 1892 and hold it in 1895).

The *North British Daily Mail* approved of Bonar Bridge as a location for the conference: 'It is singularly appropriate at this state of the agitation,' it said. 'Sutherland stands out pre-eminently above all other counties in

Scotland for eviction and clearance.' The land-reform movement in the county was 'immensely strong', with twenty-two branch associations and a membership of 3,000 overall.

The agenda and organisation of the conference showed ample evidence of the political identity that the League had attained in a few short years. Indeed, by the time of Bonar Bridge it was on the brink of constituting itself as an independent political party in the Highlands. Until then, its organisational nature had been that of a single-issue mass campaign, with all the strengths and weaknesses of that form. Now, however, it was to re-shape itself, with a formal structure and rule book. And though this new form was not to survive long – due to wider political considerations and the alteration of its mass-basis within two or three years of the passing of the Crofters' Act – the programme adopted at Bonar Bridge says much for the League's confidence at the time, as well as for enduring themes in Highland political life. Not least of these were the game laws, and what they were taken to symbolise (or their obverse, poaching, and the repudiation its practice also symbolised).

The principal slogans of the conference were simple. Firstly, the restoration to the Highland people of their native land on equitable conditions and the resistance by every constitutional method of the depopulation of the Highlands by eviction, forced emigration, or any other means. Secondly, the abolition of the game laws. Thirdly, the emendation of the laws relating to sea, loch and river fishing. Fourthly, the restoration to the people of their foreshore rights.

There was also a new organisational structure adopted at Bonar Bridge, which suggests the extent to which the League was moving beyond a single-issue mass movement. A twenty-five-strong executive was to be formed, for instance, along with district councils and county boards, the latter responsible for the selection of parliamentary candidates. A pan-Celtic league was also to be established, 'for mutual co-operation in securing necessary reforms and promoting the welfare of the Celtic people'; while delegates were to be chosen with a view to promotional touring in England, North America and the colonies.

There was also a very impressive body of Highland and pro-Highland talent present among the 300 delegates. From Parliament there were the 'Crofter Members' of Dr Clark, Dr MacDonald and Angus Sutherland. Stuart Glennie and Donald Murray had also come from London; while the anti-landlord Skye poetess Mary MacPherson was also present.

Among the delegates, too, were three of the Tiree men recently held until bailed in Inveraray gaol and shortly to be gaoled again at Edinburgh following their court appearance there. And the underlying tone of the conference was voiced by one of the delegates from Mull, one MacPhail, when he told his listeners that 'the core of England was rotten with Toryism and to be rid of these Tories they must have Home Rule the sooner the better'.

John MacPherson of Glendale was also present: 'He believed that they had compressed the work of a century into four years.' Another Glendale delegate boasted of how, eighteen months earlier, he would have been gaoled for taking a fish from the river there; but of how no one now dared interfere with him when he did so, for they had 'already broken the back of landlordism in Skye'.

(Yet again, the game laws – and game poaching – as repudiation, covert or otherwise, of the cultural legitimacy of the landlord élite!)

From Lewis, meanwhile, a delegate described the Crofters' Act as no more than a 'device to stave off the evil day for landlords', for what they wanted was 'more land for those who have too little, and some for those who have none at all'. Among other speakers were John Murdoch, and the Revd Donald MacCallum. And at one stage the conference adjourned to take part in a 3,000-strong procession, in which Ross and Sutherland men carried a banner inscribed, 'Men of Kincardine, remember Glencalvie, Greenyards and Culrain'. At a rally which followed this march, Dr Clark declared that the Crofters' Act was entirely inadequate to redress the grievances of the Highland people, and insisted that no legislation would be satisfactory unless it provided for the restoration of the land to the people. Fraser-MacIntosh, meanwhile, demanded for Scotland 'full control of her domestic concerns by means of a separate parliament'; and there were further resolutions on the Game Laws and deer-forests.

But the landlords were still prepared to fight. Even as the conference drew to a close, the authorities in Argyll were preparing to drag the men of Tiree to court and gaol. And from the south of England, the gunship *Humber* was taking her departure from Portsmouth, with 100 marines embarked, bound towards the Hebrides.

The day following her departure, the police committee of Inverness-shire met. It became evident that yet another police expedition to Skye was under way, for the purpose of giving protection to officers serving writs for arrears. Within hours of the police committee convening in Inverness, the news had reached Portree: 'The rumour spread rapidly, causing quite a flutter of excitement among the prominent parties connected with the Land League.' The local branch of the League nevertheless met to hear their delegates report on the Bonar Bridge conference, which had been 'another nail in the landlord coffin'.

Three days later the *Humber* was 'hourly expected', and 'great excitement prevailed' in the town: 'The news spread rapidly throughout the island. The excitement, which was at a very high pitch before then, was intensified.' But first the steamer *Glencoe* arrived at Portree from Strome carring Ivory himself. He was quickly recognised and 'followed all the way to the Royal Hotel, the crowd hooting and yelling all the time'.

By this time the Crofters' Commission was ready to begin the long process of reviewing crofters' rents around the Highlands. It was scheduled to begin operations at Wick in the middle of October, where in addition to the 300 applications already received, it would also adjudicate on Sir Robert Sinclair's crofting rents – which he had recently refused to reduce. Its deliberations formed an essential backdrop to the agitation throughout the years from 1886 to 1888. The crofters' movement was thus in the difficult tactical position of imminent, if partial, redress on the one hand, and coercion on the other. Of that second strand, Skye was to be cockpit towards the end of 1886.

In fact, sheriff-officers had been expected to begin serving, or attempting to serve, writs prior to the arrival of the *Humber* and Ivory on the *Glencoe*. But they then refused to proceed, as they considered the police then available to them no match for the forces likely to oppose their attempt, and had thus chosen to wait for the arrival of the *Humber's* marines.

In Sconser, meanwhile, on the very morning that the *Humber* was steaming for Portree, the crofters there found some of Lord MacDonald's deer among their crops, about which traditional depradation they had complained so bitterly to the Napier Commission. (Readers might need reminding that to this day landlords have the exclusive right to shoot deer, and penalties are severe for anyone inclined to test this exclusivity. Landlords do not, however, own the deer; and are not therefore, in law, responsible for any damage that the deer might cause.) A large crowd of men, women and boys drove the deer into the sea, where they were captured by boat, towed ashore and then slaughtered. (For crofters, on a Highland estate, in broad daylight, to behave in this manner today would be considered revolutionary, if not psychotic; in the 1880s it was at least an act of unspeakable sedition – and eloquent testimony to the extent to which active anti-landlordism had grown in Skye since the trouble at Braes just four years earlier.) By then it had become known that on the day Ivory reached the island, its landlords had agreed to end their rates-strike and pay off their arrears, 'in order to avoid the service of writs on themselves'.

Meanwhile the Presbytery of Skye had met at Portree to resume consideration of charges against the Revd Donald MacCallum. This followed their censure of him the previous March 'for his connection with the crofters' agitation', and for his 'incitement of the crofters to violence and class hatred'. On this occasion, after acrimonious debate, MacCallum was again censured for writing to the newspapers to dispute, it was claimed, the accuracy of the Presbytery minutes from the previous March. A sideshow to the military invasion, it speaks eloquently enough of the strains that agitation was causing in the Church of Scotland. It was also a prologue to further trials for MacCallum in the coming weeks.

As to the invasion itself, the *North British Daily Mail* persuasively editorialised that it had all been got up by the Skye landlords as a trick to get their rents from the crofters:

It will be remembered that the landlords refused to pay their poor and school rates on the grounds that they had not received the rents upon which the rates were assessed. Of course, the withholding of the rates was illegal; but few persons imagined at the time what a beautiful bit of legal procedure the landlords intended their illegal action to bring about. They made out lists of arrears were due; list which somehow did not show by whom the arrears were due, but gave the impression that the crofters were the offenders, and that nothing but force would put an end to their defiance of the law. Inquiries in parliament, however, brought out the fact that the landlords owed by far the largest part of the arrears. In the parish of Portree, for instance, the crofters owed only £47 for arrears, while the landlords owed £336. So the armed force has been sent; and what has happened? On the very day the expedition arrived at the island the lairds paid their rates, leaving the expedition to be directed entirely against the crofters for the small amount they owe. But for what purpose then did the lairds get the expedition there? Not to serve writs for rates, but to serve writs for rent. It is evident that the landlords were not only well organised, but were kept well informed. How did the landlords know the day the expedition would arrive? But as the crofters have not paid their insignificant amount of rates – not having had the chance which was given to the landlords – the expedition goes on, and the opportunity is obtained for serving the rent writs under its protection. It is all very clever. One week of a local parliament in Scotland would smash up the rotten system.

Trick or not, the *Humber* was shortly to leave Portree for Glendale, having embarked seventy-five marines, thirty police, and two sheriff-officers and attendants. The vessel reached Colbost in Loch Dunvegan at noon and landed her soldiers, 'armed to the teeth', shortly afterwards.

And the next day, Ivory's expedition turned its attention to the village of Stein on the estate of Waternish, where writs were served again for arrears of rates and rent. With the *Humber* lying in Lochbay, there was no overt opposition, although the cattle of the township had earlier been driven to the hill to avoid any chance of poinding.

The *North British Daily Mail* observed, 'Every village and hamlet throughout Skye is permeated with the doctrines of the Land League. The land-reform agitation now has a grip of the entire island. Stein is no exception. A number of the inhabitants are Radicals and sturdy land reformers.' Some fifty summary warrants and summonses were served in the Stein district, and the following day another fifty warrants were served in Glendale, Roag and Edinbane. And it was reported, not perhaps without justice, that 'several crofters will shortly be evicted from their holdings at the point of the bayonet, and should this be done, it is feared there will be a general uprising throughout the length and breadth of the island'.

The next Monday the military expedition travelled to Uig, where around twenty-five warrants were served for arrears of rent and rates in Kilmuir and Kilmaluag.

Still, there had been no violent response from the crofters – despite the clear pro-crofter nature of the evidence unveiled in the press, whose corps of reporters trailed Ivory around Skye, and whose reports were not considered by him to be favourable to the landlords. In fact his co-operation was denied to all but the correspondent of *The Scotsman*.

Ivory also moved against Valtos and Lealt, where the record of landlord–tenant conflict and the spirit of social relations in the Highlands over the previous century is caught in one paragraph:

> Valtos has a notorious reputation for the persistency and in many cases the violence with which it has kept alive the land war. The crofters have been harshly dealt with by the proprietor, and by exhorbitant rents and excessive sub-division of crofts the people have been reduced to the verge of starvation. In 1854, when Fraser purchased Kilmuir, the township of Valtos paid a gross rental of £48. The rent some years afterwards was raised to £94.

As Peter MacDonald had complained to the Napier Commission, 'The principal cause of our grievance is the repeated raising of our rent. We pray that the Royal Commission will give us the land in a way that we can live on, and in such a way that the proprietor cannot raise our rents or remove us.'

Meanwhile, as the sheriff-officers served notices at Sconser and Breakish the following day, the Crofters' Commission held its first hearing at Dornoch. The majority of the applicants were crofters from the estate of a Mr Sutherland of Skibo; and his response to the crofters' claims and demands was to typify another forty years of landlord-obstruction of land-reform in the Highlands. Sutherland appeared in person to argue that his estate did not fall within the provisions of the Crofters' Act, as he had 'already warned the crofters from their holdings'. But the significance of this was not confined to Skibo, of course; these proceedings would in full be available to the crofters of Skye, through the daily press, within a day, or two at the most.

By this time, Ivory had served notices all over the MacDonald estates in Skye. The day that the Tiree land-raiders appeared in court in Edinburgh, Ivory left Skye for a few days, leaving its crofters to anticipate the arrival of the Crofters' Commission – for already hundreds of them were demanding a stay of any evictions and rent-payments until the commissioners had visited the island (very clearly indeed, the proceedings of the commission were followed with detailed interest!).

The Scotsman meantime suggested that John MacPherson had been paying his rent in secret, but 300 Land Leaguers met in the Colbost schoolhouse to deny the claim with appropriate scorn.

Until this stage, Ivory's expedition had passed fairly peacefully. But on Monday, 25 October, the press announced latest developments with shrieking headlines – 'exciting scenes on Skye', 'desperate resistance of crofters', 'writs served at point of bayonet'; and reports of deforcement and arrests. The scene of the violence was again Kilmuir, the expedition having left Uig early in the morning with eleven police and seventeen marines to protect the sheriff-officer in serving charges of decrees obtained in the Portree sheriff court on crofters in the townships on the western side of the estate.

At Borneskitaig, 'fighting broke out, involving a large number of people in the township. This fighting lasted for nearly an hour, with the police and sheriff kicked and pelted with mud, until the writs were served at the point of bayonets and six crofters arrested.' And the following day a sheriff-officer was again deforced while serving a writ for arrears of rent in Garalapin, on land owned by Lord MacDonald.

By this time Ivory was on his way back to the island. He arrived the following day, and took seventy-five marines and thirteen police to Kilmuir, to conduct arrests for deforcement. When they reached Herbusta, however, they found the township deserted. After a diligent search and questioning of children, they apprehended one cowherd and a Mrs MacMillan, who were both then taken off to Portree under marine guard. And the next day Ivory was back at Herbusta, at midnight; but all the men wanted for deforcement were in hiding and not one was to be found, despite Ivory arriving in the township at 1 a.m. and searching the houses for two hours.

On the 29 October, however, Ivory's force did arrest eight men and a woman on Lord MacDonald's townships in the vicinity of Garalapin, in connection with the deforcement of the sheriff-officer the previous week.

The *North British Daily Mail's* editorial said that Ivory's actions were clearly illegal, though 'destined to mark an epoch for the land movement':

> The whole process of serving writs for rents in Skye has been illegal from beginning to end. In places which come within the Crofters' Act all question of rent are by that Act held in abeyance until decided by the Crofters' Commission. Skye comes within the Act. The formal document signifying that fact was signed by the Secretary for Scotland on the 18th of this month . . . Skye has been under the Act since the 18th inst. and the writs for rent were not begun to be served till after that date. The service has therefore been illegal; and sheriff Ivory has been raiding the island not only in a lawless manner, but on a lawless errand, while the crofters have only resisted unlawful proceedings.

Throughout November the sheriff nevertheless went on with his work, poinding possessions from Broadford to Staffin. In consequence of his conduct, thirty-three members of the Skye Volunteer Corps tendered their resignations, so reducing its numbers that it was likely to become extinct: 'The Mutiny Act was dangled in the faces of the men, but they have refused to be intimidated.'

Ivory journeyed to Braes with forty marines and a dozen police. Later, at Broadford, they found the road blocked with stones, and two boys were arrested. Then another midnight raid was launched against Herbusta – again without success. As a result, crofters' meetings were banned; but this did not stop them. Ivory, in short, was not prepared to surrender Skye without a fight. And at the beginning of November, John Nicolson of Portree was arrested on charges of defaming and insulting the sheriff.

Nicolson had written to the pro-crofter press, claiming to have witnessed Ivory in Portree post office, 'endeavouring to press the telegraphist to disclose the names of persons who had occasion to send messages through the office in November of 1884, when the first military expedition visited the island' (trying, in other words, to break the Land League system of communication from the mainland to Skye, and within the island itself). And in the middle of November, J.G. MacKay, 'one of the most prominent leaders of the land movement in the island', was also arrested on a charge of defaming and insulting Ivory. MacKay, the author of several pamphlets on the land question, was said to have defamed Ivory in a letter published in the *Inverness Courier*. According to the *North British Daily Mail*, he had called the sheriff a 'judicial monster'. (The following day's paper, incidentally, reported a meeting of Highlanders resident in South Africa, 'condemning in the strongest of terms the Duke of Argyll' and the conduct of Highland landlords in general.)

The landlords of Skye at this point tried a manoeuvre. They jointly appealed to Ivory to proceed no further; and on 11 November Lord MacDonald, Fraser of Kilmuir, Robertson of Greshornish and MacDonald of Waternish had their solicitor announce in the Portree sheriff court that they had decided to suspend further action in the matter of recovering rent arrears – on condition, however, that the crofters consigned two-thirds of those arrears to that court. The landlords also announced that they were prepared to abide by any decision of the Crofters' Commission. In fact, they had little option but to do so anyway. The crofters, therefore, spurned the offer. They considered it a trick and believed that consigning the money would be equivalent to paying it. Ivory consequently voyaged yet again to Glendale with marines and police, and also to the north end of the island. At Stein two vessels anchored offshore and forces were landed to locate and arrest the Revd Donald MacCallum – a 'man of considerable intellectual ability' and one who had a 'thorough grip of the land agitation'. Since becoming minister of Waternish established church, he had 'taken an active part in indoctrinating the islanders with the principles of the Land League'. And in Glendale, John MacPherson was also arrested.

MacCallum was to have preached in the Stenscholl church the following Sunday. Instead he was in gaol in Portree along with John MacPherson. But when bailed on Monday, he returned to Stenscholl and delivered his Sunday sermon then. Perhaps understandably, J.G. MacKay wrote to the *North British Daily Mail*, saying that the struggle in Skye was now at an acute stage: 'Landlordism is making its strongest and last pull; it is playing its last card, and it is time for the masses to rise up.'

And in fact, the Ivory expedition was coming rapidly to a close. In London a crofters' delegation was pressing the case of the crofters in Skye; while in simple financial terms Ivory's invasion, quite apart from its cost to county and central funds, had been a failure. It had also been a disaster in terms of publicity – 'Midnight raids worthy of Zululand have been the order of the night, and Sheriff Ivory has had a judicial and martial debauch,' in the words of one account.

Despite the gunboats, marines and police, not much money had been collected. 'Seventy-five marines collected between them £200 in rent. The arrears still due, or supposed to be due, are £19,500. If it takes seventy-five men and a sheriff thirty days to collect £200, how many will it take to collect £19,500?' demanded one observer. (In fact, said the *North British Daily Mail*, money collected for rates – due to the authorities – was actually being debited for rent – due to the landlords: the rates-collectors being also the estate-factors.)

In short, Ivory had failed once again on Skye. And as the government was not prepared to force the issue, the sheriff returned home, though in the week of his going it was reported that a two-month-old baby had been poinded in lieu of rent. 'The baby's value was declared by competent appraisers to be the equivalent of 2p, and to be the property of the complainer, Lord MacDonald. At the same time, a collie puppy was valued at the equivalent of 5p and a graip at the equivalent of 10p.' Given the prevailing conditions, the significance of the report lay not in its accuracy (it was denied) but in the publicity it attained; and the extent to which it was seen at least to be accurate in spirit. For many, both within the Highlands and without, it was certainly that.

At the beginning of December, the marines left Skye too, bound for Chatham. There remained the matter of court cases for those crofters arrested during the Ivory campaign. Shortly before Christmas, six men from Bornaskitaig appeared in court in Edinburgh charged with mobbing, rioting and assault. They drew six months each. And on 28 December, another batch of Skye crofters left Portree for court in Edinburgh.

Ivory, however, had failed to crush agitation in the island, while as in Skye, an upsurge in anti-landlord direct action across the Minch in Lewis can only have been fuelled by the ongoing proceedings of the Crofters'

Commission. The commission, after all, was still touring the Highlands, examining (which would mean reducing) crofters' rents – to intense interest on the part of the crofters themselves, and with an effect similar to that of the Napier Commission tour. Initially a matter of some debate and doubt, the commission's membership was approved of by MacFarlane and Fraser-MacIntosh; and by October it was in Sutherland, to hear the claims of seventy crofters with regard to the rent they were paying.

No one had expected it to favour the landlords. As the *North British Daily Mail* editorialised, 'According to the Act, a landlord may apply to have fair rents fixed for his land, but it is somewhat significant that not one of them have as yet troubled the Commission with an application.'

The same paper extensively covered individual crofter applications with regard to land and housing. For instance, it reported the case of Andrew MacKay, applying on behalf of his mother, with regard to a croft of four acres of arable and two of outrun. 'His grandfather was the first tenant. He came there in 1812, at the time of the Sutherland clearances. There was then no arable land at all, the whole of the place being moorland. All the arable ground has been reclaimed by his family on the croft.' Meanwhile at Shean, beyond Invershin, the croft of Hector Forbes, was 'little better' than the surrounding moorland:

> The house was the most miserable one which up till then the commissioners had seen. Situated on a damp foundation, built up for perhaps a foot and a half, with loose water-worn stones, on the top of which are constructed rude walls of peat, and covered with a rude thatching of broom, the house presented an appearance which it was difficult to associate with a habitation intended for the abode of man.

Diligently, the *Mail*'s reporters followed the commission throughout November. Their despatches never failed to underline, *inter alia*, the extent to which so many witnesses simply refused to give evidence except through the medium of the commission's Gaelic-language interpreters.

By the beginning of November the commissioners had moved to consider applications from tenants of various proprietors in Sutherland, despite attempts to thwart its work by the landlords. At Gruids, for instance, on land owned by Lady Matheson of Lewis, an attempt was made to persuade the crofters to spurn the protection of the Crofters' Act, and thus of the commission. This persuasion, however, they ignored; and their evidence was given by the local Land League leader William Black, who had also given evidence before Lord Napier.

According to one report, Black had been subject to an eviction attempt. But his neighbours from Lairg, Rosehall, Bonar Bridge, 'and many other districts', assembled 'to his aid and made such a determined resistance that the officers of the law were forced to decamp without effecting their purpose'. Once again, the evidence heard sustained that collective sense of injustice, that collective vision of redress, that had in the previous decade been heard with increasing volume across the Highlands. Its central theme was the old one of: the land for the people.

However by that Christmas the commission, acutely aware of the continuing agitation in Skye and elsewhere, was drawing favourable comment from pro-crofter sources; not least by dint of its decision to thwart landlord attempts to circumvent the spirit of the Act by getting their crofters to sign leases. The commission ruled in this respect that only leases of more than one year (precisely the sort of crofting lease a landlord would avoid) would render the Act inapplicable.

The perceived pro-crofter rulings of the commission had a dual effect across the Highlands. Early adjudications tended to serve as an incitement to crofters everywhere to have high expectations of the commission when it reached their area, thereby serving also as an encouragement to sustained agitation until such time as it did.

So once again there was trouble on Skye – at Elishader in Kilmuir – with the (by now) usual disturbance when sheriff-officers attempted to force payment of rent arrears. And just weeks later, further trouble erupted on Lord MacDonald's lands in south Skye, at Sconser. In March, with the Crofters' Commission in the island and taking evidence, the Sconser people readily admitted that 'on more than one occasion of late they had driven deer found among their corn into the sea, where the animals were caught by fishing boat, the spoil being equally divided'.

By now, in the spring of 1887, having won security of tenure in law and being in the process of winning rent-reductions, the land movement was in the course of moving towards the demand of the return of the land increasingly under deer-forest. Towards the end of the year, this would re-appear in spectacular form. But meanwhile, the Act of the previous summer was amended, again in the crofters' favour; an amendment of which even *The Times* approved:

> By the Crofters' Act of last year, power is given to the crofter to apply to the commission to have a fair rent fixed. But during the period between the date of application, and the final decision of the commission, it is possible according to a judgement of the Scotch courts, for the landlord to make the crofter a bankrupt for non-payment of arrears of rent, and so expel him from the holding and deprive him of the benefits of the Act. This would in reality be an evasion of the statute; for the commission is expressly authorised to stop all proceedings for removal of the crofter in respect of non-payment till the application is determined.

The Times therefore approved of the amendment, which allowed the

A CROFTER FAMILY IN POOLEWE
Edinburgh City Libraries

JOHN MACPHERSON, BY 1883 NATIONALLY
KNOWN AS THE 'GLENDALE MARTYR'
Illustrated London News

THE AVTHORITIES READ THE RIOT ACT, AT AIGNISH FARM, ISLE OF LEWIS, 1888
Illustrated London News

POLICE AND MARINES TACKLE PROTESTING CROFTERS ON LEWIS
Illustrated London News

WOMEN PLAYED A MAJOR ROLE IN MANY OF THE LAND-
CENTRED DISPUTES IN HIGHLAND HISTORY
Illustrated London News

JOHN MACPHERSON ADDRESSES A
LAND LEAGUE MEETING IN SKYE
Illustrated London News

DR RODERICK
MACDONALD,
CROFTERS' MP
FOR ROSS AND
CROMARTY
*Illustrated London
News*

J. MACDONALD-
CAMERON,
CROFTERS' MP
FOR WICK
*Illustrated London
News*

BALALLAN CAIRN, HONOURING THE PARK DEER RAIDERS
© Eòlas

LORD BROCKET MEETS ADOLF HITLER AT NUREMBERG, 1938,
ON THE LATTER'S BIRTHDAY; LORD McGOWAN LOOKS ON
Herald Picture Library

THE KNOYDART LAND-PEGGERS STUDY THE INTERDICT
SERVED ON THEM, 1948
Herald Picture Library

SCENE FROM THE BALELONE LAND-RAID, 1952
Herald Picture Library

DOUGALD MACKINNON AND DOLLY FERGUSON UNVEIL
THE PLAQUE TO MARK THE ISLE OF EIGG HERITAGE TRUST'S
BUY-OUT, JUNE 1997
Courtesy of *Press & Journal*

ALLAꞐ ꞪACRAE OF
ASSYꞐ†
© John Paul Photography

FACAL BHO'N CHEANNARD

†HE CUL†URAL
IꞐ†ERFACE
*West Highland
Free Press*

"Hello, House of Lords? . . . I want to introduce a Bill ending security of tenure for crofters."

commission to postpone any attempt to bankrupt a crofter – by delaying an action for recovery of rent, until the commission had a chance to lower it.

In parliament too, the work of the Crofters' Commission was being raised. The member for Ross and Cromarty urged the government to appoint more valuers, to speed up its work. In May the member for Caithness was reporting in the Commons press coverage of crofters' grievances in Skye, with particular attention to the availability of the land lying under sheep and deer. As these reports said of the commissioners' work on the island, the visit of the commission caused a 'great deal of excitement' in the township: 'The people crowded out to meet them and followed them from croft to croft, with long tales of their grievances.' At various points of inspection the commissioners were met by 'groups of men who urged them to give the crofters more land. It was in vain that the commissioners pointed out that under the present Act they had no power to create new crofts, even if the land were available'.

Thus the government was asked, in anticipation of legislation still many years distant, to empower the commission to form new townships and holdings to relieve such congestion. But the government would not do so.

The strains induced by concession on the one hand and attempted coercion on the other, along with attempts to restructure it as a formal progressive political party in the Highlands, were by now having a noticeable and public effect on the Land League. Acrimonious debate began to surface in the columns of the *North British Daily Mail*, particularly at the approach of the 1887 League conference, which was to be held at Oban in September and was intended to unite 'under one name and one organisation all societies advocating land law and other reforms in the Highlands'.

Once again, however, the established leaders were in attendance at the meeting. Among them were Dr Clark, Dr MacDonald, D.H. MacFarlane, Donald MacCallum, Donald Murray, John MacPherson, Stuart Glennie, and John Murdoch – most of whom formed the new executive. Generally, the view of the conference was that the original Act was no more than 'an instalment of justice'. The now familiar call for a Scottish parliament was made; it was agreed that the land question in the Highlands 'would not be settled until they had a Scottish Legislature and a Scottish Executive'. As Stuart Glennie advocated, it was time to establish a Scottish National League (again, anticipating events by many years) with its object 'the securing of Home Rule for Scotland to achieve a satisfactory settlement of the land question, which they could not get as long as they were overruled by English members of parliament'. Suitably enough, another speaker was Donald MacRae of Lewis, whose name was soon to be associated in a major way with the land movement there, and who warned that Lewis would 'fight rather than surrender'.

Shortly before the island had this opportunity however, there was to be the celebrated case in Sutherland of the fugitive Land Leaguer Hugh Kerr, as a result of trouble at Clashmore in Lochinver deriving from a crofters' decision to seize a local farm. The farm was duly seized and it transpired that the steading of the farm had been destroyed by fire – 'singularly enough', in the words of *The Scotsman*. Some days earlier a barn and byre at Glendhu had also been burnt to the ground – 'As yet, no cause has been publicly assigned of the origin of the fire.'

A correspondent in the *North British Daily Mail* observed that if there were less deer in the Highlands there might be room for more men 'and fewer Cockneys and German Princelings'; while at Land League meetings throughout the district, raids on deer-forests were under discussion. Similar action was also being discussed with reference to the Winans deer-forests in Ross-shire and Inverness-shire. A detachment of crofters connected with the League was reported in Beauly, canvassing for support: the plan was being 'seriously discussed by both cottars and crofters who have been evicted out of Strathglass and neighbouring glens'.

At the beginning of December, therefore, eleven policemen and forty men of the Royal Scots arrived at Lochinver, aboard the gunboat *Jackal*. They were under the command of the chief constable and sheriff of Sutherland, who had for the past week been in urgent communication with London and Edinburgh regarding events in Assynt. After an 'exceedingly stormy passage' the gunboat reached Lochinver, the party marched for Clashmore, and managed one arrest. But Hugh Kerr, a well-known and popular local League leader, had disappeared into the hills – with a symbolism unlikely to have gone unnoticed by the indigenous population of his district, of the Highlands, or of Scotland.

The prospect of a raid on the Winans deer-forest was still being discussed. In the middle of December a special meeting of the Lovat Land League was held at Kilmorack. It was denied that moves were afoot to organise a mass raid, but also denied were claims that the estate was so well guarded that the League could not take it if it wanted to.

Clearly, crofter consciousness was at a high pitch. It was encouraged, doubtless, by the continuing and widely publicised work of the Crofters' Commission, with even the traditionally pro-landlord *Scotsman* showing signs of criticising some landlords. As the paper said:

> Whatever may be thought of the Crofters' Act in its bearing on the relation between landlord and tenant, there will be a general conviction that it has been the means of doing good in the case of the Clyth tenants. The commissioners in that case have reduced the rents on an average of 50 per cent, and have wiped off 82 per cent of the arrears. It was shown that there had been the most unmerciful screwing-up of rents, and that practices had been resorted to as to arrears which were on the sharp side.

THE MASS MOVEMENT IN ACTION

In Assynt, meantime, affairs at Clashmore were 'assuming a very serious aspect'. The week before Christmas, the chief constable and ten of his men were billeted in the factor's house. Two had already been assaulted and stoned; dykes had been torn down; and three days before Christmas, the *Seahorse* arrived at Lochinver under cover of darkness. Forty marines helped serve interdicts relating to the seizure of the Clashmore farm; but 'nothing of Hugh Kerr's whereabouts are known, though the general impression is that he is in hiding not far from the township'. *The Times*, meanwhile, reported that fires at more than one of the Duke's farm-steadings had 'aroused suspicion of incendiarism'.

By the following week, the Glasgow Sutherlandshire Association was meeting in Glasgow to consider an appeal from the people of Stoer 'narrating the grievances which caused the present rising in the Clashmore district, and appealing for funds in support of the families of the imprisoned crofters'. Among the speakers was Angus Sutherland, MP.

At the beginning of February, the trial of the Clashmore people opened in Edinburgh. Nine women had smashed open a gate to the farm, and assaulted the factor; and later a fifty-strong crowd had surrounded a valuer with the warning that no farmer would be allowed on the land – 'for the people were going to take it for themselves'. Three of the accused were found guilty, among them the wife of Hugh Kerr. He, however, remained at liberty. As one paper noted, he had for months evaded capture, police surveillance, midnight raids and military expedition.

Elsewhere in Assynt, meanwhile, a 'raid on the Canisp deer-forest was in contemplation', while the crofters around Scourie were 'making ready for another raid on part of the Reay forest'. The Duke of Sutherland's agents believed that if something was not done soon to protect the forests, 'very serious consequences may shortly follow'.

Kerr, meantime, remained free – a Land League organiser on the run, his wife in gaol in Edinburgh for anti-landlord agitation, her husband giving interviews from a cave to a sympathetic press! The authorities spent over £1,500 trying to capture him, but without success. And when he finally surrendered to them, he was given one month in gaol – a light sentence in comparison to the sentences awarded Lewis men that winter for raiding the deer-forests and farms of their own island.

In Lewis, of course, land hunger was acute, and the popular response to deer-forests equally acute. Along with the deer-forests went large-scale popular destitution. By the onset of winter in 1887–88, much of the crofter and cottar population was on the edge of starvation. And yet in the district of Lochs, Lady Matheson had let her 40,000-acre deer-forest to an Englishman called Platt. Popular demand for more land was intense; but for years the estate had refused to concede it. Six years earlier, when the lease of the land now occupied by deer was on the eve of expiry, Lady Matheson had refused a petititon that at least some of it be given to the people. Two years later, she had again refused a similar petition.

By 1882, Lady Matheson's tenant at Park was A.C. Sellar, of the Patrick Sellar family. Two years later his sheep-farming activities gave way to deer, like another thirty or so sheep farms during the decade. In January 1887, however, a new schoolteacher had come to the area. Donald MacRae (who was to be a delegate to the forthcoming Oban conference of the League) had been expelled from his position at Rosskeen for involvement in the agitation there. At the beginning of November, MacRae had convened a meeting at Balallan schoolhouse, where it was decided to occupy the Park deer-forest. Within the fortnight the raid began. Leaving their townships early in the morning, the crofters, were 'supplied with guns. They had flags flying, and a piper headed the Balallan contingent.'

How many deer were killed in the forest is open to question; but for the authorities, the fact of the raid alone was alarming enough. The local sheriff warned that there was 'civil war in Lochs'; the tenant of the forest put his yacht at the disposal of the authorities; and the police in Stornoway were followed through the town by a large, and unfriendly, contingent of crofters and their supporters. Central to the awareness of the raiders was an 1881 petition to Lady Matheson for an apportionment of the land occupied by the forest; it had taken her until 1883 to reject the petition. The formation of the forest, according to one report, had involved the destruction of forty or fifty crofting townships, and the land could now support two or three hundred of the raiders. According to the same report, 1,500 of the 6,000 people in Lochs had taken part in the raid and 200 deer had been killed (which was absolutely not the case), with some butchered and cooked at a raiders' camp in the forest.

Within a day or two of entry to the forest, men from Harris had arrived. Great excitement, it was reported, prevailed in Balallan, with 'sentries posted at various points commanding views of the district'. As a result, eighty-two men and five officers of the Royal Scots were despatched from Glasgow for Lewis, and three carriages were made ready for them at Inverness station so that they and their equipment might be conveyed without delay to Strome and thence on to Stornoway. It was also reported, 'The crofters all over the island are unanimous in approval of the course adopted by the Lochs people. Large meetings are being held all over the west side of Lewis at which the new plan of campaign is warmly discussed.'

On arrival in Dingwall, the Royal Scots (who before dawn that morning had marched down from their barracks in Maryhill to Glasgow's Queen Street Station, doubtless observed closely by the crofters' friends in the city as they did so), were greeted by an angry crowd. And when the *Ajax* left the Clyde with 400 marines on board bound for Stornoway, her departure and destination were urgently telegraphed ahead. In the event she was disabled and nearly wrecked on the trip north – a symbolism that would scarcely have gone unappreciated in Lewis and the wider Highlands.

Confronted with this major demonstration of force, however, the raiders promptly withdrew from the forest; and it quickly transpired that the raid had been a highly-organised tactic to draw national attention to the question of Lady Matheson's Park, and Lady Matheson's hungry tenants. The authorities had been informed beforehand of the raid and its leading participants were ready to co-operate fully, having themselves arrested and brought to court: 'The leader of the movement in the Lochs parish is the schoolmaster of Balallan, Donald MacRae.'

Thus nine men soon afterwards surrendered to the authorities at Stornoway and were charged with incitement to intimidation. They included MacRae, of whom one report said: 'It is clear that the officials of the Castle are determined to crush him. He is a dangerous man on an estate such as Lady Matheson's, where the people are starving.'

In the face of this destitution, however, the landlords had nothing better to offer their tenants than the traditional remedy of emigration. A colonial agent was at this time in London, 'prosecuting a scheme for the assisted emigration of Highland crofters'. These putative emigrants would be expected to repay, 'on easy terms' the 'sum necessary to set them up in their new allotments'. The Marquis of Lorne had already expressed 'keen support for the whole idea'. Further enthusiasm was 'eagerly anticipated' from the Duke of Argyll – and Lady Matheson.

In Lewis, consequently, the Park example was being copied. On the last day of November, cottars from Ness and Barvas marched to the sheep farm at Galston and warned the tenant there that when his lease had expired they were going to take forcible possession of the place – which 'measured eight miles by six, all of which was formerly cultivated by crofters who were evicted. They gave the tenant warning to sell off his stock and prepare to emigrate.'

Shortly afterwards, the last of the men wanted in connection with the Park raid surrendered; but at the same time the land-leaguers of Lochs met to consider their next move. The meeting began with the expulsion of suspected informers, continued with congratulations to the men charged as a result of the raid, and concluded with a threat to reoccupy the Park forest.

So at the end of that week, a detachment of marines was again bound towards Lewis. These came from Plymouth aboard the *Seahorse*, with 100 rounds of ball cartridge per man. The *Jackal* was under recreational orders for Loch Shell, as the officers had been invited to a few days' shooting of such deer as were left in Park by Mrs Platt, wife of the shooting-tenant.

While the results of the Crofters' Commission in North Uist were reported, and a rent reduction of 28 per cent ordered, the *Seahorse* was arriving at Stornoway; the *Jackal* was lying at Eishken; and the Marquis of Lothian was arguing that 'people were so desperately poor in Lewis that they could be nothing but better off if they would only emigrate'.

His counsel, unsurprisingly, went unheeded in Lewis. On the shortest day of the year 4,300 cottars from Borve, Shader and Barvas marched to Galston sheep farm, surveyed the lands, and warned the tenant to leave as soon as his lease expired the following March. The contingents were 'headed by pipers and flags in military order'; in Skye, land-leaguers were meeting outdoors in a snowstorm to express sympathy with the raiders in Lewis.

The following Saturday, Christmas Eve, on the other side of the island 1,000 crofters and cottars of Point marched on the Aignish sheep-farm, yet again with flags and pipers, to warn the farmer to get out within fourteen days. They then marched on to the Melbost sheep-farm, tenanted by a relation of the Aignish farmer, with a similar threat. On 29 December a Land League meeting drew crofters and cottars from throughout the district; and it was agreed that, a week or so later, the stock of the farmers would be driven away, and replaced by crofters' stock.

Four days later a proclamation under the terms of the Riot Act was posted widely throughout the neighbourhood prohibiting such a raid. Unperturbed, a 300-strong deputation presented itself on the steps of Lady Matheson's castle to demand the farms. She refused and suggested emigration. At a mass meeting later that day in Stornoway, 'strong and passionate language was freely used'.

In Edinburgh, the trial of the Park raiders was scheduled for the opening weeks of the new year. Donald MacRae announced that he would be calling as a witness Lady Matheson. The island was by now 'in a seriously disturbed condition; the reply which the people got from the proprietrix will not tend in any way to allay the turbulent feeling that is abroad'.

The following Monday, therefore, the raid on Aignish took place, with a party of Royal Scots in reserve and thirty-six marines from the *Seahorse* stationed at the farmhouse. Soon after dawn, a police scout observed by telescope that 'there was great excitement and stir among the townships', and that people were moving to a nearby hill, where a standard was already flying. By noon, the brow of this hill was 'gradually blackening'; and then the crowd rushed down, spreading across the farm, and driving the stock before it. Bayonets were fixed; the Riot Act read; the Royal Scots summoned; and thirteen crofters arrested. That night, thirty-three marines and twelve police guarded the farmhouse.

On the following Tuesday, the rifles in the Stornoway premises of the local Volunteer company were disabled and the ammunition taken aboard the *Seahorse*; while it was reported that the farm of Galston, on the west side of Lewis, would shortly be raided. Mass deputations to the Matheson castle were now almost a daily affair; one 150-strong group of Coll crofters was turned away with the suggestion that its members should emigrate. As a result, the *Forester* was provisioning on the Clyde, and embarking marines for Lewis. The Aignish people however, unrepentant, gave notice that in five weeks 1,000 men would begin cultivation of the Aignish farm. There were also fears of raiding at Carloway and Shawbost; and from Uig it was reported that raids were also being planned.

In the middle of January, the thirteen arrested Aignish raiders were taken aboard the *Jackal* bound for Dingwall gaol, under escort of marines and police. Amid rumours the previous evening of a rescue bid, the men were embarked at 2 a.m. That same day the raiders from Park were on their way to trial in Edinburgh; 400 yards of dyke had been destroyed at Galston; and at Dalbeg farm, in Barvas, there had been threats made and police sent for.

There had also been some destruction of fences at Dell. And at Linshader, in the parish of Uig, 500 had marched from Tolsta, Dun, Carloway, Breasclete and Callernish. At Garrynahine, they warned the tenant of the sheep farm there to clear out at once, and then proceeded to deliver the same message to the farmer at Linshadder.

On the Monday, the trial of the Park raiders began in Edinburgh. The jury heard of how 130 men had marched from Gravir behind a red flag; how, in a crowd of around 150, there were perhaps fifty firearms (mostly old single-barrelled muzzle-loading shotguns and rifles); how the raiders established their camp in the forest, and how they then began the destruction of the deer.

The agent for the defence noted that the forest extended to 150 square miles; wondered how 150 men could mob and riot over as many square miles; and secured a not guilty verdict. By that evening news of the acquittal had reached even the most remote corners of Lochs. Elsewhere in the island there had been further raiding that same day, with fifty men from Borve destroying a mile of boundary fence at the Galston farm, in the process overpowering a dozen police set there to guard it. The *Seahorse* was sent to Galston with sixty marines and a contingent of the Royal Scots set off to march to the farm. Even as the jury was re-entering the court in Edinburgh, the *Seahorse* was landing her marines at Port of Ness. The next day at dawn, eighty marines and Royal Scots, along with forty police, raided Borve, where 'Land League doctrines have a firm hold'. They arrested six men who had been identified by the local farmer as League activists.

That same week, the example of Lewis was being followed elsewhere. In Skye, the Braes Land League met to demand the division among them of Lord MacDonald's Glennargilt farm. In Glendale, the people were demanding the division of Bracadale and Minginish. And in Ross-shire, 'an attempt may be made on the deer-forest of Kildermorie, on the estate of Munro-Ferguson of Novar; the authorities have been warned of the affair'.

In Lewis, meantime, the Park raiders returned to a triumphant welcome, with bonfires on every hilltop in Lochs. The Borve men were released from custody on grounds of insufficient identification; and a deputation from Back called on Lady Matheson to demand the division among them of the farm at Gress, reading aloud to her a letter with the sharply precautionary conclusion: 'In the case of a refusal it is hard to say what the result will be.'

Donald MacRae was in London, on Land League business, and was interviewed by the city's *Evening Star* at length. 'The schoolmaster of Balallan is in town. He is a famous man in Lewis and not unknown here. In his own island and parish he is the guide and inspirer of the land war, and the leading spirit of that powerful and active body, the Highland Land League. The land for the people, not for the landlords or the deer, and room on it for those who cling to their native soil, is the programme.'

By the end of the month, crofters and cottars in Breasclete and Tolsta were demanding the restoration of the sheep farms at Linshadder and Garynahine. At Coll fences were being destroyed; while to the south, in Barra, a mass-meeting at Castlebay was demanding more land. In Skye Lord MacDonald was taking court action against crofters for non-payment of rent. And on the mainland, a meeting in Brora protested against the recent increase in the county police force, 'as it is only fitted to augment the agitation which is its cause'. In Beauly an enthusiastic meeting of crofters and cottars was held, 'in connection with the Highland Land League, and had reason to rejoice at the recent acquittal of their Lewis brethren, the Park deer raiders'. At Ullapool a similar meeting agreed to 'not rest satisfied until the land which lay in close proximity to them was restored'. The six deer-forests in the parish of Lochbroom ran to 25,000 acres: 'It was agreed to continue the agitation until they secured some of the land in the six neighbouring forests.'

Still, the landlords urged their tenants to emigrate. Hugh Matheson, nephew of the late Sir James, wrote to *The Times* claiming that the poverty of the people was their own fault, as a result of overcrowding themselves on the land left over from deer-forests and sheep farms.

In Lochcarron, however, the local League met to collect money for Lewis, and hear a speaker remind them that 'they had been agitating constitutionally for too long a period. The only remedy for a redress of their grievances lay in their taking possession of the land at an early date.' This, one of the largest League meetings ever in the district, also agreed to prepare for raids in two neighbouring deer-forests. In Skye the tenants at Sconser warned that unless they were granted 'lands now under deer', they would simply take them; while in Kilmuir the tenants of six townships met to discuss similar action. In Greenock 2,000 people met to advise 'every crofter and cottar to set their faces firmly against any scheme of emigration while an acre of fertile land remains out of cultivation, and devoted to sporting purposes'.

And from the New Zealand Gaelic Society money was despatched to Charles Cameron, owner of the *North British Daily Mail*, 'conveying to you the thanks of the Highlanders of this part of the world for your powerful advocacy of the crofter cause'. Those who had subscribed to the appeal identified their origins as: Orkney, Shetland, Lewis, Argyll, Iona, Arran, Lochalsh, Arisaig, Applecross, Tiree, North Uist, Barra, Aberfeldy, Kerrera, Bonar Bridge, Dingwall, Fort William and Mull.

By then, the Aignish men were appearing in Edinburgh on trial. The Stornoway police superintendent told of how the Royal Scots had bayonet-charged the crowd; of how the authorities' warning-posters distributed prior to the raid had been removed; and of how a Stornoway shopkeeper, who was displaying one, had had his windows smashed. Newall, the tenant, told of how the day before Christmas he had met a mob, hundreds strong, carrying a red flag, and of how he was warned that he had fourteen days to get off his farm.

The trial went to a second day. Lord Craighill summed up strongly against the prisoners. The jury found them guilty but recommended leniency; the gallery cheered; and Craighill warned that if they persisted, he would have them thrown out. Having already demonstrated a dislike of Gaelic in his court, Craighill lost no time in imposing sentences of between six and fifteen months – at which the gallery duly hissed. As the *North British Daily Mail* noted, 'The hissing begun there has already spread over the whole of Scotland. Unless something better than gunboats and soldiers and gaols can be offered to the crofters very quickly, the government will find that they have heavy work before them in the Highlands.'

Certainly, the sentences passed in Edinburgh did not dissuade further agitation. The Land League again planned to send fund-raising delegates to the colonies and the Americas. Among these were Donald MacRae, John Murdoch, Angus Sutherland, John MacPherson and Alexander MacKenzie.

In Skye, crofters at Valtos agreed that 'the time for asking was past, the time for taking had come'. In Portree the Land League met to denounce 'with horror and indignation the sentences passed on the Lewis crofters and the manner in which non-English speaking witnesses for the defence in the recent trials were terrorised and browbeaten in court'. Staffin and Valtos tenants met on the sheep farm at Duntulm – 'chiefly made up of crofter townships cleared in the last thirty years' – and warned that they would soon take direct action too.

In Lewis, Lady Matheson received a threatening letter. She sent it to the post office, with the instructions that it be displayed on public view. Meetings in Skye and Sutherland were denouncing the Aignish sentences. Thirty yards of boundary dyke between the farm of Dalmore, Carloway and the township of Garinen were torn down. Lady Matheson received another threatening letter of 'abominable and scandalous content'. The Land League executive met at Dingwall, to denounce the sentences on the Aignish raiders. Two constables were now patrolling the grounds of Stornoway Castle at night; and incoming boats to the harbour watched, for fear of 'agitators' arriving in connection with the issue that had required her ladyship's police protection.

The Mull Land League denounced the Aignish sentences. In Ross-shire, a mass meeting agreed unanimously in favour of a popular invasion of deer-forests in the county on 12 August, to shoot the deer, 'in presence of the sportsmen'. The Alness Land League presented Donald MacRae with a purse of money in connection with his services to the movement. And towards the end of February, the *Seahorse* was sent to Bayble to assist in the arrest of two men wanted in connection with the recent riot at Aignish.

The Crofters' Act, therefore, and the work of the Crofters' Commission, had not stilled agitation. But they had acted, if anything, as a spur to further popular efforts to reclaim the land of the Highlands for the common, native, people of those Highlands. And at the back of it all – the popular demonstrations led by defiant pipers, the red flags, the speeches at conference and cornstack – ran one swift and central undercurrent: the repudiation of landlordism, in its various dimensions, both in the Highlands and throughout Scotland. In the words of one editorial on events in the Hebrides: 'We thus have a Scotch vote of 37 against 11 (Scots) Tories, but the voice of Scotland is silenced and overpowered by an English Tory majority, which treats the grave crisis in Lewis with indifference and contempt. Who shall say after this that Scotland receives justice at the hands of the Imperial Parliament?'

ΠΙΠΕ
ΤΗΕ ΜΟΥΕΜΕΠΤ REFORMS

'For many years the Duke of Argyll has posed as the model
Highland laird. If anyone ventured to say a word about the poverty
of the crofters, the duke was ever ready to declare that they were a
lazy lot and that their miserable condition was due to their own
improvidence. As to their being rack-rented – there was no bounds
to his indignation at such a suggestion. But the idol has fallen. Fair
rents have been fixed by the Crofters' Commission on the Ross of
Mull.'

From around 1890 the course of land agitation in the Highlands was
complicated by considerations of economic change in the wider world, of
political developments at a British level and of an increasing
identification of the land issue with the forces of organised Labour and
nationalism. The '90s also witnessed a relative decline of the Land League
from a mass campaign to a single-issue pressure group that still
represented popular opinion in the Highlands, but whose leadership was
contested by radical Liberals on the one hand and nationalists and
socialists on the other.

This was hardly surprising. The land question was central to the early
Labour movement. And this movement in turn – certainly in Scotland –
saw itself in the context, at least, of some sort of assertive national identity
in egalitarian form. As early as 1843 the *Glasgow Herald* was denouncing
'noxious socialists' at Glasgow Green. A few years later the Chartist
Feargus O'Connor was telling the House of Commons that labour was the
source of all wealth, while the Chartist convention of 1851 declared that
land was the inalienable inheritance of all mankind: 'The nationalisation
of the land is the only true basis of national prosperity'. That same year
advocates of land-nationalisation could be heard on every street corner;
and a year later still, the commissioner for mines was demanding that
something be done to 'prevent the spread of socialism in the mining
districts of Scotland'.

These ideas were clearly of a highly infectious nature. In the late 1840s,
for instance, one Lanarkshire coal company imported some seventy

starving tenants from Tiree, that crucible of unfettered Argathelian progress in the inner Hebrides: 'Only one week did they work ere they struck for an increase of 4/-, which, being refused, they marched away, led by a piper.' And by the time of the 1868 general election – despite the absence of direct workers' representation in parliament – the labour movement in Scotland was reportedly obsessed with the land question.

The political biographies of the land-agitators give some idea of the links between the land, labour and national movements. The Highlander Alexander Cameron, for instance, one-time secretary to Robert Owen and a founder of Glasgow Trades Council, was a land-nationaliser. In Ireland in the later part of the century, the National Agricultural Labourers' Union was calling for radical reform and opposition to absentee landlords; its proceedings were widely reported in the Scottish press. (One of its leaders, P.J. Smyth, MP for West Meath, had in the 1850s masterminded the escape of John Mitchel from his Tasmanian exile.)

Henry George (who met Michael Davitt, founder of the Irish Land League in New York) was welcomed by Parnell in Ireland before crossing to England to meet Labour pioneers like A.R. Wallace and H.M. Hyndman. He was, at least, an important influence behind the 1882 resolution of the Trades Union Congress in favour of land nationalisation. He also met Dr G.B. Clark, soon to be a leader of the Crofters' Party in the House of Commons. In the still-mighty Liberal Party, the increasingly powerful radical wing was calling for land-reform in the Highlands (and elsewhere). The Glasgow faction of these radicals included Charles Cameron, the crofters' champion and publisher of the *North British Daily Mail*; while in the Highlands Fraser-MacIntosh also enjoyed a long connection with the radical wing of the Liberals. The Scottish Liberal Association had in fact been formed to press for, among other things, land-reform in the Highlands.

John Murdoch's first article on the subject of land had appeared in the *Bolton Free Press* in the 1840s. Through the editor of the New York paper *Irish World*, he came in contact with Michael Davitt. In turn Davitt, via Murdoch, toured the coalfields of Scotland proposing that the land be nationalised. When the miners of Lanarkshire formed a Scottish Anti-Royalty League and a Labour League, he endeavoured to affiliate them to the Scottish Land Restoration League. That restoration league ran six candidates in Glasgow in the 1885 general election. Murdoch was one of them, and he would later stand as a Land and Labour candidate in the Partick division, then home to many city-based Highlanders. During the famous 1888 Mid-Lanark by-election, he campaigned for Keir Hardie. A few weeks later the Scottish Labour Party was formed, with G.B. Clark becoming vice-president, along with Shaw Maxwell. At the same time the Scottish Land Restoration League affiliated to the new party. R.B. Cunninghame Grahame (first president of the National Party of Scotland in 1928) was president.

Within a year of the Mid-Lanark election, the Scottish Liberal Association was demanding radical changes to the Crofters' Act and expressing the opinion that 'Home Rule should be granted to Scotland, so that the Scottish people should have the sole control and management of their own national affairs'. The first chairman of the Scottish Home Rule Association had been John Stuart Blackie. From 1892 it was Erskine of Marr, a notable nationalist and Highland champion in the coming years. Meanwhile the Fife People's League was demanding nationalisation of the land and Home Rule; and a string of Labour leaders continued to identify crofters' rights with wider socialist aspirations in the context of Home Rule.

On the economic front, meanwhile, the last decade of the century was marked by a downturn in sheep farming and a rise in deer-afforestation. Even by the 1880s, the end of the boom-times was in sight for many sheep farmers. Not least, this was on account of the rapacity with which they had exploited hill grazing land throughout the nineteenth century – in effect, profiteering from value accumulated in the land over many years of sustainable agricultural practices.

Growing foreign competition, and the deterioration of land consequent on these decades of over-grazing and over-stocking, meant that by the 1880s prices were down to 60 per cent of what they had been in the '70s – and less than half of what they had been ten years earlier. Many farmers were desperate to get out. By the mid-'80s, sheep were disappearing from large stretches of the Highlands while estate income from sheep-farming went into free-fall.

In the 1870s, thirty new deer-forests came into being, and by the early years of the following decade there were no less than ninety-nine of these so-called forests in the Highlands, covering two million acres. No longer did they comprise, as in the early years, high and largely barren land. Now, they encroached on low-lying and relatively fertile land that could have sustained crofters; but the sporting tenants could pay more rent, or the sporting owners could simply do without any tenants at all. Thus by 1912 the acreage under deer in the Highlands was an astonishing three and a half million acres.

In terms of British politics, the last years of the nineteenth century and the early years of the next were witness to the slow, if irreversible, growth of great changes. In the Liberals, Gladstone slipped from view at last, and Rosebery beat off Harcourt to succeed him. Campbell-Bannerman took the leadership in 1899; while important names of the near future, among them Asquith and Haldane, were already coming to the fore.

The Liberal party was still the principal home of radicals. The breakthrough of an independent Labour party was still some way in the future. In the Highlands, particularly, the Liberals enjoyed a wide measure of popular support. This support, allied to the agitation of the radicals within and without Liberal ranks, tended to ensure that Liberal administrations were sympathetic to the crofters' cause. In turn, a number of Conservative leaders would also come to the view that there was a case for state intervention in the Highlands in the same cause.

Thus in 1890 the Walpole Commission recommended expenditure on a comprehensive fisheries infrastructure among other things; and within two years £240,000 had been earmarked for investment in the area. The Crofters' Commission, meanwhile, was reducing rents by up to 50 per cent around the Highlands and cancelling much of the crofters' arrears. And in 1892 the government gave the new county councils the power to acquire land for smallholdings (though in the event these powers were largely worthless).

In that same year – and much more importantly – the government established the Deer-Forest Commission, with a view to identifying such lands under sheep and deer as could be used for land-settlement purposes. The Commission reported in 1895. It took the view that in the Highlands there were 440,000 acres suitable for the extension of existing holdings and a further 790,000 acres appropriate for the creation of new crofts.

In the 1895 general election, both major parties promised the Highlands a land-settlement programme. And in 1897 the government established the Congested Districts Board (CDB), which was charged with making more land available to crofters. It managed, however, to create just 500 new holdings in the first seven years of its existence. In 1907 the Scottish Secretary John Sinclair, Baron Pentland from 1909, attempted (in an echo of Henry George) further reform with a land valuation bill: it was, however, instantly destroyed by the House of Lords.

Nevertheless, 1911 finally saw the Small Landholders' Act on the Statute Book (it came into operation on All Fools' Day the following year). The Act abolished the Crofters' Commission (a new one was set up in 1955) and the CDB. The duties of the former passed to the Scottish Land Court, and of the latter to the Board of Agriculture for Scotland.

The Act re-designated crofters as smallholders and extended to the rest of Scotland many of the provisions of the original 1886 legislation. It also gave the Board of Agriculture a budget of £200,000 and some land-settlement powers. Its details were something of a magnet for obstructive landlords and their lawyers, however. Much use was made of the right of appeal in the Act, by way of special case, to the Court of Session. In the first five years, twenty such cases were heard.

Simultaneous with these developments, the established currents of nationalism and socialism continued to run strongly through the land-reform movement in the years before the Great War. Nationalism was reflected primarily in the demand for Home Rule. It was a demand that found a ready audience in sections of the Liberals, as well as in the various groupings attempting to form an independent political organisation of the working class. The first Scottish Home Rule Association, for instance, which ran from 1886 to 1918, published during the 1890s a dozen pamphlets arguing its case. In 1912 the Young Scots Society published its *Sixty Points for Scottish Home Rule*. In 1892 John Stuart Blackie published from Glasgow a slim pamphlet, *The Union of 1707 and its Results*, while in the pre-war years another eighteen titles, some of them very substantial, also appeared. Pro-Home Rule periodicals in circulation in this period included the *Scottish Review, Scottish Patriot, British Federalist, Fiery Cross*, the *Scottish Nationalist*, the *Young Scot, Guth na Bliadhna, Scottish Nation, Scotia, Alba*, and *The Thistle*.

Prominent nationalists included G.B. Clark and Cunninghame Graham, who helped bring to an overt and active sympathy for Home Rule both Highland leaders of land-reform and leaders of the labour movement. The Scottish Home Rule Association included in its leadership the likes of not just Clark, Fraser-MacIntosh and Alexander MacKenzie, but Cunninghame Graham, the miners' leader, Robert Smillie, and Keir Hardie. Another was the future Prime Minister Ramsay MacDonald, secretary of the London branch for a number of years, and from the early years of the new century an activist in the ranks of the new Labour Party.

For Labour, meantime, the process of growth was slow but steady in these years. In the early 1890s the Independent Labour Party was founded, with Keir Hardie as chairman; but though it ran twenty-eight candidates in the 1895 general election, not one was returned. Not until 1900 and afterwards, with the formation of the Labour Representation Committee, did Labour start to make major strides as a parliamentary party independent of the Liberals – traditional haven for Radicals. In the 1900 election the Labour Representation Committee returned but two members (one of them Hardie); in 1906 it returned thirty, signalling its conversion to the Labour Party, with Keir Hardie as chairman.

The Highland land question in these years, therefore, and as a direct result of the crofters' agitation, became part of mainstream British politics and an organic part of the reform movement in Britain. The crofters might not have won popular ownership and control of the land under deer; but at least they had won the argument in favour of it.

As early as 1879, after all, Gladstone had conceded that the compulsory acquisition of the land was an 'adequate public object . . . admissible, and so far sound in principle'. And some years later, Rosebery would admit that further legislation on the crofting question was needed, and promise that a future Liberal government would indeed meet crofters' demand for more land.

In the same period both English and Scottish land reform associations, with radicals of various hues in their leaderships, were targeting the punitive taxation of land values, notably at local levels. Their agitational paper 'The Single Tax' first appeared in 1894. Associated with the movement were established names like Clark, Cunninghame Graham and Shaw Maxwell; while great Labour names like Tom Mann and Sidney Webb also helped lead the movement towards the new century. By 1895 the Scottish Land Restoration League was pressuring Glasgow City Council to apply land taxation within its boundaries. And in the Glasgow municipal elections of 1896, of the seventy-five candidates no less a number than forty-nine were land-taxers.

Against this complex and fluid background the Highland Land League began to disintegrate, its traditional functions dispersed, if not dissipated, upon a wider stage of political affairs. In Morvern, for instance, the district branch of the League stopped meeting in 1889 and collapsed altogether three years later. At length, the same sort of thing was to occur elsewhere.

But public opinion in the Highlands remained strongly favourable to the aspirations that the League had represented, and that favour did not expire overnight. In 1889 an entirely Highland executive (signalling the end to all vestiges of Edinburgh and London influence) was elected, basing itself in Dingwall. It at once began to prepare for the elections to the new county councils, scheduled for the following year. But in the general parliamentary election of two years later, John MacKay, one of the League's founders, stood as a Liberal Unionist against Angus Sutherland who was running as a Liberal and Land League candidate; while no less a figure than Fraser-MacIntosh was also opposed on behalf of the Land League.

And at the League conference the following year a split was inevitable. G.B. Clark forced the issue by denouncing Liberal domination of the League. The Liberal J.G. MacKay of Portree won the presidency by one vote, however, at which Clark and supporters walked out. They re-formed the Highland Land Law Reform Association (by which title the Land League was formally known until it adopted, in 1886, the name that everyone used anyway). Clark was supported by D.H. MacFarlane, who had been re-elected as MP for Argyll the previous year, along with J. Galloway Weir – a founder member of the 'old' Highland Land Law Reform Association, who had replaced Roderick MacDonald as Ross-shire MP in 1892. This new Association, however, lasted only for three years. By this time the Land League itself was foundering too. (In 1909, the League was reconstituted as an open arm of the Labour movement by Thomas Johnston, with G.B. Clark as president.)

But though the nature of the organisational representation of popular grievances was to change substantially from the 1890s onwards, the substance of those grievances did not. The crofters, after all, had not enough of the land, while the cottars had little or none of it. And while growing millions of acres were under deer, the aspiration was still 'the land for the people'.

Land agitation therefore continued throughout the last ten years of the nineteenth century, characterised by demands and forms of struggle that were by this stage known intimately to the common people across the

Highlands. For the previous fourteen years, after all, anti-landlord agitation had been incessant on the mainland and in the islands, as the government's 1888 return of agrarian offences committed since 1874 makes very clear.

The report runs from an assault and breach of the peace at Bernera in 1874 through to the case of Hugh Kerr drawing a sentence of sixty days for deforcement, mobbing assault and breach of the peace in 1888. Between these, respectively the first and the last entries in the return, appear many others: malicious mischief in Uist, deforcement and assault at Braes, mobbing and rioting at Rogart, assault at Dunvegan, deforcement at Valtos, rioting at Glendale, breach of the peace at Stoneybridge, mobbing at Waternish, deforcement in Lochs, breach of the peace at Uig, breach of interdict at Rogart; along with a catalogue of similar incidents occurring in the years between from Tiree, Gruids, Kilmuir, Argyll, Creich, Clashmore, and at Park, Aignish and Borve in Lewis.

However, by 1888 – though the extraordinary public wrangle between Sheriff Ivory and the Valtos crofters Norman Stewart and John Beaton was still exercising the minds of parliament – the prevailing orthodoxy, in Westminster if not in the collective consciousness of Highland landlordism, was that if the Highlander could not be entirely repressed or driven or bribed into emigration, the government had better look to the matter with a view to doing something about it. Emigration remained dear to the authorities, as might be expected. A government plan to arrange a 'colonisation scheme for the crofters and cottars of the western Highlands and Islands' was proposed; and the reports of the commission that was charged with the scheme record its success, or otherwise, over the sixteen years from 1890.

Of course emigration, whether funded by the state or the landlords, did not commend itself as a solution to anything in the view of the crofters. The state accordingly set about informing itself and its agencies via a series of public enquiries on the exact nature of social affairs in the Highlands of Scotland. First of these was an official report on the condition of the Lewis cottars, which was followed within two years by another high-level committee of inquiry into 'matters affecting the interests of the population' of the area. And at the turn of the century a further study was published, comparing social conditions on Lewis with those prevailing in the early 1880s.

But no single report of the period, official or otherwise, caught the flavour of the continuing land question in the Highlands quite as well as that of the Deer-Forest Commission. In many ways similar in nature and importance to the Napier Commission, it found that around two million acres of the Highlands were under one hundred or so deer-forests. Among these could be found that of the Duke of Sutherland, with 145,000 acres under deer in that county (the Duchess had another 35,000 acres in Ross-shire); that of Lochiel with 32,000 acres in Inverness and Argyll; that of Lord Lovat with around 80,000 acres in Inverness; that of Lord MacDonald, by now down to a paltry 10,000 acres of Skye; that of Lady Matheson (resident by now in the south of France) with 34,000 acres in Lewis; that of Munro Ferguson with 3,000 acres at Kildermorie; that of A.J. Balfour with 30,000 acres at Strathconon; and that of the Duke of Portland with 36,000 acres at Langwell in Caithness.

The efforts of the commission emphasised the extraordinary extent to which the land surface of the Highlands was increasingly dedicated to the recreational destruction of red deer. In its report and appendix the commission suggested ways by which such land could be dedicated to crofting use. Just one page of the appendix indicates, for instance, that the commission thought suitable for new or enlarged crofters' holdings about 14,000 acres on E.S. Bowlby's estate of Knoydart; while in Arisaig over 2,000 acres were thought suitable for new holdings; and on Lord Lovat's estate in North Morar, almost 700 acres of the Bourblach grazings were nominated as suitable for addition to existing crofters' land.

By now the 'eviction mania' of earlier years was passing, largely as a result of the Crofters' Act (while small victories were also being recorded in the courts with regard to rights-of-way). Still, however, the *Oban Times* could report that the threat of summary eviction was continuing to 'cast its evil blight over the peaceful inhabitants of Lismore and the humble tillers of the soil around Loch Nell'. In this case, a portion of the Barcaldine estate had been purchased by a Mrs Ogilvie of Sussex, following the departure of two farmers. While she had 'only entered into possession in November', her efforts 'to oust the tenants on the estate have been vigorously prosecuted and persistent'.

By the 1890s, nevertheless, the traditional sort of unfettered eviction was increasingly a thing of the past – the great bulwark of the 1886 Crofters' Act serving to preserve the crofting community from much of the tyranny of earlier decades. Indeed, a new rhythm had entered the anti-landlord agitation in the Highlands. It was reflected notably in the fate of the Land League (a pre-eminent example of an institution falling necessary victim to its own success). The League had blossomed as a response to agitation rather than as an inspiration of that agitation. Though it won widespread support very quickly, it was in essence a single-issue campaign, serving as a focus for indigenous agitation on the ground. It shared, as an organisation, in the victories of the 1880s; and as a result of those victories it was prey to the pressures and strains of any successful single-issue campaigning organisation. The logic of its existence led it to develop towards a formal, party-type association, thus provoking questions as to its stance with regard to the established parties. It was driven, or at least its leaders were driven, to involvement in national issues; and hence national issues became an issue in League politics. Unsurprisingly, it could not, in the form that it had established during the

1880s, survive the pressures of the complex historical situation of which it was part.

Nevertheless it continued to run parliamentary candidates. In Argyll, D.H. MacFarlane, who had won the seat in 1885 and lost it the following year, took the seat back in 1892 as a Liberal/Crofter (though he would lose it again in 1895). In Caithness Dr Clark, under one banner or another, held the seat from 1885, through the elections of 1886, 1892, and 1895. Clark lost the nomination for the seat for the 1900 election as a result of his support for the Boer, however; and in that election the land-banner was formally carried by F.C. Auld, founder and candidate of the Land Law Reform Association of Caithness. He lost.

In Inverness-shire Charles Fraser-MacIntosh, who had held the seat in 1885 and 1886, was replaced for the 1892 election by D. MacGregor, candidate of the Inverness-shire Land League. But from 1895, when it was lost by the crofters, until the end of the Great War, no further candidate stood in the name of the League. In Ross-shire Dr MacDonald had represented the seat in 1885 and 1886. From 1892 J.G. Weir, standing then as a Liberal/Crofter but afterwards simply as a Liberal, held the seat in 1895, 1900, 1906 and 1910. On his death in that year, Ian MacPherson (who would later write an introduction to a reprint of Alexander MacKenzie's history of the Highland clearances) took over.

In Sutherland the electoral record of land-reform candidates was patchy. Angus Sutherland had contested the constituency in 1885 without success. Though he did win it the following year and held it until 1892, he then resigned it. J. MacLeod took it as a Liberal/Crofter in 1894 and held it the following year as a simple Liberal; but in 1900 he was beaten – by one of the Leveson-Gower family. In short, both the scope and form of anti-landlordism changed during the 1890s, partly as a result of increasing government interest in Highland affairs and Highland votes – signified by the Scottish Secretary Lord Lothian's tour of inspection in the autumn of 1889, which was inspired by 'a view to improving the lot of its inhabitants'.

The very public activities of the Crofters' Commission also helped adapt the nature of agitation; and indeed, the depth of agitation. Its proceedings constituted an important element in crofting affairs throughout the last decade of the nineteenth century, and in particular for the early part of that decade, with its first rulings firing expectation and morale throughout the Highland area.

But still the fabric of Scottish affairs remained at times strangely suggestive of earlier days. In the first month of the century's last decade, for instance, the MP for the Partick constituency died. Educated at Rugby and Balliol, an Edinburgh advocate married to the daughter of the landlord of Morvern, he was none other than Patrick Sellar's son, Craig – in whom, it may fairly be said, the manifold blessings of clearance, 'improvement' and constructive hobbyism had most generously been invested.

In the month of his departure, meanwhile, the executive of the Land League met in Dingwall to reappoint Donald MacRae as organising secretary and to urge crofters to support land-reform candidates in the forthcoming county council elections. On Lewis the crofters of Lochs were reported to be making ready to take possession for cultivation of the Park deer-forest. Elsewhere, reports were being received of destitution among crofters who had, or who had been, emigrated to Canada:

> The present position of many of the families sent here under the auspices of Lady Cathcart, speculative land companies and the government, should be a sufficient warning to those at home to stay and face the ills they know rather than come here and face the ills they know not.

The districts referred to were at Cathcart and Wapella, to which Uist people had been driven prior to the appointment of the Napier Commission back in the early '80s.

In February 1890, following the urging of the Land League executive, land-reform candidates in general swept the elections for the county councils in the Highlands. In Sutherland, Land League candidates took seventeen of the nineteen seats. League candidates also won every seat in the Hebrides, while in Skye they enjoyed a majority of two to one over their opponents. As a result, the League quickly began to use the new Highland councils as platforms for land-reform. All of them (except Argyll, the only one to have returned a pro-landlord majority) petitioned parliament to implement the Land League programme.

Within weeks of the election, the crofters of the parish of Canisbay in Caithness were laying claim to land in the district. On Jura the Crofters' Commission held a court for local tenants, 'at which their chief grievance seemed to be the encroachment of the deer-forest and consequent restriction of their pasture and loss of stock-land'.

That April, a deputation to the factor for Lovat estates was led by one Hugh Fraser, president of the Lovat Land League. The deputation requested that the crofters be given the use of a local hill, for which they were prepared to pay a reasonable rent. The factor refused on the grounds that the land in question was let to Lord Winborne; at which the crofters announced that they would simply go to the Crofters' Commission, 'who'll give us our rights, of which we were unjustly deprived years ago'.

That same month a Land League meeting in Uist was addressed by Donald MacRae. He urged all present to persevere in the agitation for more land and a further reduction in rent. At the close of the meeting, a committee for each township in the district was elected. It was announced that a mass meeting would shortly be convened, 'with a view to further action', at which Donald MacFarlane would speak.

Shortly afterwards the Duke of Sutherland announced that he was to clear the extensive sheep farms of Melness, Siberscross and Clebrig and turn them into a deer-forest. On Knoydart, Baird announced the same type of plan. Meanwhile the Crofters' Commission had been busy on the Duke of Argyll's estate in the Ross of Mull:

> The Ross of Mull crofters complained very much of rack-renting before the Royal Commission in 1883 and from the finding of sheriff Brand's court it would appear that they were somewhat justified in their complaints. In the 47 cases in which fair rents have just been fixed the crofters got an average reduction of 39 per cent, and have had over 63 per cent of their arrears wiped off. For many years the Duke of Argyll has posed as the model Highland laird. If anyone ventured to say a word about the poverty of the crofters, the duke was ever ready to declare that they were a lazy lot and that their miserable condition was due to their own improvidence. As to their being rack-rented – there was no bounds to his indignation at such a suggestion. But the idol has fallen. Fair rents have been fixed by the Crofters' Commission on the Ross of Mull.

That June the MP for Ross and Cromarty, Dr MacDonald, was addressing the annual meeting of the county association of the Land League. And a matter of weeks later some of his constituents on Berneray were raiding Borve farm on the island, knocking down a stable and burning out a stackyard, in a conflict that would run into the autumn (and return later in the decade).

The following spring forty or fifty men raided Park deer forest, as they had threatened a year earlier, and began to prepare the once-cleared township of Ornsay for cultivation. Thirty-two of the men were subsequently gaoled, but briefly. On the mainland fierce evictions, though rarer than before, were still taking place – as on the Brahan estate that summer, with assault on, and the deforcement of, an eviction party. In the Hebrides, meanwhile, Lady Matheson returned to Lewis 'for the first time in some years'.

In Lochcarron twenty crofters petitioned the Crofters' Commission for more land. The factor, called as a witness by the crofters' representative Donald MacRae, conceded that the land in question had been taken from the township fourteen years earlier, without compensation. In Lochs, meanwhile, as a result of the commission's decisions, the rents of 'forty-eight small holdings in Ranish' were reduced by 'over 41 per cent' on average. And in Barra the commission had ordered an average reduction of 38 per cent on the holdings of 136 crofters.

The *Glasgow Weekly Mail* noted during the last week of the year:

> On the whole of Lady Cathcart's Long Island estates which comprise South Uist, Benbecula, Barra and several small islands,

there are 998 crofters whose cases have been dealt with during various visits of the commission. The average reduction of rent granted over the whole is slightly over 30 per cent. They were due £27,338 of arrears, of which the commissioners have cancelled £20,967 . . . A liberal concession of land is being offered to the crofter tenants on the well-known estate of Kilmuir in Skye, by Mr G.A. Baird of Stichill, who acquired the estate three years ago.

In short, the balance of class-forces had changed in the Highlands by the 1890s, the work of the Crofters' Commission both encouraging expectation and stifling active protest on the scale of the previous decade; while the focus of agitation swung to the question, not so much of security of tenure, but of recovery of land from sheep and deer by means of formal political action. The scale of direct action therefore dipped, though in the spring of 1892 there was trouble at Clashmore in Sutherland, with fences and dykes again destroyed, and the chief constable of the county writing in some alarm to his superiors in Edinburgh. That same month, too, the crofters in the north of Lewis were meeting to demand legislation empowering the Crofters' Commission to increase holdings and to give new holdings to those without any land at all.

At precisely the same time, the Duke of Portland was taking over the shootings of Dunbeath Castle, extending his deer-forest lands to almost 80,000 acres. And that August, on Skye a sheriff-officer and party attempting an eviction were assaulted and deforced in the traditional way.

Back on the mainland, the Winans deer-forests were drawing attention again. Winans had not shot anything on them for five years, nor had anyone else been allowed to, and the deer were multiplying alarmingly. This was a 'novelty in congested populations', in the sardonic words of one report. 'There can be no doubt as to the public scandal of so much land being kept uncultivated and useless,' it went on, 'when thousands of crofters are being kept in poverty because of the smallness of their crofts. Some parts of the deer-forests might be tilled and large parts might be used for the grazing of crofters' stock.'

On Skye, meanwhile, Lord MacDonald was taking court action for eviction against five of his tenants in Snizort. Three of them were widows. And in Glendale a mass meeting of crofters and cottars was promising further united action with regard to the land question in the Highlands.

At Dunrobin the Duke of Sutherland's funeral was proceeding to the tune of the usual lamentations (though his sons were absent on account of a small but splendidly vicious tiff over the London and North Western Railway shares). That October the Land League met, once again at Portree, for its annual conference: fifteen resolutions called for a radical reform of matters relating to the land question. It was also agreed to reappoint Donald MacRae as full-time organiser.

In the previous three months the press, in particular MacKenzie's *Scottish Highlander*, had been keeping the land question firmly in the public eye. In July, for instance, the paper had carried front-page statements from its favoured candidates for the 1892 parliamentary election. Among them was Fraser-MacIntosh, for Inverness, whose views were 'unchanged since the 1885 election on the subject of deer-forests, game laws, and rights of salmon fishing in river estuaries and arms of the sea'. J.G. Weir was another, who had been the unanimous choice of candidate by the Highland Land League.

That same month the paper was covering Lady Matheson and the crofters of Lewis, while in August it was reporting a case of deforcement in Skye, at Lynedale, and paying continuing attention to the fate of the crofters evicted to Canada from the Gordon Cathcart estates on South Uist. It reported legal action against Donald MacRae and J.G.Weir's tour of Lewis, as well as publicising a lengthy series then running in the *People's Journal* on the subject of 'men or deer in the Scottish glens?'. The *Scottish Highlander* also reported further court action by Lord MacDonald against the crofters of Skye; tenant meetings at Glendale demanding more land; and the death, and legal battles accompanying it, of the Duke of Sutherland.

Along with a sideswipe at the Church of Scotland and its historical relationship with Highland landlordism ('the established church and the land-question: better late than never'), the *Scottish Highlander* covered at length the September conference of the League. Stories telegraphed from Portree reported the presence at the conference of Mary MacPherson, the anti-landlord Gaelic poetess, and the absence (due to sickness) of Michael Davitt. A report also noted that at the 1885 conference in Portree there had been ten times as many people present, but added defiantly, 'No settlement of the land question in the Highlands can be regarded as final which does not clearly recognise and fully embody the inherent and historic rights of the Highland people to their native soil.'

Comment and correspondence relating to the conference continued throughout that autumn. The *Scottish Highlander* also campaigned for Land League county council candidates, carrying an 'address to Highlanders' by the League president on 'the man to vote for', with subsequent comment on the results. It then turned its close attention to the appointment of the Deer-Forest Commission (the proceedings of which it would follow closely in the coming years). It also monitored and reported the response to the appointment of the commission by both crofters and landlords – the latter very promptly convening in Inverness to discuss its implications.

Similar themes dominated throughout that winter and into the following year. In Kilmuir the people of the district were 'on the march for more land', walking in procession with pipers to the scene of a cleared township to demand it. In Inverness the Land League was setting up a stream of crofter-witnesses to appear before the Deer-Forest Commission. In Glendale and Valtos crofters were demanding 'their rights' and more land. In Arnisdale, on the shores of Loch Hourn, the local branch of the League was also demanding land. In Argyll the duke was evicting crofters. Throughout Skye the people were busy appointing delegates to appear before the commission, its visitation to the island then being imminent. The dowager Duchess of Sutherland was gaoled in Holloway, convicted on contempt of court charges relating to a who-gets-what struggle over the late duke's will. And the *Scottish Highlander* continued to publicise the record of the MacLeod landlords with regard to evictions on Skye, along with extensive coverage of the work of the Deer-Forest Commission in the same island.

By mid-decade, while the authorities continued to concern themselves with land-agitation matters across the Highlands, the same themes of land-hunger and crofter militancy remained apparent. In January 1896, for instance, the Glendale branch of the League was still active, meeting to elect office-bearers and hear reports, with John MacPherson in the chair. The following month the House of Commons was yet again debating the 'crofter question'. In March, Sheriff Ivory was once again falling out with Inverness-shire county council, occasioning some acid comment. By the end of April Lady Matheson, widow of Sir James, was dead and buried at last.

In May the Crofters' Commission was at work in Torridon. In June, the Duke of Sutherland was in the Court of Session with regard to salmon poaching and 'Sir John Orde's crowbar brigade' was evicting tenants in Uist – a matter which would also surface shortly in the House of Commons. In September there were further evictions in Badenoch, with houses reportedly burnt down. In September, also, the League met at Stornoway for its fourteenth annual conference, an event to which the *Scottish Highlander* gave extensive coverage.

Towards the end of the decade, too, the land question and related matters continued to exercise public interest. By then, however, the leaders of twenty years earlier were quitting the scene. The death of MacKenzie came at the beginning of 1898, and that of Mary MacPherson towards the end of the same year.

The gentry, old and new, against whose doings both MacKenzie and MacPherson had so long campaigned, still traded in estates as before. Strathaird on Skye sold for £19,000 to the owner of Eigg. The same laird would within months be in conflict with his Eigg tenants, whom he had 'migrated' from Galmisdale to Laig, and who were approaching the Crofters' Commission as a result. Meanwhile the Duchess of Sutherland visited the Hebrides, Andrew Carnegie bought Skibo Castle and the bottled-sauce millionaire Perrins was busy turning Ardross Castle into a habitation suitable for a man of his resources (and evident tastes).

But the causes and conflicts of earlier decades were still to be seen, albeit on a less generalised, or at least less acute, scale. Crofters in Wester Ross were still destroying deer-fences, and still being interdicted, and still calling on leaders of the land-reform movement (in this case, Donald MacRae) to represent them. Elsewhere in the Highlands, crofters were raising Court of Session actions against their landlord. Dr G.B. Clark addressed the Caithness Land League, to the effect that 'landlordism has performed no useful function and it is bound to go because it is a burden on the land'. And in the Black Isle there was a 'threatened agitation' following a meeting of the League: 'There has been a revival of the crofters' agitation in Ross-shire.'

Many other such conflicts occurred, if on a local scale, right through to the end of the century. But as a decade in the history of land-agitation, the 1890s represented something of an interregnum. It had opened in hope; and that hope had been sustained by the judgements of the Crofters' Commission, the findings of the Deer-Forest Commission, and (in its closing years) by the work of the CDB. The price of this hope had been a downturn in agitation of a mass character, in a decade where the lines of development were more obscure and complex than before, and where the forward march of progress proved to be less obvious and less simple that it had earlier seemed.

Yet popular aspiration and expectation remained as high, or higher even, than formerly. Both, though, remained unmet by the end of the 1890s. For the land movement in the Highlands, the century therefore closed on a note of unrequited hope. But the new twentieth century that now opened did so on a new note – albeit in an older and familiar tune.

TEN

A NEW LAND LEAGUE

'They openly go about stating their determination to stand by one another, and on no account to yield up one inch of the land seized, holding that it is better to go to prison than suffer longer as they are doing, seeing their families starving before their eyes. The position of affairs is serious, the unrest spreading rapidly.'

———❦———

The twentieth century opened with the death of Victoria, the succession of Edward VII and general elections carried along on a strong tide of imperialist sentiment. The war with the Boers in South Africa was the principal focus of enthusiasm (though the vexed question of Ireland and her independence was never far from the centre of things).

But it was a significant sign of the effect that land agitation in the Highlands had exerted over the previous twenty years that the manifesto of the Labour Representation Committee was pledged to the 'nationalisation of land'; while even the Liberal manifesto contained the encouraging, if not exactly specific, phrase, 'so long as our Land Laws are unreformed'. In the event, Conservatives and Liberal Unionists took 403 seats in the House of Commons and the Liberals 183, with three seats going to Labour and Independent Labour members.

The results in the Highlands also reflected the political warfare over issues unconcerned with the land question. Inverness Burghs was contested by a Liberal and a Liberal Unionist, the latter taking the seat. A Conservative beat a Liberal in Wick Burghs and Argyll. In Caithness a Liberal beat a Conservative and two Independent Liberals. (One of them was G.B. Clark, the other F.C. Auld, running as a joint candidate of the Land Law Reform Association of Caithness.) In Inverness-shire a Liberal also held off the Conservatives. In Orkney and Shetland a Liberal Unionist took the seat from a Liberal. In Ross and Cromarty, J.G. Weir for the Liberals held off a Conservative; and in Sutherland a Liberal Unionist saw off a Liberal.

But the old refrain of 'the land for the people' could still insistently be heard in Highland politics in the first decade or so of the century. In the

154

years leading to the Great War this demand for land was accompanied by a steady rise in deer-afforestation; landlord obstruction of popular aspiration; a failure of government agencies to effect significant land-reform in the crofting counties; and the increasing, formal identification of the Highland land question with the young Labour movement in Scotland. (By 1900 at least 50,000 people in Glasgow alone can, considering the effects of continuing Highland immigration to the city, be calculated as having been Gaelic speakers.)

For the Highland élite, meanwhile, the dawn of the new century promised an age at least as generous in its charms and advantages as that which had preceded it. By the autumn of 1900, for instance, the recreational 'sporting season' in the Highlands was well under way: 'excellent sport' was reported from the vicinity of Dunrobin, from the Ben Alder forest, from the Glenquoich deer-forest, and from Argyll – where the gentry were congregating in their lodges and steam-yachts, among them the earls of Harrowby and Dufferin – and from Badenoch, where Lord Southampton and guests had obliterated three and a half hundred brace of grouse in four days. Shortly afterwards too, in Lewis, Major Duncan Matheson, by now in control of the estate, was importing 140 deer from England in order to improve the stock of his forests. At the same point the *Oban Times* was carrying an advertisement from the MacDonald estates on Skye offering for let the farms of Boreraig and Suisnish, in the parish of Strath, extending to 3,000 acres and carrying a Cheviot stock of 800.

In this sense at least, little or nothing had changed; and thus from the very opening of the century there was to be a steady stream, at times bursting into spate, of anti-landlord direct action in the Highlands. It was one that would run strongly right up until the opening of the Great War itself.

Over the first five years of the period, agitation was concentrated in the outer and inner Hebrides. In Barra, for instance, there was a marked upsurge of agitation towards the end of 1900, which culminated on 15 September in the 'forcible seizure of the farm of Northbay'. Two thousand people were living on the island's 25,000 acres, while three quarters of those acres were in the possession of just three farmers – 'their portion being principally arable land and pasture of a very fine description'.

The people, meantime, were 'housed in a deplorable manner. The miserable patches of rock and peat cultivated by them cannot be called land, but for want of better they raise their yearly supply of potatoes as best they can in such patches.' Since the beginning of the previous decade, under the 1892 legislation purporting to give county councils the power to acquire land for settlement purposes, the tenants at Northbay had been petitioning for more land. They had eventually 'endeavoured to obtain by enforcement of the compulsory clauses of the Allotments Act by the County Council of Inverness some amelioration of their wretched conditions but the influence of landlordism in the county council proved too strong'. After five years of complaining, the parish council of Barra finally warned of a 'cottar upheaval through its refusal to give justice'.

The people had already petitioned the CDB to come to their aid, but the Board had replied that it was powerless to help. And thus:

> The whole fishing and cottar population has risen, seized the farm, divided it into lots for crofts and house sites, and cast lots for the different portions. They openly go about stating their determination to stand by one another, and on no account to yield up one inch of the land seized, holding that it is better to go to prison than suffer longer as they are doing, seeing their families starving before their eyes. The position of affairs is serious, the unrest spreading rapidly. There is abundance of land in Barra suitable for house sites and crofter holdings, and the people express their entire willingness to pay a just rent for such.

Commenting on the failure of the CDB to live up to its declared purpose of providing land for the people, the *Oban Times* condemned the Board and demanded legislation on the basis of the recommendations of the Deer-Forest Commission. It was a condemnation all the more damning, given that the Board was just three years old, and that its birth had been welcomed as a premonition of great hope.

Spurned by both Board and county council, the Northbay land-raiders also petitioned the island's owner, Lady Gordon Cathcart – though without much hope, given the long-established nature of the Gordon–Cathcart regime in the southern isles. As Thomas Johnston was to observe just nine years later, she could be presumed to be, through marriage, a 'genuine Huntly Gordon of the real old tooth-and-talon breed. While still on the sunny side of twenty summers [she] married John Gordon of Cluny. In 1880, two years after Mr Gordon's death, she married Sir Reginald Cathcart. Lady Gordon Cathcart has not visited Barra for some thirty years.' Thus within a fortnight of the raid on Northbay, Gordon Cathcart's lawyers were writing to the Congested Districts Board, urging them to put a stop to the raiding in whatever way possible (the presumption being that neither she nor they thought that a police–military force could be acquired).

She was, however, decisively thwarted on this occasion, though at some considerable cost to the public purse. The following spring, the CDB bought Northbay farm and some of the nearby farm of Eoligarry, amounting to almost 3,000 acres of land, from which just under sixty holdings were to be formed. In other words, the raid had resulted in a very clear and certain victory for the raiders despite the obstruction of the landlord and the weakness of statute and official agency. This lesson was not to be lost on the rest of the Hebrides either.

During that same winter there was trouble at Sconser on Skye, scene over the best part of thirty years of anti-landlord direct action on the part of crofting tenants. In October Lord MacDonald's factor, who had acquired a sheriff's order empowering him to remove crofters' stock from Sconser, wrote to the chief constable of the county in some alarm:

> I am convinced that as soon as I proceed to carry out the sheriff's order these crofters will be up in arms and use force to prevent me. With a force of thirty police I do not think that a riot would be attempted but this, I am convinced, is the only means of preventing one, so I write to ask if you can oblige me by supplying me with such a force.

The chief constable replied to the effect that he would consult with the sheriff of the county. The sheriff advised that it would be better to despatch a sheriff-officer first. If (or when) that officer was deforced then a party of police could be considered.

At the end of October the factor reported again to the chief constable. He had, as advised, sent a sheriff-officer to Sconser. The officer had, however, managed to serve only half of his notices, 'when the people apparently found out the reason of his visit, upon which the township gathered round and stones and dirt were thrown'. Dogs also were set on him, but evidently did not touch him. 'The people told him that for his own sake he had better stop and further said that if anyone came to remove sheep, half a dozen of them would never return.' The sheriff-officer, meanwhile, complained to the procurator-fiscal, in a clear attempt to involve the police. He demanded the eviction of five crofters who had 'caused an irritancy of their tenancy'. He claimed his party had been 'accosted' by about a dozen men:

> These men at once adopted a threatening attitude and told us that we had come far enough, that they wanted no more of our papers, and if we were wise for ourselves, that we had better return the way we had come as quickly as possible. As I saw the crowd was increasing and getting more threatening I displayed my Badge of Office and Wand of Peace and declared myself deforced. A mob of about 40 women and children [came] after us and over a dozen collie dogs, which they hounded upon us.

He also attempted to implicate the local teacher: 'My own opinion was that the scholars of the school were let out for the purpose of following and annoying us. They followed us for about a mile on the road and besmirched us with clods and mud and everything filthy they could.'

The sheriff-officer took particular care to report that when he asked the crowd whether they would prevent him serving his notices (a standard procedure, or manoeuvre, by which he could simply prove deforcement in court if anyone had answered in the affirmative) the local teacher called out to the people to remain silent. This they did. As a result, the procurator fiscal thought it uncertain whether the officer had, in law, been deforced at all. The sheriff-officer complained about all of this to the factor, who urged him to go to the police as a means of bringing some discreet pressure to bear on the chief constable.

As a result of what clearly seems to have been a conspiracy on the part of minor officialdom to bring in the police and crush crofter resistance at Sconser, the police inspector at Portree wired in code to both the chief constable at Inverness and the procurator fiscal at Strathpeffer. And in the middle of November, the chief constable (still MacHardy) wrote to the factor that the sheriff had granted permission for a police expedition to Sconser, scheduled for the middle of January, 'in order to allow full time for conciliatory influences to operate'. In December, however, the matter of the imminent assault was raised in parliament, with questions directed towards the Lord Advocate. The authorities at once backed down. The estate offered the Sconser people land at Boreraig and Suisnish (from which, of course, tenants had been cleared only a few decades earlier). In Sconser, as at Northbay, the common people had won; and if their victory was a small one on the Highland scale it was, at least, a mighty one in Sconser.

Meantime, the spirit of agitation was undimmed in North Uist. There 'the cottars have been clamouring for land for a generation or two back and, having lost all faith in the working of the CDB, openly declare that they are forced to revolt in order to obtain sufficient pieces of land to live on'. There were several hundred cottar families involved. Many of them had applied to the Deer-Forest Commission, the County Council and the Congested Districts Board for land. A small estate had recently come on the market. The people had applied to the Board for it to be divided among them, but the Board had rejected the demand, claiming that the land was unsuitable. This reply 'exasperated' the cottars:

> A great number of them went in a body on Saturday to part of the lands of the estate and marked out small crofts for themselves. One cottar said it was quite clear to him that the only way to get the Congested Districts Board to work sensibly was for the people everywhere to break the law. They declared they would seize and hold the land by force, no matter how many of them had to go to prison. Several cottars referred to their sons and brothers fighting in South Africa. Further developments are anxiously looked for, as many crofters are to join in with them in order to get better lands than those they have.

And within a week the spirit of 'unrest and agitation' over the seizure of the land, at Griminish and Vallay, was spreading throughout the island. 'On Tuesday night a great meeting of crofters and landless cottars was held at Bayhead, representatives from various townships being present.' The chairman, Norman MacDonald, a cottar of Bayhead, reminded his audience that 'over half a century ago their forefathers were ruthlessly evicted from their homes at Griminish to make way for sheep farmers'. For nearly a generation they had been agitating to have the land returned. They wanted the farms of Vallay, Griminish, and Scalpaig, and would take them and keep them, unless the CDB swiftly bought out the landlord, Campbell Orde (who had in any case been trying to sell the farms for more than two years). Thus the people would again petition the CDB and parliament; but 'unless a speedy, favourable reply' was got, 'forcible measures' would be taken.

In various parts of Lewis, too, there was a popular demand for holdings – not least on the farms at Aignish and Gress, notable locations of land-seizure twenty years later. The CDB approved of the scheme to divide the farms into holdings. Major Matheson, however, disagreed. To cede the farms as crofts would render the land subject to the protection of the Crofters' Act and thus closed to their free exploitation on the open market. It would also encumber the major's island with the sort of 'kinsmen' then fighting the Empire's cause in South Africa. And so the Board was 'accordingly unable to take any further steps in the matter'.

There was also further trouble on Bernera, scene of the great anti-landlord riot of 1874. Seven years earlier, the island's cottars had asked the Deer-Forest Commission to have the farm of Croir divided among them, and since then applications had been made to both landlord and factor. Therefore towards the end of April, getting no satisfactory response from either government agency or landlord, 'a number of cottar-fishermen took possession of the farm and marked it off in lots. They seem determined to retain possession.'

In due course, the land-raiders on Croir received notices of interdict from Matheson. In open defiance, they responded by planting potatoes on the land that they had marked out for repossession. The matter was raised in the House of Commons, but the Lord Advocate announced he was not prepared to introduce legislation 'to increase facilities already given as regards the acquisition of land in the congested districts of the Highlands'. And thus, before the month was out, 'the hunger for more land all over the island estate is now developing into an open revolt at the refusal by the responsible authorities to give any heed to the solicitations of poverty-stricken cottars and crofters for patches of land to live upon'.

By now, the remaining sheep farms in the Highlands were on the brink of an acute crisis, with land increasingly being turned to deer. 'The price of blackface wool has fallen to a minimum, the larger farms cannot find tenants, and landlords all over the country are transforming vast tracts of pasture land into deer-forests,' in the words of the *Oban Times*.

The popular demand for these 'vast tracts of pasture' remained as high as ever; but the CDB was unable to satisfy it. It had originally been appointed for a five-year term, but after just three years its performance was drawing the fire of the Highland press:

> With more than half of its life having expired, we should be able to reckon on the completion of nearly one half of its duties. We do not think the people of the congested areas will take that view. If it proceeds during the next two years at the leisurely pace of the last three, it will at the end of its term leave the Highlands with the problems of congested districts untouched at its foundations. We can only have congestion eradicated by the thinning out of the people over the land. It is a first duty of the Board to bring congestion to an end, and judged by that duty, its three years' administration has come painfully short of the mark.

As a result, agitation extended to South Uist, at Iochdar, where the estate factor had demanded that the crofters erect a protective fence between their patches of land and the contiguous Griminish farm (upon which, clearly, the crofters had been allowing their stock to graze). This demand, however, 'revealed to the crofters that there was no intention of relieving their present poverty-stricken condition, and the largest meeting ever to take place on the land question in South Uist was at once held'. Restoration of the land had commenced at the beginning of the new century, and it would not stop until 'complete restoration had taken place'.

There was also trouble in the townships of Suishvale, Howbeg and Howmore, where the tenants of Gordon Cathcart met to decide how to 'force' land from the estate, and to hold a demonstration against 'the tyrannical laws which subject cottars and small crofters to starvation when ample ground is available'. Thus a great crowd headed by pipers marched on the farm of Bornish and marked it out in crofter holdings; 'resolutions' were then passed by the marchers to the effect that 'after 25 years asking peaceably for land, their application being unheeded, they resolved to delay no longer in taking such lands'.

In May 1903 the farms of Milton and Ormiclate were seized and apportioned among the people who were preparing the land for cultivation, and were determined 'to retain forcible possession'. And within a week, twenty-five cottars from Stoneybridge had taken possession of the Bornish farm and divided it among themselves, in time for the spring planting of crops.

Nor were these short-lived incidents. Indeed, the agitation in South Uist continued unabated over the following three years, by which time the crofters of Howbeg were marching 'in procession, with flags flying and headed by pipers, to the farms of Ormiclate and Bornish, and again took possession'. Twenty-one holdings were pegged out and temporary huts made ready, for use when they commenced cultivation. On the same afternoon the crofters of Stoneybridge marched to the Ormiclate machair, near Loch Olay, and divided it into thirty holdings. They had in fact first seized this land, the best in the district, during the winter of 1883–84; at the time of the passing of the Crofters' Act in 1886 they had asked to be given it, but were debarred by the restrictive conditions imposed by the estate that accompanied its offer.

In December 1904 they again asked to be given it. But again Gordon Cathcart refused. It was of course a fact that 'in the early years of last century the machair had been part of the Stoneybridge crofters' holdings, but they were dispossessed and the land added to the Ormiclate farm'. The farm, along with that at Bornish, ran to 20,000 acres of hill and low ground, 'in every sense suitable for settling crofters'. Great unrest reportedly prevailed among the cottar class 'who have made up their minds to hold the lands they have seized against all comers. They are determined that they will have the land for themselves. It is said that the cottars of Iochdar and Daliburgh districts, who are reported to be restless, will also soon seize the large farms of Gerinish, Drimore and Milton.' In that event 'the whole of the island of South Uist will be in their hands'.

During this period there were numerous other incidents both on the mainland and the Inner Hebrides – not least in Tiree, where crofters and cottars once again asked for land. The Duke of Argyll, however, counselled them as follows: 'You should enlist in the Naval Reserve. There are very many lowland farmers anxious to get workers now. I am also willing to assist in getting good lands for those who may like to join their friends in New Zealand and Canada.'

And in Skye, by the winter of 1905–06, agitation was also in the ascendant, on a scale suggestive of twenty years earlier – as a steady stream of press stories and reports to the authorities indicate only too clearly. The *Inverness Courier*, for instance, was reporting mass meetings at the Quiraing that February; the *Highland Times* wrote of expected raids at Snizort the following month; and *The Scotsman* throughout March and April reported trouble at Uig and planned raids at Kilmuir ('discontent, disturbance, and lawlessness are once again appearing in the crofter country').

And on the wider scale of national affairs, the land question had continued to exercise the interest of significant sections of Scottish public and political opinion.

Though as early as January 1900 the nationalist quarterly *Scottish Review* was lamenting (in an article on the taxation of land values) that 'Home Rule is dead or dying', nationalist publications continued to give prominence to land-reform. For example the very first issue of the occasional *Fiery Cross* announced, 'We will advocate the restoration of the people to the land of their fathers.'

Nor did the subject escape the notice of the monthly *Scottish Patriot*. As the 1903 'sporting season' in the Highlands got under way, it published a full tabloid page showing the extent of deer-forests in Scotland, illustrating in graphic form the extraordinary degree to which the common people, particularly in Inverness-shire and Ross-shire, had been driven to the coastal margins of the land in the cause of deer-forests. Two months later, in an article on 'the land monopoly', it was explaining how the Congested Districts Board 'betrays its trust'.

Throughout the following year it campaigned on the land question in general, and in particular on rights-of-way in Blair Atholl under the heading of 'The Duke of Atholl as a Land Grabber'. It opened this campaign with a reference to a celebrated dispute away back in the previous century: 'There are still Robertsons alive who remember their clansman Dundonnachie and the case of the bridge-toll. The question of the land in Scotland and especially in the Highlands is the leading question in Scotland at the present day.' Throughout the summer and autumn of that year, the periodical sustained a campaign fighting-fund raised by public subscription on the issue.

And that same winter the nationalist *Guth na Bliadhna* observed:

> It is really monstrous that huge tracts of the Highlands and Islands should be denuded of their inhabitants in order to make room for deer; and we beg leave to remark that were this country governed at home instead of at Westminster, a state of affairs so humiliating and depressing, so morally unsound and so economically wrong as this is, would never have been suffered to endure, much less to attain to its present scandalous dimension. From one-seventh to one-sixth of Scotland belongs to red deer.

The continuing interest in the land question, and its continuing identification with issues of class and nationality, was reflected in the 1906 general election, when the Liberals took 399 seats, the Conservatives (inclusing 25 Liberal Unionists) 156 and Labour 29 seats. Only the Labour manifesto, however, specifically mentioned the land, asserting that 'overcrowding continues while the land goes to waste. Increasing land values go to the people who haven't earned them.' In each of Inverness and Sutherland, a Liberal beat a Liberal Unionist. In Wick a Conservative beat a Liberal. In each of Inverness-shire, Orkney and Shetland, and Argyll and Caithness, a Liberal beat a Conservative. And in Ross and Cromarty the Liberal J.G. Weir also beat off the Conservatives. Radicalism in Labour form, in other words, was nowhere near a breakthrough in the Highlands. For the time being (and for rather a long time to come) the Liberals were secure in the Highlands, if increasingly nowhere else.

But for the vanguard of the Labour movement land remained central to its perception of the future. That perception was given focus and direction by, above all, Thomas Johnston's wonderful weekly, the *Forward*. Founded in 1906, *Forward* was to become almost at once a paper unequalled (with the exception of the *West Highland Free Press*) by any other in twentieth-century Scotland. Most of its early contributors and production journalists were Fabians, but they included Roland Muirhead, who – along with Dr G.B. Clark – was often to rescue the title from financial disaster. The Irish connection was maintained by having James Connolly as Dublin correspondent; and the socialist connection by the likes of writers and organisers such as John Wheatley, whose principal strategic vision was to tie the Irish working-class vote to Labour in Scotland. Wheatley's adoption of socialism had coincided with the launch of *Forward*. John Maclean was another contributor.

In its first two or three years, *Forward* devoted regular space to coverage of the land question, including the theories of Henry George (of which it was highly critical) which were still influential at municipal level in the west of Scotland. It also scrutinised the proceedings in parliament of legislation on the land question, for the Liberal government of 1906 was committed to an ambitious if unspecific programme of land-reform. Many Liberals, however, not to mention the Conservatives and the House of Lords, were opposed to any such reform. By the end of 1906 *Forward* was republishing House of Commons voting lists on a clause of the Land Tenure Bill, which clause proposed to enact that the consent of landlords was not necessary or required for certain improvements made by tenants to holdings. Of those voting, only two Scots were in favour. One was Labour, the other the Liberal member for Sutherland. And a week later *Forward* could editorialise:

> The present government came into power pledged to Land-Reform, and it has begun the task of redeeming its pledges, so far as Scotland is concerned, by framing the Small Holdings Bill. Even men who stand aloof from party politics are genuinely surprised at such legislation proceeding from a Cabinet that is largely composed of capitalists, lairds and lawyers.

The surprise was not misplaced. By the following July the Bill was 'being mangled in committee', according to *Forward*; while the same edition reported the vote on the proposal of the Labour leader, Arthur Henderson, to abolish the House of Lords. (Those voting against the motion included the members for Argyll, Inverness, Caithness, Inverness-shire, Sutherland, and Ross and Cromarty: proof positive to *Forward* that the Highlands needed independent Labour representation in parliament.)

The hegemony of the lairds and lawyers in parliament was matched on the ground in Argyll. In November, *Forward* was reporting that of the fifty-seven members of Argyll County Council, thirty-nine were landlords and factors and another eight were merchants, farmers, ministers and lawyers. Of the eighteen-strong small-holdings committee of the council, sixteen members were either landlords or factors. Every large estate in the county was directly represented on the committee by either a landlord or his factor; while the Duke of Argyll's estate was represented by two factors.

Popular demand for the land nevertheless remained a strong undercurrent to affairs in the Highlands. In the winter of 1906–07, a Highland Crofters and Cottars Association was established: 'We cannot afford any longer to be dominated by a gang of obstructive Peers, most of them English, some of them Scots. The aim of the Highland Crofters and Cottars Association is to restore the land to the people and the people to the land.'

And the *Oban Times* was still campaigning on land-reform, demanding that the powers of the Congested Districts Board be 'considerably extended, so as to include among other things, the power of compulsory purchase of land, at present used for the purposes of sport, in order to extend existing small agricultural holdings and to create new ones'. By way of support for this, the raiders at Bornish and Ormiclate farms were by the middle of March, 1906, simply cultivating the land. Further, a 'large number of crofters and cottars from Iochdar and Lower Carnan' then marched in procession to the farms of Gaerinish and Drimore, and took possession. 'The farms were formerly in the occupation of their fathers and grandfathers, and the ruins of the dwellings are still to be seen.'

That spring, the chief topic of conversation in Highland communities was the proposed new legislation on the land question. And as pro-crofter members pressed their case in the Commons, all eyes were on the latest developments in the long-running Vatersay dispute.

As the landless and land-hungry in the north of Barra had wished for land in that part of the island, so those in the south, around Castlebay, had longed for land in the island of Vatersay. Referring to Barra, after all, the Napier Commission of twenty-odd years earlier had reported, 'The cause of the prevailing poverty is easily arrived at; it is the want of land. The land is particularly hilly and rocky, yet there is enough of good land, if it were divided among the people.'

In September 1900, therefore, Vatersay had been raided by Castlebay area people. The island was the second largest farm on the Cathcart estate, and had been scheduled by the Deer-Forest Commission as suitable for crofter settlement. Twenty cottars from Glen and Kentangaval warned the Cathcart factor that 'dire poverty would not permit them to wait longer', and that if a favourable answer was not given to their request for land, they would go ahead and take possession of it. 'If you require time to consider your decision,' they wrote to the factor, 'we are willing to wait for fifteen days, but if a favourable answer is not forthcoming within that time we give you fair notice that we will take action without it.' Five hundred people waited a whole day in Castlebay for the factor's answer; Vatersay was then invaded and pegged out.

And the following spring, Vatersay was again raided. 'Six large fishing boats laden with fishermen and cottars crossed to Vatersay and took formal possession.'

In 1903 the CDB finally bought just sixty acres of the island, Lady Cathcart making a handsome profit from the sale, and the land was divided into fifty potato plots. This, however, failed to still agitation, and in 1906 there was yet another raid on Vatersay, with fifty cottars landing in February, ferrying stock over from Barra throughout the summer and building homes for their families. By the following year, they had completed twenty such houses, and showed every determination of staying on the island for good. The CDB therefore asked Cathcart to establish a crofting township on Vatersay. Cathcart refused and offered to sell the entire island to them – at a huge profit to herself, and at a price that the Board could not in any case afford. The estate then took legal action against the raiders, for Cathcart had 'carried concession beyond all reasonable limit' and, as she told the authorities, 'such a combination as now exists for taking and keeping violent possession of private property constitutes a condition equivalent to anarchy or to civil riot'.

In June, ten of the Vatersay raiders appeared in court in Edinburgh at the complaint of Cathcart, 'with the concurrence of the Lord Advocate', to answer charges that they had in breach of interdict remained in occupation of the land taken. The Lord Justice Clerk gave them all two months in Calton Gaol for refusing to give an undertaking that they would leave the island. The men were, however, released early and returned home, where they proceeded directly to Vatersay to commence cultivation. By the autumn, the CDB had agreed to buy the island for £6,250 (a price all the raiders believed to be extortionate). This went ahead despite a last-ditch attempt by Cathcart to thwart the settlement, on the grounds that there was not enough rain on the island.

Agitation on Barra was not stilled, however, and in March 1909 the landless people in the north of the island – 'being utterly despondent of getting land' and having petitioned the authorities without redress – raided the Ardmore part of Eoligarry. Glendale in South Uist had also been lately raided and there were 'also rumours that a raid is imminent on Milton Farm'.

Throughout this period, *Forward* kept up its agitation on the land question, with the clear purpose of promoting anti-landlord direct action in the Highlands. It was, in this respect, a direct successor to *The Highlander* and the *Scottish Highlander*. But in two other respects, at least, it was different. Firstly, it was driven by a vision of the land question as an all-Scottish issue; secondly, it commanded a very clear vision of the solution to land-hunger, namely nationalisation of the land. However, in journalistic brilliance *Forward* was a formidable match for John Murdoch's *Highlander* (though it missed, perhaps, something of Murdoch's concern for the integrality of a distinctive Highland culture to Scottish politics); and in these early years of the twentieth century, *Forward* easily deployed a greater degree of influence on the land-agitation than any other title.

Quite apart from its series on 'Our Noble Families', which ran throughout the first half of 1909, *Forward* gave space to the cause of large-scale timber-growing versus deer-afforestation; reported popular agitation on a rights-of-way issue in the Vale of Leven; and campaigned against the continuing influence of Henry George's theories on land taxation. It also printed the voting records of selected Scottish MPs, among them those of the Liberals John Ainsworth for Argyll, Munro-Ferguson, Annan Bryce for Inverness, and John Dewar for Inverness-shire. It printed with dismissive scorn an invitation from the Marquis of Tullibardine for Thomas Johnston to visit the Atholl Forest during the grouse season. (Johnston nevertheless despatched an undercover 'special commissioner' to Atholl, whose reports ran under the headline, 'Breadalbane Clearances going on now!'.)

It printed an appeal from six Uist crofters at Dalbeg (which suggests that the paper was certainly circulating in the Hebrides). It publicised the effects of exclusion from the Crofters' Act on Arran and reported the unanimous support of Shetland County Council for land-nationalisation. It introduced John Wheatley, 'president of the Catholic Socialist Society', on land-monopoly, the Revd Malcolm MacCallum of Muckairn on deer-forests versus crofters, and G.B. Clark on the Highland land question. It attacked the government's record on land-reform (in a review of three years of Liberal administration). And, towards the end of the year, *Forward* launched the first of what would be many attacks on the Liberal MP for Caithness, Harmsworth, a London newspaper owner (and owner of the *Northern Ensign*).

But it was to the re-formation of the Highland Land League that much of the weekly tabloid's energies were devoted in the second half of 1909. This, clearly, had been planned for some time and the journal's sustained coverage was to form the impetus for the launch of the new organisation. On 3 July 1909 the paper carried a long letter from Alistair Sutherland, a one-time delegate to the 1884 conference of the 'old' Land League, which included the observation that 'there are not wanting signs of an impending upheaval in the Highland of Scotland'. This sort of upheaval was, to the editors of *Forward*, 'the crofters' only hope'.

The following week the paper carried a half-page appeal, headlined in Gaelic with the slogan of the 'old' Land League: 'shoulder to shoulder'. Signed by 'The Editor', it called for a new Highland Land League, to 'carry on a militant propaganda especially in the non-crofting counties'.

A week later, the political basis of the proposed new League became clear: its slogan (and how appropriate that word is!) would be 'no landlord need apply'. *Forward* published two columns explaining why the League would be separate entirely from the Liberals. They were written by Hamish MacRae, grandson of a Sutherland evictee and headlined 'The traitors who mis-represent us'.

Correspondence and reports were carried at length in each of the next five issues; while on 28 August the paper carried two columns on 'The Highland Land League – an appeal to working men', as token of its clear orientation to the Labour movement. And a week after that, Johnston spelled out this orientation more clearly, with reports of the League's formal inauguration.

Its president was G.B. Clark; its vice-president was Thomas Johnston; Roland Muirhead of Bridge of Weir was treasurer; and Alexander Mowat of Glasgow's Partick district was secretary. The constitution proposed 'to bring about the restoration of the people to the soil' and to abolish deer-forests and 'pluralist farmers'; while a key clause referred to 'the ownership and control of land by the State'. It added that all new candidates endorsed or supported by the League were to sign the constitution of the Labour Party.

Thus a week later, *Forward* was reporting that Keir Hardie would tour the Highlands for the new League. A week after that, in the course of the 'great Budget demonstration' in Glasgow when 100,000 workers marched, there was a Highland Land League contingent with banner, platform and its own speakers in Glasgow Green. Two months later the League had produced its first pamphlet on the landlord problem.

In the Highlands, meanwhile, and particularly on the western seaboard, anti-landlordism was unabated. On Tiree the demand was unbroken for further land-reform; in Uist the Milton farm, if not broken up quickly, was under threat of seizure; and in Lewis, a local farm had been seized by the cottars of Shawbost as early as May. Indeed, by the following month 'neither persecution nor threats of imprisonment can seemingly avail anything in preventing illegal seizures of land by the cottars of the Western Isles'. The Dalbeg farm was still under occupation – 'It is reported that the whole of the landless population of the island are extending their sympathy and support' – while there was also talk of raids on Harris. From Lewis the cottars of Back, Coll and Vatisker wrote to warn that unless they were given land, they would take it for themselves on the first day of the following October. Yet again the Commons discussed the land question in the Highlands, in a 'debate that should be an object lesson to crofters and their friends'; and by the end of the year, the agitation for land was as strong as ever on Skye.

The new year opened (and closed) with a general election. In the first, in which the Liberals took 511 seats (compared to 273 for the Conservatives) Labour got 40 seats. The Labour manifesto had declared, 'The country has allowed landowners to pocket millions of pounds every year in the shape of unearned increment. Our present system of landownership has devastated our countryside. The land for the people!' In the second election, the Conservatives took 273 seats, the Liberals 271 and Labour 42; once again, land-reform had been high on the Labour programme. (The Conservatives had been more worried about threats to the unelected second chamber – 'behind the Single Chamber conspiracy lurks Socialism and Home Rule' – as token of the looming 'constitutional crisis' over the power of veto exercised by the House of Lords.)

In Scotland, in the first of these elections, the Liberals took 54 per cent of the vote, the Conservatives and Liberal Unionists 40 per cent and Labour just 5 per cent. In the second, the Liberals again took 54 per cent, the Conservatives and Liberals Unionists just under 43 per cent, and Labour just over 3 per cent. This was to be the last general election until 1918; and in it, the continuing hegemony of the Liberal Party in Scotland is clearly seen. In the Highlands this hegemony was particularly marked, Liberals winning every seat in each of both elections. (As to Highland by-elections, there was one in Ross and Cromarty in 1911, another in Wick in 1913, and a third in Inverness-shire in 1917. The Liberals took them all.)

In the face of this, however, Johnston's *Forward* agitated with rare persistence. Throughout 1910 it ran a long series of 'rambling recollections' by G.B. Clark, including a piece on 'how we roused the Highlands', 'the curse of English dominance', 'the fight for the crofters and the Crofters' Act' and 'how we beat the landlords'. There were many other such pieces.

But the greatest effort went into promoting the League. In the first general election of that year, for instance, it was planned to run C.A. Paterson in Caithness. In the event he did not run, on account of the hold 'Harmsworth and his money' had on the constituency, with his 'paid man in every parish'. By the spring, however, an 'effective summer campaign' was being organised, while the annual meeting of the League returned as office bearers G.B. Clark, C.A. Paterson, Thomas Johnston and the Revd Malcolm MacCallum of Muckairn.

The new League was active in Mull and Caithness too, where one meeting drew a crowd of close to a thousand people (though it went unreported in Harmsworth's *Northern Ensign*), and where four branches were in operation. Speakers were also despatched to Fort William, Skye, Raasay, Islay, Banff and Argyll, in which county there were active branches at Campbeltown and Carradale. Branches would also shortly be formed in Edinburgh and Dundee. Towards the end of the year the League would draft a parliamentary bill to amend the 1897 Congested Districts Act – or 'Home Colonisation Bill', as G.B. Clark styled it.

That winter also saw the first of a long series of Highland Land League Papers, written for the most part by John Fullarton Armour. Among their titles were, 'What the League will Do', 'The Emigration Evil',

'Afforestation: is there a landlord conspiracy afoot?', 'The Congested Districts Board', 'The Sutherlands', 'The Killing of the English Land Act' and 'The Liberal Treachery on the Land Bill'.

And though *Forward*'s weekly reporting of events on the ground in the Highlands never matched that of its predecessors (and may not have been intended to), nevertheless a close watch was kept on events in the Hebrides. In April 1910, for instance, the paper was reporting a meeting at Idrigill, where it was decided to take by force the farm at Scudaburgh, with a copy of the resolution being despatched to the CDB.

Idrigill, of course, remained a hotbed of anti-landlordism. The authorities were receiving (coded) messages by telegraph to the effect that 'the ground officer says crofters threatened him with grievous bodily damage if ever he accompanied a sheriff-officer again'. Following this, the procurator wrote to the sheriff:

> The very active part which the women took in the disturbance is perhaps the most regrettable feature of the whole case. The animosity shown to sheriff-officers in the old land agitation of the early '80s was very marked. I believe in every case practically in which they were resisted the plan was adopted, which was followed at Idrigill, of putting the women (and frequently children) in front of the crowd and getting them to pelt the officers. It therefore seems to me to be necessary that such action should now be taken as will make it plain to the people of Idrigill that they will not escape the consequences of their conduct. Otherwise, there is only too good reason to fear that the spirit of lawlessness will spread. It is a most infectious disease and in Skye at all events I feel sure that for some time to come it will not be safe for any sheriff-officer to attempt to execute a warrant.

The procurator also urged the sheriff that the 'ringleaders' they proceeded to select must not be judged by a Skye jury. And thus the Scottish press was shortly reporting, 'Skye crofters sentenced, heavy penalties for contempt, great sensation in the island, relief fund for imprisoned men'. The sentences, however, made little difference. The people of Idrigill, and from throughout Kilmuir, defiantly marched in procession to a mass meeting on Biallach Hill, overlooking Uig – on a spot where Henry George had made a speech twenty-five years earlier calling for land-reform – and made it plain that their defiance was the equal of punitive action in the law courts.

The next four years were characterised, therefore, by a continuing trickle of agitation, mainly in the western Highlands; by the manoeuvres and debates surrounding the Small Landholders' Act of 1911; by the popular perception that the provisions of that legislation were inadequate; and by continuing efforts to build the League as an integral part of the Labour movement (though John Wilson, for three years an editor of the nationalist *Scottish Patriot*, was a member of the League too).

These efforts were not without success, although the League never attained (even if it so aspired to) the mass character of the 1880s. But the Labour movement was slowly making political progress at local as well as national level. In May 1911, following the death of Galloway Weir, the MP for Ross and Cromarty (who had taken it over from Dr Roderick Macdonald in 1892 as a Liberal/Crofter), the League even considered running its own candidate – though in the event Ian MacPherson for the Liberals beat off a Conservative in a straight fight. A month later, however, *Forward* editorialised:

> There is in the Highlands enough political sentiment of an advanced type to give Scotland in the House of Commons a group of land reformers, working on independent lines, and with land nationalisation as their goal. The Socialist who comes in contact with the Highlands for the first time is astonished at the widespread convictions on the land question which are Socialist in nature.

That same month with delegates from every county in Scotland present, the annual meeting of the Highland Land League unanimously agreed to alter its name to the Scottish Land League. It also decided to delete the clause tying the League down to the Labour Party in parliament. Any representation the League might have there in future 'should be independent of all political parties'.

The secretary of the renamed League was C.A. Paterson, who quickly announced that he would contest Argyll at the next parliamentary election as a Liberal and Land Law Reform candidate (having been adopted as such by the Liberal association in the north of the county, though he was clearly a land-nationaliser). But by the following spring the League, though it had the urban areas of Scotland covered, was appealing for money for a rural organiser: 'The control of the Highlands lies with the Liberal Whips, who find there safe seats for alien reactionaries.'

Meanwhile the League and *Forward* kept pressing the land question in the Scottish Labour movement, with G.B. Clark arguing that the Labour Party 'must now make a bold bid to capture the imagination of the working class on the Land Question'. The long-delayed small landholders' legislation (its author's name satirised without mercy by *Forward*) was also working its way through parliament. Some leading Liberals attempted to sabotage it and Paterson denounced, in *Forward*, 'Munro Ferguson's latest landlord trick'.

'Kepting' Sinclair's proposals had twice gone through the Commons in 1907 and 1908 but had been on both occasions destroyed in the Lords.

Now, however, with the ending of the Lords' veto, these proposals were on the point of enactment, for they were reintroduced as a private measure with government support. The Crofters' Commission and Congested Districts Board would be replaced with Land Court and Board of Agriculture.

The League and *Forward* scarcely welcomed the legislation, in August 1911. The paper gave the issue an extraordinary amount of space and prominence, all of it hostile. The legislation represented 'the government's great betrayal of Scotland', according to Paterson. By the following January *Forward* was reporting what it called 'the first fruits of the land-bill treachery', and two months later the Revd Malcolm MacCallum was bitterly criticising the 'Liberal Land Court'. That May the paper editorialised, 'The first meeting of the Scottish Land Court takes place this week at Tain when the Landholders' Act will start on its voyage. We have now to create the conditions which will make land nationalisation easy.'

Meanwhile the League was active in Caithness, complete with county organiser; while *Forward*, very much in the spirit of MacKenzie and Murdoch with regard to the Napier Commission, followed the progress of the Land Court carefully, and carried a series of exposures of 'landlord extortion and fraud' across the country.

Nor did the new Board of Agriculture escape censure. In April 1913 Paterson wrote in *Forward* that 'the Board of Agriculture have been trying to negotiate with landlords for the creation of new smallholdings'. The landlords had acted 'according to the traditions of landlordism – blocking any scheme for the benefit of the people except on receiving extortionate blackmail'. And by the summer of 1914 *Forward* was reporting the 'failure of the Small Landholders' Act'.

With *Forward*'s 'appeal from the Hebrides: the disappearance of the Gael', and 'advice to tenants before the Land Court', went reports of the people of Point in Lewis petitioning the Board of Agriculture for smallholdings; for the Board was very quickly awash with demands for land. This demand, however, the Board was in no position to satisfy quickly (if at all). By the end of 1913 the 700-acre farm of Reef in Lewis was raided by the cottars of Valtos and Kneep, in the parish of Uig. They were 'apparently exasperated at the delay of the Board of Agriculture in dealing with their applications for smallholdings'.

Reef had once been a crofting township and had been raided in 1883. Some of the raiders then had been gaoled, their stock sold to pay their legal expenses. Now, however, the raid had not so much been premeditated, 'but was the coming to a head of the discontent that has been seething in the district for some time past. The fear is entertained that the outbreak at Reef is only the beginning of agrarian trouble in the island.'

The following spring, therefore, with the Commons discussing changes to the recent legislation, eleven of the Reef raiders were sent to gaol for six weeks each. Major Matheson had let it be known that he would not press for punishment if the raiders would promise no longer to raid. But to this they would not agree.

That winter, indeed, raiding went on in the Hebrides. In the spring of 1914 raiders had seized Taransay island (off Harris), planted forty barrels of potatoes, fenced their crops, and 'now seem to look upon the raided ground as their own. It is reported that building operations have also started.'

By now, however, Europe was poised on the brink of war. The Balkans were the fuse, their people having tired of the arrangements of that great peace with honour cobbled at the Congress of Berlin back in 1878. With the distant tap of the recruitment drum growing ever more urgent over the continent, the German and Austrian waiters toiling in the hotels of Oban were being summoned home by telegraph. Still, the *Oban Times* found space for a letter whose author knew even then of 'Highland clearances as bad as any that have happened in the past':

> I know of men being turned out of the Highlands today, for no other reason than the whim of a laird, and knowing this, can you wonder that a movement is afoot, and gaining ground rapidly, to organise the Highlanders in city and clachan, to fight once more for the cause which the *Oban Times* has so strenuously advocated?

In Lewis, crofters were demanding to know why not one acre of land had yet been given them under the smallholders' legislation: 'A feeling of keen disappointment is threatening to assume a serious aspect.' The expectations inspired by that legislation had been 'chilled almost out of existence'; and on all sides, there was 'ample evidence of a coming revolt'.

With three and a half million acres of the Highlands now under deer – compared with just two million at the time of the Deer-Forest Commission twenty years earlier – it was not surprising that another letter-writer to the *Oban Times* could suggest that 'all ardent advocates of land-reform should see to it that "the heather is kept burning". A thoroughgoing land agitation on land matters seems urgently called for.'

That letter appeared at the end of June. Just a matter of weeks later, Europe was at war.

Within twenty-four hours of the declaration of hostilities, over 2,000 people met at Helmsdale, the strath of Kildonan behind them. On the platform was the Inverness journalist Hassan, president of the Inverness Trades Council and son of Laurence, one-time acquaintance of John Dillon and Michael Davitt. Along with him was Joseph MacLeod, doyen of the land reform struggle of earlier years, who proposed a strong motion on 'the land to the people'.

But the meeting also supported the war, 'secure in the hope that the "holy crusade" of their fathers would soon be answered and the land restored to the people'. Three days later *Forward* attacked Highland landlords in general, and in particular 'the English capitalist who represents Caithness in Parliament'.

But by now it was all too late for this sort of class and cultural consciousness. For the jingoism of those that met that day, the price would be heavy. And the first instalments were due almost at once.

ELEVEN

WAR AND THE PROMISE OF LAND

'It is doubtful if the Kaiser himself ever rose to such a height of intolerant impertinence and almighty self-importance as the Duke of Argyll does in his appeal. One would have thought that the Duke would approach these people timidly, saying "I am the representative of a class who bled the Highlands almost white". But there is nothing of that strain about the Duke's appeal.'

———

It is a matter for cautionary reflection that the armies of the continental powers bore far greater casualties in the First World War than the British. Many communities, urban and rural – the countryside as usual the lush granary of fodder for forced-service armies – in Germany and France and Russia suffered terrible devastation. Some civilian populations directly experienced desperate depredations as well. While two million Poles served in the conscript armies of Russia and Germany and Austria, for example, their national territory was site of the greatest battles of the eastern front. The Polish figure for military dead was something around 450,000; for civilians it was much, much higher. In the five years from 1914, the population – calculated on the basis of the territory of the inter-war republic – fell by four and a half million, or almost 15 per cent.

Overall British military mortality was paltry by this sort of standard. But the war still cut swathes through the ruling classes, the intelligentsia, and the ranks of the industrial worker and the countryside worker alike.

Britain's total of war dead was 745,000. A 1921 parliamentary return simply divided it by ten (in proportion to Scotland's share of the British population) to propose a figure of 74,000 for Scotland's war dead. But the National War Memorial had suggested in a White Paper a year earlier that the figure was over 100,000. And Scottish territorial battalions, which involved a far higher proportion of potential recruits than south of the Border, and which were largely rural in composition, took dreadful losses – especially in the campaigns of 1915.

Some commentators in the '20s argued that Scotland endured worse proportionate losses than any other part of the Empire, and that of these losses the Highland share was the greatest. The dead, of course, were overwhelmingly private soldiers: one officer died for every thirteen men.

Certainly, the Highland contribution was a significant one. By the spring of 1915 some 4,500 men were away from Lewis on military service. The fifty-four families in Lower Shader had as many men at the front; the twenty-six families in Ballantrashul had twenty-five men there; and the sixteen families of mid-Borve had eighteen men away. From Lewis almost 7,000 men joined the forces (and the mortality rate for Lewis, according to one contemporary report, was half as high again as that for all Imperial forces).

On the mainland, the three seaboard parishes of Wester Ross had seventy-six men killed out of 367 serving: a mortality rate of over 20 per cent. Out of 100 local men in the Seaforth and Cameron regiments, the death rate was 35 per cent, or just about three times the Imperial average. 'Here is the record of the rural school at Auchtertyre in Ross in 1897. On roll, 48; remained in parish, 1; in next parish, 1; returned from abroad, 2; died young, 4; killed in Great War, 5; at sea, 1; emigration to other parts of Highlands, 4; other parts of UK, 10; overseas, 20.'

Many Highland formations were part of the 51st Highland territorial division, a 'flying division' usually in the thick of action. Three times, its intervention saved the general situation on the Western Front, albeit at some cost: around 1,500 men 'lost' at Festubert; 8,500 at the Somme; 2,500 on the Ancre; 2,500 at Cambrai; 5,000 at Morchies-Bapaume; and 2,000 at Rheims, for instance.

From the parish of Inverness alone 700 men died. The pattern across the Highlands was similar:

> In quiet country places the losses of war were most felt. The percentage of killed in the Empire's forces was 12, but seldom, if indeed ever, were the losses sustained by any Scottish community, urban or rural, so low. Many districts, for example south-west Ross, showed figures for killed of over 23 per cent of those serving. Villages like Dornie and Bundalloch lost one young man out of every three. Of 102 local young men joining the Seaforths and the Camerons from the three parishes of Kintail, Lochalsh and Glenshiel, thirty-six were killed. Such figures were not exceptional. As one moves through the Scottish countryside and looks at the little parish or village memorials, one cannot but realise what irreparable damage was done to the fabric of rural life.

Two of the casualties sustained in the early days of the war were the sons of the ill-starred family that owned the Arisaig estate. The younger, Stuart, was twenty-five and a lieutenant with the first battalion of the Camerons when he went off to war in August 1914. Within four weeks he was missing, presumed killed, with the Expeditionary Force on the Aisne. Two months before his departure his brother William, aged twenty-six, educated at Marlborough and Oxford, had been married in Westminster and had honeymooned at Arisaig House (that many-windowed mansion beside the beach from which the Young Pretender left for France), being drawn there from the station in a carriage dragged by the tenants. A lieutenant with the second battalion, Camerons, William was killed at Ypres on the evening of 22 February 1915.

Others were to survive, though at some cost. In 1914 Jock MacKenzie of Ardgay left with the Seaforths, not returning until his demobilisation in 1919. In one action he saw his original battalion, of over five hundred men, lose 80 per cent of its strength. Wounded badly and gassed later that same year, he lay helpless in a mound of dead and dying until a French soldier found him and gave him a shot of rum, which revived him. Three days of crawling and resting between the lines (during which time he was also wounded by shrapnel) took him to a 'forward dressing station' in the Imperial lines, as these famous charnel houses were known. MacKenzie survived the war. As late as 1981, he still had three German bullets lodged in his body. He also continued to suffer once a year from the effects of gas. He would at once go to the end of his croft with a half-bottle of rum, drink it, and be violently sick; but recover from the effects of the gas. As a small boy, he had lived beside two very old women, both of whom had been crippled as young girls in the Greenyards anti-landlord riot of the previous century.

And in North Morar at the start of the Great War, there was a large enough community at the head of Loch Morar for two shinty teams to play, according to one man who was brought up there prior to going to Gallipoli with the Lovat Scouts. (Today, as for many years past, the area is a deer-forest without any resident population.)

If cautionary voices identified these sorts of consequences in 1914, however, they were largely drowned in the clamorous orgy of jingoism with which the Highland gentry – and others – greeted the outbreak of war. In the *Inverness Courier*, for instance, the editor James Barron assured his readers that the 'savage pretensions' of Germany had to be 'reduced to impotence'. Within months, in May 1915 at Festubert, the 4th Camerons were 'losing' 13 officers and 238 men from the lesser, though no less necessary, ranks. And at Loos that autumn the soldiers of the Highland battalions were slaughtered (Barron's son among them).

Such casualty rates did not go unnoticed on the Home Front. Even by the middle of 1915 the children of the Easter Ross towns were taking care to pretend that they did not see telegraph-boys in the streets (but all the same watched in irresistible terror the home for which they headed). In some families in Skye – and elsewhere – many sons were 'lost'. From Portree alone, twenty-six men were 'lost' on the night of 17 May 1915, at Festubert. Lord Lovat, in letters to his wife, urged her to get round the crofters on the estate in the cause of morale. The King's message to the Highland Mounted Brigade on their departure for service overseas caught the spirit of the thing: 'I feel sure that the great and traditional fighting reputation of Scotsmen will be more than safe with you and that your Brigade will spare no effort in the interests of the Empire's cause to bring this war to a victorious conclusion.'

The Highland gentry, naturally enough, were prominent in this crusade from the promised land of modern romance; albeit in the officer corps. A century and a half of radical land-centred agitation had not altered that elegant old balance of responsibility. When the 5th Seaforths marched away from Dingwall with the guns of the fleet crying out over Cromarty and the Union Flag a-swagger on every dunghill steeple, the Duke of Sutherland was their honorary colonel. By 1918 they had 'lost' 870 men. Cameron of Lochiel, meanwhile, commanded the 5th Camerons, while 'the MacKintosh of MacKintosh' led that same regiment's third battalion; and Lord Lovat took his Scouts with the Highland Mounted Brigade to Gallipoli's Chocolate Hill (where a number of them still lie, gravestones distinguished by Gaelic inscriptions).

As the stream of volunteers for walk-on parts in this grand drama of great-power competition dried up, conscription followed. By the spring of 1917 few appeals against conscription were being granted in the Highlands. Some men – or boys, rather more accurately – were allowed to remain at home, but only until the spring planting was completed. Many old people faced the prospect of having to get in the harvest that autumn on their own. Staple foodstuffs were everywhere in short supply: the rich, indeed, being urged to eat expensive foods that the poor might have more potatoes to consume.

Still, there were important consolations. The Scottish Secretary announced that, 'where the hottest of the fighting has been, there the Highland regiments have been found. After the war every Highland soldier who desires to do so should settle in the homelands and not be shipped to the colonies.'

By the spring of 1918 matters were so serious that the Board of Agriculture was urging people in the Highlands to grow more food. Under the Defence of the Realm Act, it even made an order authorising the killing of a deer by the occupier of an agricultural holding, if such a deer was trespassing on his grazings or causing injury to his crops. It evidently required a European war to amend the operation of the game laws in the Highlands – and then on a temporary and emergency basis.

What the effect of all this was on the Highlands is not easy to identity with much precision. Military mismanagement (and by the pre-war landed classes at that) can hardly have improved popular opinion of them. But the evidence is in short supply, though some suggestion is available from the private war-diary of the Catholic chaplain to the Lovat Scouts at Gallipoli. Hugh Cameron had been priest in Castlebay on the

outbreak of war. Aged forty, he was shortly in Gallipoli and noted towards
the end of the disastrous campaign there:

> Rumours of evacuation. The sooner the better. None of us will be
> sorry to leave this damned hole of a graveyard where so many
> brave men have fallen in vain. This is for my own use and I can put
> down my own thoughts for they are the thoughts of all of us. From
> start to finish Gallipoli has been a most abominably managed
> business. Had the fine material available been properly handled
> we should long ago have been in Stamboul instead of holding
> three miles of flat dominated on three sides by the enemy. We
> were up on those heights more than once and bad leadership in
> high places lost them to us. That is what makes the temper of the
> army so bitter.

Another survivor of the Great War said of South Uist:

> The country was bled white. Where I come from there were seven
> men killed, it was the same all over the Highlands, it suffered an
> awful lot of casualties. The first regiment of Lovat Scouts, they were
> practically all of them Gaelic speakers – but the Highlands were
> never the same afterwards. You didn't have the same type of men.
> There's no question, the war made a huge difference. There were
> some houses in Uist that lost three and four sons, there was just the
> mother left and so on, and the place deteriorated. There was hardly
> a family that didn't lose someone – there was a gloom on them all
> after it.

Despite this, however, the land question remained firmly on the domestic
political agenda; and increasingly so as the war drew to a close and the
dangerous cry of 'the land for the people' (for this time they were in
uniform) was heard again. Food shortages alone drew the attention of the
state to underused land resources, and cast light on the possibility of a
peacetime reorganisation of land use, tenure, and ownership. By the
summer of 1916 the matter of post-war land settlement in Scotland was
being raised in the Commons; and by that autumn the government's
Acquisition of Land Bill was making its way through parliament. A year
later 'yet another parliamentary land-reform group' was constituted with
the view that 'the land question must occupy first place in all schemes of
social reconstruction after the war'.

And by 1918, the London press was reporting on agitation in
Sutherland, Tiree and Skye, along with the proceedings of a deputation
from the Scottish Smallholders' Association to Lewis, Sutherland and
Caithness. The Association, and its journal the *Scottish Smallholder*, had
been campaigning for post-war land settlement, and changes to the 1911

Small Landholders' Act, since at least 1917. So too had *Land Values*, the journal of the campaign for the taxation of land values, then in its twenty-fourth year of publication. *Land Values*, though published out of London, gave sustained coverage to the land question in the Highlands throughout the last year of the war. It had an active Highland branch based in Inverness, which occupied its time by sending pamphlets on the land question to the soldiers at the front. By February 1918 it was denouncing the 1911 Act as 'already a dead letter in Scotland. The search for land has proved absolutely vain and it is impossible to get suitable land except by paying exorbitant compensation.' Even *The Times* carried reports from South Uist on Lady Gordon Cathcart's interdiction of her crofters. It also reported from North Uist on Sir John Orde's legal contest with the Board of Agriculture before the Land Court; and on the despatch to prison – at the very moment of Germany's last great offensive on the Western Front – of crofters from Sutherland.

In part at least, this public attention was due to continuing agitation in the Scottish radical and nationalist press on the land issue. In 1914, *The Thistle* was anouncing the nomination of a crofter parliamentary candidate for Inverness-shire (though with the coming of war the election was abandoned), and reporting, 'The Small Landholders' Act has neither created, nor met, a demand for land in Scotland.'

Later that year the same journal was covering the extent to which Highland estates accustomed to 'traditional' owners were falling into the hands of what it called 'alien capitalists'. It also reported a private member's Bill in parliament designed to amend the Small Landholders' Act. *The Thistle* added, 'It has now been in operation for two years. No fewer than 8,000 applications for new holdings or for enlargements to existing holdings have been made, and less than 300 of these have been dealt with. In eighteen counties there are altogether 3,599,744 acres of deer-forests.'

The following year the author of the failed private member's Bill was writing a *Thistle* piece on the 'paralysis of Scottish land-reform'. Commenting on the third annual report of the Board of Agriculture, he observed: 'Four years have passed and only 434 new holdings have actually been created. Truly a miserable record. A landlord opposition in Scotland persistently dogs the progress of the Act by recourse to every legal expedient to defeat its end.'

From Inverness, the *Highland News* was also distinctly anti-landlord in tone by the early months of the war. Of the Duke of Argyll's appeal for recruits, for instance, it observed:

> It is doubtful if the Kaiser himself ever rose to such a height of intolerant impertinence and almighty self-importance as the Duke of Argyll does in his appeal. One would have thought that the Duke would approach these people timidly, saying, 'I am the

representative of a class who bled the Highlands almost white.' But there is nothing of that strain about the Duke's appeal.

And by March 1915, on an attempt to repossess crofters' land in the parish of Clyne by the honorary colonel of the Seaforth Highlanders, the *Highland News* could observe: 'The House of Sutherland is at its grim work again. It may be using more civilised weapons – perhaps the law courts in place of the crowbar and the torch – but the one thing that matters is the same; the people are to be dispossessed.'

Nor did *Forward* lose sight of the land question. The sixth edition of *Our Noble Families* appeared in February 1915, the paper billing it as 'a valuable, unimpeachable and imperishable record of aristocratic tyranny, oppression and land thieving in Scotland – it proves that all the Huns do not live across the Ocean'. (Within just eighteen months it was once again sold out.) During the remainder of that year *Forward* ran a series of articles on 'the land and the war'; 'the land after the war'; and (in April the following year) on 'patriotic landlords – landlord robbery of Board of Agriculture money'.

By 1916 *The Thistle* was warning, in an article on post-war land settlement, that 'the young men have learnt much during their sojourn in the trenches'. And *Guth na Bliadhna*, in an article on 'the conduct of the land agitation since 1884', was observing that 'the movement that culminated in the adhesion of the Scottish land reformers of the 1880s to the Liberals was a fatal mistake in political tactics'.

A year later *Forward* was reporting that the Scottish Land Court was 'paralysed'. And Thomas Johnston was writing, 'The extraordinary story of how the Scottish Land Act of 1911 has been secretly paralysed in the midst of the great war of liberation – surely to God there's a limit to what the people of Scotland are going to stand!'

Nor had the Land League, despite the pressures of war, disappeared from the scene. The *Forward*-backed Scottish Land League does indeed appear to have sunk by the spring of 1915; but by then (and from the end of 1913) a new Highland Land League, with a Gaelic rather than Labour orientation, had been constituted. Within a month its London-based secretary, G.J. Bruce, was writing in *The Times* on deer-forest devastation of agricultural land in Sutherland. By the following year, Bruce was occupying the columns of *Highland News* on the Duke of Sutherland's efforts to evict an eighty-three-year-old man, with three sons in the army, from land at Cnocan to add it to a grouse-moor. By 1916 *Forward* was reporting 'the communiqué of the Highland Land League' on affairs in Sutherland.

By this point in the war the League was under fire from jingoists on account of having appealed for money, on the behalf of crofters, from Highlanders in British colonies – 'thus undermining Imperial resolve'. Nor did it take long for the League to become embroiled (as tradition might be thought to have dictated) between nationalists and socialists; although by this point both were moving, rather unsteadily, one unto the other.

By 1918, indeed, at a delegate meeting of the League in Glasgow, it was decided that it would affiliate to the Labour Party in Scotland and would run with Labour joint candidates in all the Highland constituencies at the first general election. *Guth na Bliadhna* added after the meeting that 'organised Labour in Scotland would be behind the movement provided Three Capital articles were vigorously supported: National Self-Determination, the Land for the People, and Native Language and Culture'.

Appropriately enough, the Celtic nationalist Erskine of Marr observed in the same edition of *Guth na Bliadhna*, in an article on the Celtic and Labour movements, that 'hitherto the Celtic movement in Scotland has not been even a popular, much less a democratic, movement. It has divided its attention between the lairdocracy on one hand and the bourgeoisie on the other.'

By March 1918, G.J. Bruce was touring Lewis. At a meeting in Stornoway the chairman was none other that what the new *Stornoway Gazette* – founded the previous year by the former Hebridean correspondent of *Highland News* – called 'that veteran fighter in the land movement, the Revd Donald MacCallum'. Other emissaries of the League were elsewhere in the Highlands and 'the popular spirit is rising everywhere'. The League's programme, consisting of 'the Three Essentials, Autonomy for Scotland, the Land for the People, and Native (as opposed to English or Feudal) Culture', was hailed with enthusiasm and adopted by great numbers, wherever it has been expounded and preached'.

By September that year, and the war all but over, the Scottish advisory council of the Labour party had met in Glasgow and 'expressed its approval of a vigorous democratic policy, based on the recognition of national autonomy for Scotland [and] "the land for the people"'. A joint committee of the Labour party in Scotland and the Highland Land League had been appointed:

> [It] will shortly issue an appeal to the Scottish people for support in an effort to secure the return, in as many Scottish constituencies as possible, of candidates favourable to autonomy for Scotland and the land for the people. Over 40 candidates have been adopted, and the candidates for the Highland constituencies nominated by the Highland Land League and the Labour organisations will shortly be announced. Already·the intimation that a big Land and Labour campaign is on foot has aroused consternation in the camps of the old political parties; and in several of the Highland constituencies there has been a shaking of the dry bones of Scottish Liberalism.

The appeal appeared shortly afterwards, styling itself 'Scotland's National Freedom Fund', with addresses at the headquarters of both the Scottish Labour Party and the Highland Land League. Old themes were apparent:

> The Scottish Labour Party and the Highland Land League, believing that Scotland's interests can best be secured by the re-establishment of the Scottish Parliament, and by the land of Scotland being owned and controlled by the Scottish state [sic], desire your support. Since the Union of Scotland with England in 1707, Scotland has experienced ever increasing difficulty in obtaining from Westminster that attention to her needs which she demands they deserve. Most of the efforts for reform made by Scotland have been spoiled or defeated by overwhelming English votes. The English people show a marked disposition to conservativism, while the Scottish people on the other hand are undoubtedly progressive in political thought and action. The result of the Union has been that Celtic culture and Scottish ideals are discouraged, while the tendency is for the ideals and culture of England to be thrust upon our country. Large areas of Scottish land have been denuded of people in order to provide sporting grounds for the idle rich.

In the autumn of 1917, meanwhile, the Bolsheviks had grabbed power in Russia and – by a hair's breadth – managed to keep it. The common sense of their programme of bread, peace and land must have seemed marvellously self-evident to the armies in the mud and those who waited for them at home.

In a faint – but, for the landlords, desperately worrying – echo of these events, *Forward* could headline a story, in the immediate aftermath of the Bolshevik putsch, 'Bolshevik tactics in the Highlands', and go on to record that the Highland Land League 'has its hands full at the moment. Tired of politicians' promises and the dilly-dallying of the Board of Agriculture, groups of men in the Highlands are quietly taking possession of their common heritage.' The League, *Forward* reported, was in contact with raiders on Skye, Raasay, Tiree, and Helmsdale. And a fortnight later it could assert, 'There is nothing in Industrial Capitalism to beat landlordism for naked, barefaced, impudent exploitation and tyranny.'

In fact there had been land-raiding even earlier, during the war years. In the spring of 1917, for instance, raiding took place at Kyleakin and Sconser in Skye.

In July, a spokesman for a number of people from Kyleakin who had occupied grazing land wrote to the factor for the MacDonald estates:

> We have heard quite enough about this little patch of land and there is no estate authority in Britain which can question the

legality of our taking possession of it. We will not give up the land nor pay rent though it cause bloodshed. We shall have none of your interference in this matter in future but shall have justice and more land to cultivate.

And from Sconser, the Board of Agriculture was informed that part of the deer-forest there had 'been illegally taken possession of for growing potatoes to the detriment of game preservation. This practice appears to be on the increase.' The Board had received a letter in which the crofters 'ask the Board virtually to homologate the illegal action taken by them, and the representative of the food production committee in Skye recommends that the crofters should be left in the possession of the land'. The Board's response was that it 'obviously . . . cannot act as suggested, as similar seizures of land would inevitably follow'.

The complaint about the conduct of the Sconser tenants had been brought by a firm of Edinburgh lawyers, acting for Sir Anthony Abdy, *curator bonis* (an agent appointed by the Court of Session on petition from medical authorities) for Lord MacDonald (then an inmate in an Edinburgh asylum). They complained that the Sconser forest, in the past worth £600 a year in shooting rental, was unlet and unlikely to be let 'at this late date in the year'. Some months earlier the Sconser people had asked for a part of the deer-forest, and the estate claimed to have offered the use, on unspecified conditions, of the northern part at Sligachan. In the opinion of the factor:

> The placing of cattle on this part of the forest would minimise the amount of injury to the forest as a whole. Notwithstanding this offer, several of the crofters recently put cattle on the southern part of the forest, in which is situated the sanctuary for the deer, and according to our latest information they are taking in cattle. The situation is therefore going from bad to worse. The *Curator Bonis* is naturally most unwilling to take any legal proceedings against the trespassers as his actions would certainly be misrepresented and it is by no means certain that even with a decree of the court in his favour he would be able to vindicate his legal rights. He deprecates the unwarrantable and unreasonable action of the crofters and fears that, unless the law is enforced, the mischief will spread and injury to many other interests will follow. The estate is very heavily burdened and, owing to the increase in the rate of interest on mortgages, the high rate of income tax and the fact of several of the shootings being unlet, the financial position is most serious. It will be most unfortunate if the illegal methods of the Sconser people are followed by others.

At much the same time, there was also raiding at the north end of Barra, again at Eoligarry, scene of so much agitation in the previous fifteen or so years. And by the following February, events in Tiree were being raised in the Commons. In due course the Tiree raiders got ten days each in gaol.

There was also wartime conflict in Sutherland. As early as March, 1915, the Highland Land League was calling attention to actions of the Duke of Sutherland in persecuting Highland crofters and threatening evictions. The issue related to an eviction attempt on one Joseph MacKay, whose father had been shepherd for a tenant-farmer of the Sutherlands, but who had been dismissed when the hirsel he herded had been put under deer instead. Joseph MacKay, however, insisted on remaining in his father's former cottage, and grazing his own sheep on the land around it. Meanwhile he applied to the Board for an official holding – to which the estate responded by issuing an eviction notice on him.

The secretary of the League, G.J. Bruce, wrote to the Board: 'The Duke of Sutherland, following the example of his notorious ancestor in 1815, has commenced persecuting Highland crofters and threatening evictions. One of these notices was recently exhibited by me at public meetings in Sutherland.' The eviction had been threatened the previous July, when the League had held protest meetings: 'I had several hundred men pledged to assist, and on the day the war began, we had a meeting of 2,000 in Kildonan. Our League is determined that the practices of the Sutherland family in 1815 will not be permitted in 1915.'

The estate told the Board, without any apparent sense of history, that Knockan, scene of the dispute, was 'near the march of the parishes of Clyne and Kildonan', and added the allegation, with vengeful gratuity, that MacKay's sister was the mother of an illegitimate daughter.

The authorities chose not to treat with Bruce: 'In view of the tone of Mr Bruce's letter, it seems undesirable to enter into any discussion with him.' Bruce, therefore, was simply reminded that he would 'incur a serious responsibility' if he was 'party to any resistance to the law'. Bruce was not intimidated and replied, 'I am to warn your government that if it permits or helps the forcible eviction of the old man of eighty-three, whose three sons are now serving with His Majesty's forces (North Hants Yeomanry, Seaforth Highlanders and Natal Light Horse) it may only do so over the dead bodies of MacKay and those Highlanders who will defend him.' The matter was also raised in parliament, with the Lord Advocate being asked whether the threatened eviction in wartime Sutherland constituted a breach of the Defence of the Realm Act.

That same summer, nine cottars in the township of Port Gower, in the parish of Loth, took possession of grazing land on the farm of East Garty, the property of the Duke of Sutherland. The cottars had originally tried to lease the land from the duke, but to no avail; and following the raid on the land (much of it on railway embankments) proceedings were raised in Dornoch sheriff court. The cottars were arrested in their beds at dawn and taken to Dornoch. Three of them were women, one a widow with two sons on active service; while Hugh Melville had three sons, all volunteers, in the army (two having returned from Canada to join up). Nevertheless they were all gaoled at Inverness for ten days.

The women, in fact, only served one day. The men, on their release, were met by supporters, 'to salute and honour the men for the brave stand they have made for what was their just right, and what they had been promised. Their incarceration added one more chapter to the battle for land-reform in the Highlands.' The background to the dispute concerned the tenant-farmer of the land in question, who had called in the local police prior to the raid – the local constable informing the chief constable, the procurator and the sheriff in due course that the raiders, 'following incitement by the Highland Land League', had given notice of their intention to take the land and put stock on it.

This they proceeded to do, despite padlocked gates and the presence of the police (who did not intervene). The farmer himself wrote to the authorities, complaining that he knew one of the raiders to be a Land League member. This man had threatened that 'they were going to take my farm and they were going to fight to the death – it was to be a test-case, and only the first of three in the district'. The farmer, sending his letter by registered mail, also noted that 'the horrible action of the Portgower crofters is really Ireland in Sutherland, actual Sinn Feinism, the Land League is sowing lawlessness and Sinn Feinism'. This matter also was brought up in the Commons.

Within months, of course, the war was over. The land question was clearly an important one as far as the 1918 general election went in the Highlands. The 1918 Franchise Reform Act had extended the British electorate from its 1910 level of 7.7 million to 21.4 million, greatly expanding the male working-class electorate, and adding a portion of the female population to the electoral rolls.

The Land League was by now firmly established on the Scottish political scene, in association with the Scottish Labour Party and its demand for Home Rule. One League meeting in Greenock, for instance, ended with a recital of some Gaelic songs, followed by a rendition by the choir of 'The Internationale'. From 1917 the League had been taking full-page advertisements in the nationalist press to insist that 'Scotland become again an independent nation, and that all lands, mines, and fisheries be restored to the Scottish Commonwealth'.

Full pages were also taken to list the League's leadership which by 1917 included office-bearers in Aboyne (Erskine of Marr), Durness (Revd Adam Gunn), Glasgow (Revd James Barr), Lochs (Revd Donald MacCallum), Coll (Revd Malcolm Morrison), Inverness (Revd A. MacLeod), and in London (Dr G.B. Clark and Willie Gillies). There were further office-bearers listed for Caithness, Helmsdale, Stornoway, Tain, Reay, Rogart, Oban, North Uist, Lochganvich, Balalan, Tongue, Raasay, Kyleakin and Halladale. Its objects were 'to secure Autonomy for Scotland, the return to the people for their use and enjoyment of the land taken from them and now held in large areas by nobles and other landholders in the Highlands of Scotland'.

The 1918 election was held in the middle of December. The established parties made considerable play of the extent to which they were committed to land-reform. Although the Liberals, led by Asquith, managed just one word on land in their manifesto, Labour pledged to 'free the soil from Landlordism and Reaction' and promised that 'the Labour Party means to introduce large schemes of land reorganisation, and it is fully aware that they can only be done in the teeth of the most powerful vested interests. Land nationalisation is a vital necessity. The Land is the people's.'

The manifesto of the Coalition of Bonar Law and Lloyd George also announced grand intentions with regard to the land question:

> Plans have been prepared, and will be put into execution as soon as the new Parliament assembles, whereby it will be the duty of public authorities and, if necessary, of the State itself, to acquire land on simple and economical bases for men who have served in the war, either for cottages with gardens, allotments, or small-holdings as the applicants may desire and be suited for. In addition to this, we intend to secure and to promote the further development and cultivation of allotments and smallholdings generally as far as may be required in the public interest. Arrangements have been made whereby extensive afforestation and reclamation schemes may be entered upon without delay.

Nevertheless, the League ran candidates under its own banner in Argyll (L.M. Weir); Inverness (G.J. Bruce); Ross and Cromarty (H. Munro); and the newly-created constituency of the Western Isles (H. MacCowan).

MacCowan, provost of Oban, was the nominee of the Stornoway branch of the Independent Labour Party, running with the blessing of the Highland Land League. But it was a sign of the times in the Western Isles that all three candidates called for sweeping land-reform and a 'radical transformation of the land system'. And in Inverness-shire the League candidate, G.J. Bruce, took space on the front page of the *Inverness Courier* to present his programme in Gaelic. Bruce said he had been born in a small bothy-type house to a poor crofter, the descendant of parents cleared from Strathnaver 'who had to find an exile overseas'. In 1913, he had succeeded in re-establishing the Land League:

> I fought relentlessly against the displacement of our people in favour of the German prisoners. I struggled strongly to increase the wages of the mining workforce in the Highlands. Self Rule for Scotland, the Land for the People and the People for the Land. The

fruits of the threshing blade belongs to all and the land belongs no more to one than another.

Bruce's advertisement did not prevent anti-League editorials in the *Courier*. But the paper did nevertheless report one of Bruce's meetings in the Town Hall (soon to be decorated with the 700 names of the parish dead). That report of his speech gives something of the flavour of the campaign:

> He stood for the land for the people. He had brought with him the old blue banner that had floated so often in the great assemblages in the North, when they were out for the land for the people. It had been the banner of the Highland Land League. That league was responsible for originating the agitation which led to Scotland getting all the advance in land-reform it had obtained; but they must admit that the land laws had been almost a complete failure in securing land for the people. That was proved by the last report of the Board of Agriculture for Scotland. In Inverness-shire in 1915, the total number of applicants for smallholdings was 1,339, and for enlargements 1,250, making a total of 2,589. How many did the Board of Agriculture get through? There had been granted 106 new holdings and 73 enlargements.

That, Bruce thought, was failure and nothing else but failure:

> At the outbreak of the war there were something like 8,400 applications for smallholdings in Scotland undealt with. Why should they have such vast areas of land for the blood sports of the autocrats who came to the Highlands for idle moments of each year? The present stampede election was one of the greatest scandals for which the government was responsible. Not more than sixty per cent of the soldiers would have any chance of voting. In the burgh of Inverness, twenty-six percent of the voters were absent voters. In the county there were 5,000 absent voters. The Highland regiments that had a large share in winning the war were disenfranchised. And what about land for returning soldiers? Up to May last, provision had only got as far as settling 26 soldiers on the land; and the provision consisted of giving large sums to certain big landlords for the most barren spot they could get hold of. He had in his blood a feeling of antipathy to the oppressors of the people.

In the Western Isles campaign the rhetoric was similar, though the vote was won by Donald Murray, the Liberal candidate and a strong advocate of land-reform (as his parliamentary interventions would shortly demonstrate). He also enjoyed the support of the *Stornoway Gazette,* which may have helped: 'He is the local candidate, the first in the field, and the people's choice before any other from outside of the constituency was dreamed to be possible.' On a turnout of 44 per cent of the electorate, Murray took 47 per cent of the votes cast; the Land League candidate took just over 10 per cent, or 809 votes. But Murray's election address had announced that he 'would press for a strong and effective scheme of land-reform which would result in a speedy distribution of all the available land in the Highlands and Islands among the people'. And certainly, over the next four years, he strongly supported land-raiding in the Hebrides, and became noted for his speeches in parliament on the issue of land-hunger.

In Inverness-shire too, the mainstream press favoured non-League candidates. The *Inverness Courier* denounced all the League candidates as extremist agitators and 'agents of the Invergordon dockers'. In any case they all lost, Weir in Argyll taking 19 per cent of the vote on a 52 per cent turnout, G.J. Bruce getting 27 per cent on a 37 per cent turnout, and in Ross and Cromarty Munro taking 21 per cent on a 51 per cent turnout.

On the British scale, Coalition candidates took 473 of the 707 seats in the Commons. In Scotland 54 of the 71 seats went to Coalition candidates. And in the Highlands, Coalition Liberals had taken Argyll, Caithness and Sutherland, Inverness, Ross and Cromarty, and Orkney and Shetland. Their only upset was in the Western Isles, where Murray ran as a simple Liberal. In other words, Labour was still some years short of its national electoral breakthrough. Due to the circumstance of Coalition Government it did win on a British scale – and for the first time ever won more seats, at 57, than the Liberals at 38. But in the Highlands, in coalition form or not, the old hegemony of Liberals held good.

But the wartime and immediate post-war land-raiding kept the land question firmly to the front of Highland and Scottish politics. This was notably reflected in continuing criticism of the 1911 Small Landholders' Act. As early as the first month of war, for instance, *The Thistle* had observed:

> The maleficent hand of the landlords' influence in the fashioning of the Act in the House of Lords comes out strongly in the reports connected with the sittings of the Land Court. Claims of a serious and costly character are made by the landlords whose estates are interfered with by the Court for the purposes of settlement. The Bill, as introduced by the Government, was avowedly for the purpose of re-peopling the Highlands; a great public object before which the so-called landlords' rights should have been minimised to the uttermost. Instead of this, they have been magnified to the uttermost. In one case lately reported, a large sum, considerably over £2,000, was awarded by the arbiter for depreciation of

sporting rights, on account of the settlement of crofters on a portion of the estate. And this sporting value did not arise from deer; but from the shooting of wild geese.

By the end of 1916 the Land Court, in its fifth annual report, was regretting the manner in which the Act had been 'marred and mangled' by the ingenuity of landlords' legal agents appealing Land Court decisions to the Court of Session. These decisions had effectively destroyed the usefulness of the Act. The procedure for the creation of new holdings was 'complicated and expensive'. The limits of rent and area were 'so narrow, particularly for pastoral holdings, that this Court has had to refuse to authorise schemes for new holdings, excellent in themselves and for the public interest'. The statutory element of compensation to the landlord came in for particular criticism as the Act's 'most essential defect'; and the Land Court reported 'with great regret' that the compulsory provisions of the Act had been 'rendered practically unworkable by judicial interpretation of the clause which deals with compensation to the landlord'.

By the following year *Forward* was simply dismissing the Small Landholders' Act as 'The Landlord Protection Act' (printing in the same edition its own 'land programme for the Highlands'). The essential weakness of the Act was that it gave landowners whose land the Land Court ordered to be resettled the right to claim compensation for disturbance of their 'sporting rights'. This in effect made it impossible to reclaim land from deer-forests, so huge could the claim for compensation be.

For *The Thistle* the 'ignominious failure' and 'iniquitous terms' of the Act were proof of the 'disgraceful lengths to which landlordism was allowed to go' to prevent the settlement of the people on the land:

> This short-sighted and rapacious action of the landowning class gives us a warning as to popular action in the future. The settlement of the people on the land is one of the greatest domestic questions that will come before the people when this cruel war is over and care will have to be taken that there shall be no more landowning juggling in the future. A strenuous attempt to do so will be made by the landowning and privileged classes. Of that there can be no doubt – and it must be resisted to the uttermost.

And just three months from the end of the war, *The Thistle* was reporting on 'depopulation in Glenquaich', with the comment:

> While there is an Act of Parliament which is expressly designed to give a peaceful settlement in Scotland to men of the class of crofters or small agriculturalists, and that a considerable sum of public

money has been spent in carrying out this policy, yet at the same
time landowners in the Highland districts are permitted to carry
out a policy of depopulation on portions of their estates.

Even Lord Lovat thought the Small Landholders' Act a distinctly bad piece
of legislation. 'It was bad in itself' (in other words, Lovat was implacably
opposed to any state interference in the Highlands); 'it was not too wisely
administered'; and 'it failed from the very start'.

Post-war, therefore, against a background chorus of this sort of
criticism, new legislation on land settlement was promoted. During the
course of 1919 the Land Settlement (Scotland) Bill made its way through
parliament. It was introduced there two days after the opening of the
grouse-shooting season and the Scottish Secretary moved its second
reading in the Commons the following day. *Land and Liberty* gave the
debate no less than five pages of space.

There had been small-scale legislation on the land during the war. But
the Land Settlement Act was altogether more ambitious in scale. Its
central provisions were to amend and extend the discredited 1911 Small
Landholders' Act, 'to make further provision for the acquisition of land
for the purposes of small holdings and otherwise facilitate land
settlement in Scotland'.

For Labour it was a 'great advance on anything they had yet had in
connection with land settlement': while landlord opposition to it was
strikingly muted. In the Commons only two members for Highland
constituencies spoke on the matter. For Argyll, Sir William Sutherland
offered no major complaint on it. For the Western Isles, Dr Murray
complained that it made no provision for land squatters (former raiders
now established on land to which nevertheless in law they had no right):
'People in my constituency are getting impatient and are asking when are
they going to get smallholdings?'

The Conservative Sir George Younger (for Ayr Burghs) worried that 'the
moment smallholdings are established on any property in Scotland the
capital value of the estate is reduced' – a point to which he returned in
November, when the Bill was before the Scottish Grand Committee. It
was proposed that compensation for acquired land would be paid on the
basis of the agricultural value of that land, rather than its 'sporting' value.
Younger wanted this provision deleted. The proposal was unjust and
ruthless: 'There were many natural deer-forests suitable only for sporting
purposes and bringing in large rentals, which would be destroyed if small
holdings were created on *or near them*, and something ought to be done
to mitigate the extreme loss in cases of this kind.'

But the landlords were markedly reticent in their criticism and they
mounted no significant opposition to the passage of the Bill. In the Lords,
Lovat contented himself with concern for the 'absolute power the Bill
gives to the Board of Agriculture for Scotland practically to make

bankrupt any unfortunate landowner in Northern Scotland who derives most of his revenue from sporting estates'. However for the Duke of Sutherland, with 300,000 acres to his name in the Highlands – as he reminded his peers – other considerations were uppermost:

> For 100 years the Highlands have from time to time seen a series of land agitations. They have died down only to rise again and to cause fresh unrest and trouble. Let us hope that this Bill, the fruit of a compromise with all parties, may be a way of laying that ghost which has haunted the Highland glens for so long. The Bill will go to another place and very probably will be returned in the form in which it was sent by us. A serious constitutional crisis might then arise.

But it was not considerations of constitutionality that bothered Sutherland. It was simple fear of what might happen if the landlords did not concede something, for the echo of events in Russia had resounded beyond the modest confines of pier-head and clachan. They had resounded – most alarmingly – in the drawing-rooms of lodge and castle; and the drawing-rooms had sensed the old earth tremble.

That, at least, was perfectly clear from what Sutherland told the House of Lords next:

> We remember that it is only a short time ago and a few years before the war that in Scotland, at any rate in the Highlands of Scotland, the House of Lords was looked upon with anything but favour. It was considered to be the author of all tyrannical evil. We do not wish for a similar state of affairs at the moment, when we should all be united against the evils of Bolshevism.

Thus supported – if that is the right word – the Bill received the royal assent the day before Christmas. Thirty-three years since the young David Lloyd George had listened spellbound to Michael Davitt and the new Crofter's MP of G.B. Clark speaking on the land question before the Welsh Land League among the grim slate screes of Blaenau Festiniog in north-west Wales, the state set about what it said was the resettling of the Highlands.

TWELVE

AVOID LAWYERS, CONTINUE PLOUGHING

'When facing the Germans we were filled with promises of getting land where and when we wanted, and now four years have elapsed but we are still left in the cold. The great European war was finished in about four years and the British government through the Board of Agriculture has failed in about the same time to acquire small plots of land for those to whom they were promised. Is it not time to end this farce?'

⎯⎯⎯⎯

In the wake of the First World War, the demand for land in the Highlands was as insistent as ever. And if anything, it was even more determined. In the words of one contemporary observer, 'In the crofting counties the question is fairly simple and uniform. There is a definite demand for land to be satisfied and a definite purpose to be served. The agrarian question in these counties has been prominently before the public for at least a generation.' As a result, the land question occupied a prominent place on the political agenda in the years following the Armistice.

In this period Labour – on a British scale – at last moved steadily, and decisively, ahead of the Liberals. In the 1918 election the Coalition took 473 seats; but Labour, at 57, were well ahead of the Liberals' 38. In 1922, however, when the Coalition had ended and the Conservatives took 344 seats and the Liberals 115, Labour at last had broken through to take 142 seats. The following year, Labour took 191 seats, putting it in a position to form a minority government. It lasted a year only. But though Labour fell back to 151 seats, the Liberals had crashed to 40 – the number of seats held by the Labour Party in 1910!

Throughout these years the land question commanded attention on a British political scale. In 1922 Labour's manifesto promised wide-ranging changes to the game laws, while the Liberals promised a 'comprehensive reform of the existing land system, including Taxation and Rating of Land Values'. The following year, the Liberals were demanding the development and encouragement of smallholdings, while Labour promised to 'restore to the people their lost rights in the land'. And by 1924, the Liberals were promising to 'secure to land workers the fruits of their energy and enterprise through a complete alteration in the system of land tenure'.

In the Highlands, meanwhile, the banner of radical, anti-landlord reform (carried in the 1918 general election by the Highland Land League in Argyll, Ross-shire, Inverness, and the Western Isles) was borne by the Labour Party – though not with great electoral success. Still, Labour in Argyll took 35 per cent of the vote in 1920 (represented by the Revd Malcolm MacCallum), and 23 per cent in 1924. In Inverness, Labour in 1923 and 1924 took respectively 35 per cent and 37 per cent of the vote. And in these same years the party's candidates took 24 per cent and 17 per cent in the Western Isles.

In a context where Labour had yet to establish itself fully as an enduring political force on the British stage, and where many Liberal candidates were strongly associated with land-reform, none of these performances was discreditable. And taken together, they serve to indicate the extent to which the land question and associated agitation remained central to the Highland agenda in the post-war period.

The radical and nationalist press did not fail to promote this centrality, either. By the autumn of 1921 *Land and Liberty* was reporting that one-fifth of the land area of Scotland was under deer-forests. The following year, the title covered in some detail the general election campaign in Inverness-shire. It reported with stern glee that Cameron of Lochiel had urged his tenants not to vote for Murdoch MacDonald (the National Liberal candidate) unless 'he modifies his views on the taxation of land values'. Cameron's instruction occasioned an uproar in the Scottish press. And by 1923 *Land and Liberty* was reporting a Commons debate on the despatch to Edinburgh's Calton Gaol of land-raiders from Skye. One of the speakers in this debate was the recently-elected Thomas Johnston, founder of *Forward*.

Liberty, the 'Scottish Home Rule journal', as it styled itself, also campaigned steadily on the land question. In the spring of 1920 the paper was supporting the parliamentary candidacy in Argyll of the Revd Malcolm MacCallum and asking, 'Why are the Highlands the playground of the southern capitalist?' MacCallum also enjoyed the support of *Forward*, which reported his campaign under the stirring headlines of 'class war in the Highlands', and 'carrying the socialist message through far Argyll'.

That summer *Liberty* also reported that the Highland Land League had 59 members in Coll, on Lewis. And a month later, as the Highlands were convulsed with yet another outbreak of raiding and threats against the landlords, the paper reported that a speaker from the London office of the League had addressed large May Day demonstrations in Chatham and Rochester on the subject of 'the Scottish Land-Raids'.

Early the following year, *Liberty* reported the removal of the League's headquarters from London to Greenock. And in March 1921, as token of the continuing identification of land-reform with the Home Rule cause, it reported the inaugural meeting of the Scots National League. Speakers including Erskine of Marr, Willie Gillies and Angus MacDonald, Highland Land League president. There was further token that June, this time of the close relationship between land-reform and radicalism, when Willie Gillies wrote (of John MacLean): 'It is not without significance that with scarcely one exception the doughtiest opponents of capitalist rule throughout England's cracking Empire are men of Celtic blood and Gaelic name.' Throughout the remainder of that year, *Liberty* ran lengthy monthly reports on the doings of the Highland Land League.

Meanwhile *Forward*, as well as offering its usual diligent news reporting of land-agitation in the Highlands, continued to find space for theoretical pieces from long-term land-reformers like G.B. Clark, C.A. Paterson, and the Revd Malcolm MacCallum. It also found space for an attack on the record of land-ownership in Morvern ('the Almighty of Lochaline'); and reported in extensive detail the attempts in the early 1920s to introduce nationalisation-of-land Bills to the Commons.

Of the gaoling of Skye land-raiders, meanwhile, *Forward* reported in verse:

> So Hurrah for the Highlands the Sport Estate Highlands
> Domain of the Nimrods from Piccadillee
> The working-class vermin are fast disappearin'
> The last of the clansmen in gaol at Portree.

The background to this extensive press and parliamentary attention was the continuing spate of raids in the immediate post-war period. As an official summary of the time indicates, seizures or threats of seizure of land were common from 1918 through to 1920. Incidents recorded include locations in Harris, the Uists, Shetland, Tiree, Skye, Wester Ross, Sutherland, Caithness, and at various points on Lewis; while another fifty farms across the Highlands were under the threat of imminent occupation.

A similar summary for 1922 details incidents at Forsinain in Sutherland, at Nunton in Benbecula, at Kilbride in Skye, at Newton in North Uist, at Strathaird in Skye, at Rodel in Harris, at Stimervay in Lewis, at Drimore in South Uist, at Galston in Lewis, at Pitcalnie in Ross-shire, at Scoor in Mull, at White Park in Islay, and at Glas Eilean in Harris.

In the Uists, for instance, the anti-landlord activities of groups of ex-servicemen drew extensive attention in parliament and in the press. In North Uist by early 1920 a dozen men were threatening raids, and marching behind a piper from the local premises of the Great War Comrades Association. And events at Balranald in South Uist were to draw appeals of support from public associations across the Highlands (and beyond). They included the North Argyll Liberal Association and

British Legion Branches in Inverness and Dumfries, among others.

At Balranald, thirteen men were involved. Of these, one had been four years overseas; a second disabled with the army; a third four years overseas; a fourth also overseas for a year; a fifth overseas for nearly three years; a sixth overseas and twice badly wounded; a seventh overseas and twice wounded; an eighth overseas and badly wounded; and a ninth overseas and wounded. All had been volunteers.

They had over some period of time been applying to the estate for land, and to the Board of Agriculture to take some action – but in both cases without success. In November 1920, therefore, they marched to the landlord's house, headed by a piper, and told him that they were simply going to take his land the following day. As one of them recalled a full sixty years later:

> He got very excited about that of course. But we told him to go to blazes and the next morning we were on his land. We tipped over his carts, we rounded up his sheep and cattle and drove them away. It was a week after that had happened that we were served with a sheriff's interdict forbidding us to set foot on Balranald.

The men had already written to the landlord in plainly uncompromising terms: 'We, the undersigned ex-servicemen, have decided to let your cattle have fourteen days in Paiblesgarry, but you must keep all sheep off it from now on.' And within a week of this missive the Board of Agriculture was also told that 'thirteen ex-soldiers have now raided the said farm [Paiblesgarry on Balranald] and are manuring potato ground'. They had divided it into equal shares and 'emphatically declared they would not remove'. If any proceedings were taken against them, 'they were prepared to go to prison'.

A week later the landlord was complaining to the authorities that others in the district were also ready to raid: 'The crofters on the north side of the farm are just waiting developments and watching to see what action the Board are to take.' He feared that if things went on 'as at present' there would 'undoubtedly be another raid'.

As a result the men were taken to court, and sentenced to sixty days without the option of a fine. But as there was no gaol accommodation for them, they were released. Later, however, they were indeed gaoled. Two of them were arrested while attending a Territorial Army training camp at Inverness (though the arrest nearly occasioned a riot).

The conflict, however, was not at an end. The following spring, an officer of the Board of Agriculture was writing to the Scottish Secretary to express his deep anxiety 'about the situation in the islands generally. There have been two fresh raids in the Lochmaddy district this week and the situation calls for careful, firm and very speedy action.' And on the same day the raiders themselves wrote to their anti-landlord Edinburgh lawyer, Donald Shaw, offering to withdraw from the land on condition that the landlord did not work it. This, they warned, would start trouble again, as they were 'dead set on having it' and will have it if at all possible'. The Highland Land League's secretary also pressed the Lord Advocate by letter on the case of the Balranald raiders.

There was continuing land-raiding elsewhere in the Highlands and islands too, doubtless encouraged by the small burst of hunger and destitution that victory in the Empire's cause had brought to the populace as its prize. By the spring of 1920 the press was reporting food shortages, widespread distress and starving children on Skye; and by the autumn typhoid on Lewis. Unsurprisingly, these conditions were matched by a rash of land-raids in Sutherland and the Hebrides. The implications of these new raids did not go unnoticed. In August, while the Board of Agriculture was reported as being short of funds, the House of Lords discussed the now widespread land-raiding across the Highlands.

In 1922 there was further trouble in North Uist. Ex-servicemen from Berneray raided at Cheesebay, Lochportain and Newton farm. They wrote in a confident tone to the authorities with regard to their complaints:

> Please do not think we care one straw for threats of imprisonment, for apparently without additional sufferings to what we have had on the continent of Europe, our cause will not succeed. When facing the Germans we were filled with promises of getting land where and when we wanted, and now four years have elapsed but we are still left in the cold. The great European war was finished in about four years and the British government through the Board of Agriculture has failed in about the same time to acquire small plots of land for those to whom they were promised. Is it not time to end this farce?

The Board responded with a threat that any land-raiders in North Uist or elsewhere would be struck off its list of prospective settlers.

Raiding nevertheless continued across the Highlands. On Skye, land was seized at Kilbride by ex-servicemen from Torrin. At Christmas 1920, the local Church of Scotland minister had warned the Board that a raid was being planned on a local farm. And the following April the farm in question, on the estate of Lord MacDonald, was duly raided. A full eighteen months later, however, no progress had been made by the Board in terms of making official the claims of the raiders.

As a result of this inaction, their Edinburgh lawyer (again Donald Shaw) wrote to the Scottish Secretary. 'With the exception of a few acres the whole of the arable land on Kilbride farm has been out of cultivation for a number of years,' he stated. 'All the men for whom I act are ex-servicemen. One of them had no fewer than four brothers fighting with him in France'. The estate feared involvement in the dispute. But the tenant-farmer of Kilbride went to the Court of Session and gained an interim interdict against the raiders. A sheriff-officer was, in time-honoured fashion, then deforced. And in the summer of 1923, five years after the Armistice, the village of Torrin was invaded at an early hour: 'The arrest of two disabled ex-servicemen, it is understood, has arisen from a charge of alleged deforcement on the farm of Kilbride.'

By this point there had also been trouble in the west of Skye, where the demands for land were now so advanced that 'they could not be met under personal ownership'. MacLeod of MacLeod thought it wise to agree to sell land for crofter settlement in the parish of Bracadale, 'including the well-known farms of Talisker, Gesto, Drynoch, Ullinish and Oze'.

There was also a raid at Strathaird, with some cottars taking possession of Camusunary, and pegging out seven crofts. By March 1923 they were still in possession of the land, refusing to leave, and facing court action charitably raised the previous Boxing Day. Their defence was that 'they were not in breach of moral law in laying claim to cultivate some of the lands held by their forefathers for centuries'. They had served in the 51st division and some of them had been badly wounded – 'it was only in despair of any action being taken to apply the law that they in their suffering decided to occupy'. Thus they raided the deer-forest (the tenant of which lived in London for nine months of the year) and seized land that 'had at one time been under smallholders, who were subsequently removed'. Nevertheless, they were given two-month gaol sentences – though the public outcry was so great that they were released after ten days.

That same month three Broadford land-raiders were also facing court appearances. They too were all ex-servicemen. The first had been with the Argyll and Sutherland Highlanders, the second with the Seaforths and badly wounded, and the third had lost a leg at the Somme with the Black Watch. Still they were ordered to appear before the Court of Session within a fortnight.

During this period, though raiding was particularly popular in the Western Isles, there was considerable direct action, or threats of it, on the mainland and the Inner Hebrides too. In Sutherland trouble-spots were identified at Forsinain, Blarich, Farr, Kirkton, Kinbrace and Cambusmore. From Ross-shire and western Inverness-shire they included Kishorn, Glenshiel and Coiliree, along with Arnisdale in Glenelg. From Argyll they included Mishnish, Islay, Arinagour and Arnabost on Coll, Gometra and Fidden on Mull, and parts of the Auchenreir, Fearnoch and Barnaline estates. There were also threats of land-seizure in Caithness, where the crofters were reportedly 'in revolt' at the farms of Latheron Mains and Latheronwheel Mains, at Charleston and Knockglass. There was also a case in Perthshire, at Carwhin on the Breadalbane estates.

And in the early post-war years, there were two notable cases of determined land-raiding on Raasay, which was owned by William Baird, with William Rownsley as the sporting tenant. The first of these raids began on 20 March 1920, when eight local men raided Raasay Home Farm, in the vicinity of Raasay House. They had earlier been assured that they would get land; tired of waiting for the Board to allocate it, the men simply staked out their claims, having by this point established for themselves the legal services of Donald Shaw.

The factor for Baird promptly applied to Portree sheriff court, successfully, for an interim interdict against the raiding. And a sub-commissioner for the Board of Agriculture at once informed the Scottish Secretary that the 'attitude of the applicants is in my opinion utterly unreasonable. They should not receive the very least countenance from the authorities' He went on to identify the leader of the raid as John M. MacLeod, shoemaker, Raasay: 'He is very hostile towards the factor. I have no doubt he is the author of the raids and the principles of the raiders.'

But the shoemaker of Raasay was not a man to be intimidated by courts or commissioners. MacLeod himself warned the Scottish Secretary of the results of public meetings held on Raasay and Rona on the land question in both islands. At these meetings:

> The criminal negligence of the Board was unanimously condemned. The inaction of that incompetent body is wholly responsible for all land-seizures in Scotland, many of the applications for holdings having been sent to the Board years ago. The interdicts served on the raiders are strongly resented by the islanders, 50 per cent of the male population of which went willingly to the Great War alleged to have been in defence of liberty. At the meetings it was agreed that unless the requests for holdings are granted immediately, there will be forcible possession taken of all the available land in the island.

This was not the end of the matter. In 1921 a group of men from Rona also warned the Board that they would take the law into their own hands and make a general raid on both sheep and Home Farm of Raasay, 'which is for a number of years now let to a sporting English gentleman, who rears calves with the milk we should be getting for feeding our little children'. Three months later, therefore, police reports from Portree were warning the authorities that men from Rona had lately been on Raasay measuring out plots of land. The same report quoted the factor as not regarding the matter as 'in any way serious. He does not think that the Rona men have any intention of taking forcible possession of the land. He rather thinks the matter is a piece of bluff on their part to spur on the Board of Agriculture to purchase the land for them.'

Within a week of this report, however, a raid had indeed gone ahead. As a result an interdict was taken out, but ignored; and that July the raiders deliberately failed to answer a summons to appear in court in

Portree on charges of breaching the interdict. The chief constable wired the Scottish Secretary in August, regretting he had to report that 'though the officers got into touch with all the defenders, the latter would not listen to reason, showing plainly that they would resist any attempt to take them by force, finally dispersing in different directions and defying the officers'.

As a result, the chief constable prepared to deploy the fishery cruiser *Minna* in an assault on the land-raiders, along with the two dozen policemen he supposed necessary for such an attack. The raiders were to be seized from their beds in the middle of the night; taken to Portree during the remaining hours of darkness, 'without any person being aware of what was being done'; rushed quickly through an early court; and taken thence by the *Minna* to Kyle and gaol in Inverness 'with little demonstration or trouble'. The fishery authorities, however, refused point-blank to have anything to do with the suggestion of using their vessel in the attack. A late-night police assault was still mounted, and five of the men were thereafter gaoled for six weeks. A national outcry followed.

Petitions poured into the government from across Scotland (and beyond) from branches of the Comrades of the Great War Association and numerous trades-councils – among them those of Montrose, Galashiels, Ealing, Edinburgh and Aberdeen. Letters of protest arrived from, among others, the Highland Land League in Greenock. The wives and sisters of the gaoled raiders wrote to the monarch at Buckingham Palace with a covering note from MacLeod (written on his shoemaker's bill-headings). Raasay, they said, had once 'sustained in comparative comfort a large number of smallholders but was cleared many years ago to make room for sheep or deer'. Despite the harsh treatment of generations of islanders, however, the people, on the outbreak of the Great War magnanimously forgot the injustices and insults heaped on their forefathers and had joined the forces, 'at a time when landlords found their title-deeds were of no avail in preserving their lands from danger'. Man, and not title-deeds, was 'the only hope then of the landlords'!

Inverness Trades Council demanded the release of the men. A fund was opened in the town for their dependants. A former front-line soldier with the Camerons wrote to the *Inverness Courier*:

> Apparently the holdings which parliament ordered for our landless cannot be obtained unless our people first submit to imprisonment. We want to hear no more in the Highlands of our 51st division or any division after the insults suffered by those men for foolishly fighting for landlords. We thought we were fighting for our country, but now find it was only for the landlords' country, and that when we claim any part of it we are directed to gaol. Monuments for the dead and gaol for the living!

Even a Board officer noted that there was a growing feeling throughout the west that the only way to get land was to raid it. 'From everbody's point of view a stand should be taken against the idea that raiding can be undertaken not merely with impunity but as a sure means of achieving the raiders' ends'. The Raasay raiders, meanwhile, spurned offers of a deal with the Board. They wrote to the Board to that effect, via their lawyer, while still in gaol in Inverness, towards the end of 1921. They also wrote to the Prime Minister, stating their case.

Tiree, too, remained a hotbed of anti-landlordism in the wake of the Great War. Indeed, as early as the spring of 1918 – with the conclusion of the war by no means yet certain – the matter of land-hunger was raised in the Commons. The Scottish Secretary was asked whether he was aware that the Duke of Argyll has taken proceedings to 'interdict crofters of Tiree from cultivating and producing food upon suitable but entirely idle land near their homes'; and, in view of the present food situation and the thousands of acres of suitable land lying unused by the Duke of Argyll's estates, whether he would 'take steps to enforce the cultivation of these area under the Defence of the Realm Act'.

The reply was that the duke and one of his his tenant farmers on the island had obtained perpetual interdict at Oban sheriff court, 'against certain cottars and others taking possession of the farm of Balephetrish and part of the farm of Kenovy, Tiree'. It was added that, in general, the government's agencies were 'making every effort by arranging for an increase in the food supply'.

The Board of Agriculture was also in touch with the authorities on the issue. In January the previous year – in other words, well in advance of the 1919 Land Settlement Act – applications had been received for land on the farms of Balephetrish, Reef and Crosspool. As far back as 1913, obstruction on the part of the principal farming tenant and the landlord had set back a Board plan to create more crofts on the island. And by 1918 there were 219 applications for holdings and 70 for enlargements (although 69 and 27 respectively had by then been established).

The Board sent an officer to report at first hand on the 1918 raid. He reported that he had not put himself in the way of the raiders, and only met two of them:

> From these I gathered that the feeling of the raiders is very strong and that they are determined to persist in what they have begun. They declare that even if the law checks them they will, at the first opportunity, resume. When I was there the land had been broken at eight places. Not much ploughing has been done due to bad weather but they mean to push on. There is a good deal of wild talk about gaol, and about the support they expect to receive in Glasgow where they have many friends. They say that on their arrival in Glasgow they will be met with a sympathetic crowd, flags

will be waved and there will be a general throw-down of tools. At ordinary times this might mean nothing but with so much unrest it is difficult to foresee the result. I understand they are backed up by some strong Land League body. I heard casually that a wire has been received advising them to go on ploughing but avoid lawyers. They feel that now is the time to obtain the land. There is a general movement in Tiree to get land. Personally, I do not think they will be at peace until the farms of Balephetrish and Crosspool are taken for division.

By early April, following the seizure of land at Balemartin, the authorities were being warned that the Highland Land League had resolved to do everything possible to help cottars engaged in food production and who were threatened with arrest. At the same time, the League was organising largely-attended meetings on Tiree.

And later that month eight raiders were arrested and given ten days in gaol at Oban for having taken thirteen acres of land at Balephetrish. In the Commons the Scottish Secretary was asked whether 'it is intended to continue the persecution of these men who are only voicing the demand in Scotland for access to the land for those who desire it'.

The Oban police wired the prison commissioners reporting that the sheriff recommended the men be treated as political prisoners and be allowed to wear their own clothes. The commissioners agreed, 'so long as the clothes are suitable'. Objections to the arrest of the raiders – most of whom were very old – poured in to the authorities: from the Highland Land League in Greenock and Edinburgh, from the Edinburgh Labour Party, and from the parliamentary committee of the Scottish Trades Union Congress. The raiders' lawyer, again Donald Shaw of Edinburgh, wrote about the case to Lloyd George in protest.

In due course the raiders were released – one day ahead of the end of their term, to allow them to catch the steamer home at 6 a.m. rather than having to spend six days doing nothing in Oban (as opposed to six days' land-raiding on Tiree). An anonymous civil servant scrawled on the memo requesting the early release, 'Yes; I suppose this is a land-agitation case.'

The gaol sentences had no effect on raiding on Tiree, and this continued throughout that last summer of war. The raiders complained that the crops they had planted on the raided land were being eaten by the tenant-farmer's sheep with the encouragement of the landlord. They also complained that the police had prevented these sheep being driven away. The matter of this police obstruction was duly raised in parliament, while the Cornaig division of the Highland Land League, based at Scarinish, complained bitterly about the matter to the Board of Agriculture. That summer, with the last great offensive under way on the Western Front, one of the raiders wrote to the Highland Land Settlement Association, asking,

'Why don't they take the sheep who have destroyed our crops and put them in the firing line in France?'

And by August the following year, raids were again threatened at Crosspool. One of these prospective raiders briskly wrote to the Board: 'We have waited long enough and if steps are not taken by the Board soon, we shall take possession of Crosspool by the November term.' The Board replied that land would not be available for three years. And thus at Christmas 1919, sixteen ex-servicemen of the island were once again threatening action. One of their number wrote to the authorities, 'We have gathered together and made up our minds to divide the land ourselves – until you see your way to divide the land yourselves, according to promise. This is our last communication anent the subject.' The following February, therefore, there were more raiding and assaults on Tiree.

And three years later, there was still further raiding. The Board was once more being warned: 'We are sorry that we are again forced to fight the land battle over again. But we want to notify the Board that we intend to enter and take possession of part of the farm of Cornaigmore in May.' The Scottish Secretary was also warned: 'The result is that we again must take the law into our own hands and enter the farm of Cornaigmore.'

And as late as 1926, a full forty years after the naval invasion of the island to arrest and gaol land-hungry raiders, there were again threats on Cornaigmore. The Board said that the farm did not fall within the compulsory-purchase clauses of the 1919 Land Settlement Act and nothing could therefore be done about it. Nor would the Duke of Argyll voluntarily let it be divided. The Board, then, was warned: 'Nothing will induce these men to keep quiet till they get what they have a right to. All the farm is a waste ground, neither ploughed nor stocked for the last thirty years. How long is the Board going to allow that sort of thing while others are starving in the land of their birth?'

But most notable of the land-raiding incidents in the wake of the Great War were those associated with Lewis and Harris – then owned by the richly eccentric and vastly rich English soap-boiler William Lever, Lord Leverhulme. This man had acquired Lewis (ownership of Harris came later) towards the end of the Great War from Colonel Duncan Matheson; and with his island he acquired a history of poverty, clearance, land-shortage, factorial oppression and forty-odd years of popular resistance to landlordism. One contemporary observer noted:

> Lewis and Harris suffer from literal congestion. The 30,000 people in Lewis (apart from 4,000 in Stornoway) live in 100 township villages round the coast of the island. In some respects Harris is worse off than Lewis. Harris has all its good land on the Atlantic side and on the Minch side the land is much more rocky. Yet it is among these rocks that the greater part of the population of Harris lives. What makes the situation worse in South Harris is that a great part

of the machair grazing is not even in a sheep farm, but in a deer-forest – and in the height of summer the deer may be seen on the low ground, just as they may be in the deer park at Magdalen College.

In any case, there were 'whisperings' of an 'impending change in the proprietorship of Lewis' by the closing weeks of 1917. In February 1918 Leverhulme, then aged sixty-five, formally took up ownership of the island.

That July he visited it for the first time as owner. Before the summer was over he had joined the local lodge of the freemasons; been in 'frequent conversations with representative businessmen in Stornoway'; and captured the enthusiastic support of the *Stornoway Gazette* (launched the previous year) which found his coming 'like an inrush of fresh life to the island'.

(The *Gazette* remained a staunch supporter of Leverhulme during his time as owner. *Liberty* called it 'the journalistic flunkey of Lord Leverhulme' and 'that most contemptible and servile specimen of the English press which continues to crawl in our midst. To all intents and purposes it exists for the vain glorification of the new English proprietor of Lewis.')

By the new year, Leverhulme was moving quickly. In January he was proposing ambitious development schemes for Lewis, while the following month he was negotiating for the purchase of South Harris from Lord Dunmore. He got possession of it that May for £36,000, thus becoming the second largest landowner in Scotland after the Duke of Sutherland. By July, as token of the extent to which he had to all appearances settled in, he was gifting robes and regalia for the provost and magistrates of Stornoway (in respect, no doubt, of their civic roles).

But this apparent honeymoon was not to last long; and it would founder on the old question of the land. During the Great War over 6,000 Lewismen had served in uniform. The Lewis to which they returned contained 3,000 statutory crofters and their families, along with 1,500 cottars and squatters and their families, as well as a number of deer-forests and tenanted farms.

The ex-servicemen expected to receive land – with some justice, given that the farm of Aignish had been broken up into a dozen crofters' holdings by the former owner of the island in conjuction with the CDB before the war, along with land at Uig on the west of Lewis. The Board of Agriculture had also scheduled four farms for subdivision before the outbreak of hostilities, and had applied to the Land Court for enforcement orders. But the war had put an end to these proceedings. Thus, 'very little land settlement' had been carried out in Lewis and Harris, 'which are the worst-off of all the congested districts'.

Leverhulme, however, quickly set his face against any sort of land settlement. To him, in a breathtaking failure to understand anything whatsoever about the community into which he had so grandly parachuted, it was 'irrelevant and a gross waste of public money'. Almost at once, then, he managed to split public opinion on the island. This was almost certainly his intended object.

By March 1919, with the Liberal Robert Munro as Scottish Secretary, land-raiding was under way again. The farm of Gress, in Back, was pegged-out and claimed. A month later, 'after the Communion services were over in the Back district', a number of former soldiers and sailors (The Scottish Federation of Discharged and Demobilised Sailors and Soldiers had an active branch in the island) pegged-off smallholdings for themselves on the farm of Coll, also in Back.

By April, Leverhulme's representative was visiting the ex-soldiers and raising hopes which 'may well prove the dawn of the Lewis raiders' day of anticipation'. Within a fortnight, however, there was further raiding at Balallan. There, a 'large number of disappointed applicants, ex-soldiers, demobilised sailors and others' had taken possession of a tract of land 'suitable for smallholdings. Village planning at the different proposed new settlements, viz. Brenigil, Stromas and Aline, provides not only for the allotments being shared out, but sites for a school, church, and cemetery.'

Four parties were now in play: Leverhulme with his money and alleged plans to develop the island on the basis of industrial fisheries; the raiders, demanding the crofts they had been promised by politician and statute; many of the people of Lewis who were not unnaturally in favour of Leverhulme's schemes (though not of necessity opposed to the claims of the raiders, raiding, or land settlement); and the Scottish Office.

The point at issue was Leverhulme's insistence that he would not countenance the break-up of farms which were needed, he said, to continue to provide milk for the island. For their part, the raiders were adamant that they had a right to land. As one of them, Angus Graham of Coll, wrote to the Scottish Secretary:

> We trust that you will now see the advisibility of directing the Board of Agriculture to enforce here, without further delay, the Acts of Parliament passed for the relief of the landless. Our families have suffered and are suffering severely from bad housing and from want of milk [sic], potatoes and vegetables, while there are thousands of acres on all sides of us fit for cultivation, devoted to the rearing of sheep and game.

According to Graham, Coll and Gress and a number of other extensive farms were entirely worked for the benefit of the landlord, while the raiders were unable to obtain a few acres for smallholdings:

> We are willing and have repeatedly offered to pay a fair rent for the lands needed by us. Section nine of the Land Settlement Act of 1919 enacts, 'Where the Board are satisfied that there is a demand for

smallholdings and that suitable land is available for that purpose it shall be the duty of the Board to prepare a scheme for the constitution of one or more new holdings on such lands'. So far as we are concerned the Board for which you are responsible to Parliament has not done its duty. Indeed it has failed to make any provision for us. The Board cannot deny that we have satisfied them that there is a demand by us for smallholdings or that there is suitable land available here to meet our demand. You have now the responsibility of deciding whether or not we are to receive peaceable occupation of the lands required by us and to which we are by law entitled.

The dispute continued into the following year, while Leverhulme's commitment to his proposed development of Lewis began to wane. That spring no less a veteran of crofters' struggles than the Revd Donald MacCallum was supporting the Lewis raiders in *Forward*. Thomas Johnston also visited the raiders at Coll. So too did John MacLean. (Anticipating by half a century the strategic significance of the Cold War's Iceland Gap, he offered perhaps the most perceptive of all speculative comments on Leverhulme's entire adventure in Lewis: 'I am convinced that Leverhulme is preparing Lewis and Harris for the Navy in case of war with America. Britain controls Greenland; so that by this chain she would have a continuous sweep right across the north of the Atlantic to Canada.')

In February, Coll and Gress were again raided; Leverhulme interdicted the raiders involved; the Scottish trades unions raised their voice in formal protest; warrants were issued for the arrest of the raiders; they promised a prison hunger strike; the Scottish Trade Unions Congress demanded a statement from the government with regard to its land-settlement policy; and Leverhulme without warning suddenly withdrew from the contest – abandoning his plans to 'industrialise' Lewis. The bribe, in other words, had been withdrawn, and the multi-millionaire flounced off in a fit of wounded pique.

Public meetings were held in every school on the island, at every one of which there was overwhelming support for a continuation of development. But the following year, with land agitation still ongoing, Leverhulme's schemes were at an end on the island.

He transferred his attentions to Harris, meanwhile offering every crofter in Lewis the free ownership of his or her croft. (The offer was turned down. It would have meant taking the land outwith the provisions of the 1886 Act, as amended since, and outwith the protection of the Land Court). The following year the distinguished *savonnier* put Lewis on the market ('sporting estate for tuppence an acre'). A year after that he was dead; and soon afterwards his expenditure on Harris was at an end, with the island also up for sale.

On Harris the people had promised not to demand land as long as Leverhulme's development plans were under way. At once, therefore, there was an outbreak of agitation. In the spring of 1926 the farm of Scaristaveg was raided. The next spring, following refusal to respect interdicts, the raiders were sentenced to two months in gaol. Two of them were gaoled again at the end of the year; and as late as May 1929 two raiders were once more gaoled for four months. There were too in this period raids at Borve, Bosta, and Tong.

There was also continuing agitation in Islay, Skye and Glenfinnan in Lochaber (where there was talk of a raid on the local deer-forest); while in Lewis there were reports of resistance to evictions of cottars and land squatters at Carloway. And there were also complaints from the southern isles:

> The crofters of South Uist, Benbecula and Barra hold their land under the heartless dictatorship of the Trustees of the late Lady Gordon Cathcart. This landowner left a sum of money to assist in further clearances. The Trustees, following her own example, are determined to show she was right for they use all the resources of modern terrorism to make the lives of the crofters as unbearable as possible.

But throughout the 1920s there had been a slow process of land settlement, against a background of raids and steady emigration. Deer forests remained a striking feature of Highland land use, as a 1922 government study found; and by the middle of the decade, three and a half million acres of Scotland were still under deer. So, too, was emigration prominent. In the early spring of 1924, for instance, the British Columbian government was suggesting Queen Charlotte Islands as suitable for the settlement of Hebridean emigrants. Between July and November the previous year, around 55,000 people had left Scotland for North America.

By then, of course, the great post-war emigrations from Lewis had taken place. The *Metagama* had sailed. And with the *Bendigo* went one emigrant, by the name of MacKinnon, who said according to the *Inverness Courier* that 'he had become tired of waiting for a holding, for which he had made application as an ex-serviceman'.

To 'settlement' in Scotland, of course, the landlords had for many years been inveterately obstructive and avaricious in broadly equal proportion. In the Uists, the Cathcart estate contested the settlement plans of the Board of Agriculture. On Tiree the Duke of Argyll did likewise. The island of Benbecula's 22,000 acres sustained a population of 1,200 on 233 crofts and the single farm of Nunton, itself running to just under 1,000 acres. By 1922 there were fifty-one applications for new holdings and thirty-four for enlargement of existing holdings. Delays had led to the farm being raided twice; but the Cathcart estate opposed its division on the grounds (as in the case of Vatersay earlier) that there was an inadequate water supply to it! The estate further argued that if the farm of Nunton was indeed to be divided, this should only be on the basis of the government buying the island in its entirety.

The same species of extortive obstruction was evident on Mull, at the bidding of the Duke of Argyll, with regard to Scoor Farm. Similarly on Skye, where landlords would not consent to the formation of new crofts unless at prohibitive cost, 'proceedings are impracticable on the grounds of expense owing to the existence of a mansion house and valuable sporting rights which would be rendered useless by the constitution of smallholdings'. In other words, the cost of crofts was the purchase from public funds of the entire estate, at a price set – or over which veto was exercised – by the landlord.

Thus it is scarcely surprising that the process was slow. As early as the autumn of 1920 there was a total of 13,000 applicants for smallholdings throughout Scotland, of whom 5,000 were ex-servicemen. Of these, less than 400 had been selected for a holding and a much smaller number had actually been settled. The *Inverness Courier* noted, 'It is already apparent that the Land Settlement Act of 1919 is a failure as an adequate measure for settling even the approved 5,000.' And three years later the same paper was reporting that in Skye not one holding had yet been formed in either of the congested districts of Sleat and Waternish: 'With very few exceptions all the new holdings wrung in recent years from landlordism have been the results of raids or threats of raids.'

And in the slow process of settlement popular force, or the threat of it, was the key component. On Harris, Kyles farm was finally settled in 1926. One official of the Board wrote, 'The need of the applicants for land is particularly pressing and unless early provision is made for them, they will doubtless take forcible possession.' Rodel Farm was settled in similar vein. In the words of another Board official, with regard to the purchase price demanded by the landlord, 'As this is well within our limits we can agree without any reference to the abject surrender to terrorism apparent in this application'.

Luskentyre was also broken up, under the same impetus. The authorities feared trouble, 'with consequent renewal of agitation and possible lawlessness and disorder. The King's Writ hardly runs in Harris and if land raiding starts, the situation will get out of hand. The money is being paid to buy off disorder.' A total of sixty-eight families were also resettled between 1923 and 1925 from Harris (and Lewis) at Portnalong in Skye, as a result of the Board of Agriculture having bought the North Talisker estate in 1921.

Slowly, therefore, throughout the 1920s, the work begun by the Congested Districts Board pre-war began to be reflected in resettlement at the bidding of the Board of Agriculture. In Caithness, sixty-acre holdings were the norm: 'It can safely be claimed that in no county has a greater number of more satisfactory land settlement schemes been caried out than in Caithness.'

In Barra, the Board of Agriculture bought and distributed Eoligarry, adding to the pre-war division of Vatersay by the CDB. In 1922 Raasay was acquired and the land distributed. In the Uists and Harris, too, land settlement (or rather, land resettlement) schemes went ahead, most of the land once under farms formed on cleared townships being returned to the people. In North Uist the holdings were around twenty-five acres, exclusive of outrun and share in common grazings. On Tiree the farms were finally turned over too, more than a third of the island's population winning a holding as a result. On Skye, where the CDB had formerly acquired Glendale and Kilmuir, the Board of Agriculture acquired large tracts of the island around Loch Bracadale – adding over 50,000 acres in more than 200 new holdings.

In Sutherland, as well, a number of sheep farms were broken up and distributed. And in Lewis eight farms in the south-west of the island were broken up – along with, in due course, those in the east of the island which had occasioned so much conflict and publicity in the immediate post-war years. From 1912 until the end of 1927 the Board had formed a total of 2,874 new holdings and 1,641 enlargements to holdings throughout Scotland. In the Highlands, those formed were notably in areas with a long record of determined anti-landlordism. As the 1928 report of the committee on land settlement in Scotland put it:

> The problem in the Highlands involves historical, racial, economic and social considerations. We are dealing with a community which has refused to acquiesce in any of the attempts to change the method of holding or using land which have been made in the last 150 years, and the legislature has been compelled to meet the claims it has made to be allowed to live its life in its own way.

That year the National Party of Scotland was formed, with a radical policy on the land. It was succeeded in 1934 by the Scottish National Party. The president of each was Cunninghame Graham who had, back in the 1880s, been first president of the Scottish Labour Party.

And in the 1929 general election the Labour Party, with 287 seats, became the largest party in the House of Commons. The Conservatives took 260 and the Liberals 59. Labour Party candidates, on a Home Rule platform, took 24 per cent of the vote in Argyll; 45 per cent in Inverness; 41 per cent in Ross and Cromarty; and 32 per cent in the Western Isles. In each case the candidate for the party with the largest number of seats had stood on a platform of 'the land for the people'.

John Murdoch and Alexander MacKenzie – among many others – would surely have approved.

THIRTEEN
THE CAT STROKED IS MEEK

'You Highland swine, these Hills are mine
This is all Lord Brocket's Land.'

In the aftermath of the Second World War, there were sufficient murmurings of land-centred discontent on Skye for the remaining farmers and landlords in the island to be privately concerned. And in Ross-shire there was agitation for land-raids in the spring of 1947, to have the farms requisitioned for war use at Balnagowan turned into crofts for homecoming service personnel.

In 1952 a land-raid, drawing on long-established tactical traditions, took place in North Uist. Crofters asked for help from the Department of Agriculture in an attempt to extend their holdings. They wanted land that was occupied at the time by the 850-acre Balelone farm – owned by Henry Cator of Norwich. But Cator, who owned a number of estates in various parts of the country, would not relinquish the farm. The crofters were also refused assistance from the department. They wrote to the Labour MP for the Western Isles, Malcolm MacMillan, who had taken the seat on the retiral of Ian MacPherson (author of the introduction to the second edition of Alexander MacKenzie's *Highland Clearances*). In their letter they announced:

> We are going to raid the farm of Balelone on the 28th day of November. By so doing we shall give the whole world an opportunity to judge the righteousness of our request and actions. We have nothing to hide. It is our intention to give ample warning to all parties concerned and to conduct ourselves in as orderly a manner as possible in the circumstances. This is no idle talk on our part. We are on no account going to turn back.

In the event, there was no need to. Cator – mindful, perhaps of land-agitation traditions – backed off from confrontation and in due course a successful settlement was reached.

A few years earlier, in 1948, the Lochaber Crofters' Union contested in

209

the Court of Session the resumption of croft land at Caol, near Fort William, under the leadership of Donald Kennedy of Lochyside (grandfather of Charles Kennedy, MP for Ross and Cromarty). At the time of the court action, Kennedy recalled that his great-grandfather had been one of the original settlers at Caol, having reclaimed it from bogland after his eviction from the shores of Loch Arkaig. The efforts of the Union to block the proposed resumption originated in an attempt in the immediate pre-war period, to form an all-Highland Crofters' Union. At a conference in Mallaig, in February 1939, it had been unanimously agreed to express concern at the reluctance of the authorities to 'utilise their powers of large-scale land settlement in the Highlands'. The conference had also called for a Crofters' Commission 'able to form new holdings, enlarge existing holdings and procure more land for common grazings'.

The onset of war put an end to this. In 1948 the Court of Session refused the appeal of the Lochaber Union. But the appeal, and other post-war disputes, serve to illustrate the extent to which the land question was still a living one in the 1940s. The most notable of these was the land-raid at Knoydart in 1948: that raid recalled in Hamish Henderson's celebrated song which includes the following verse:

> 'You bloody Reds,' Lord Brocket yelled,
> 'Wot's this you're doing 'ere?
> It doesn't pay ,as you'll find today,
> To insult an English peer.
> You're only Scottish half-wits,
> But I'll make you understand,
> You Highland swine, these Hills are mine,
> This is all Lord Brocket's Land.'

Knoydart had, of course, been savagely cleared in the middle of the previous century. This savagery was recognised during the Napier Commission's visit to Portree in May 1883, when it questioned the owner of Knoydart, John Baird, the thirty-one-year-old nephew of its original purchaser (the ironmaster Baird). Incidentally, one of young Baird's answers to the commissioners clearly suggests that there was resistance to this clearing.

The original Baird had acquired the estate in 1859, shortly after its clearance. By the 1880s, of its 67,000 acres from sea-level to over 3,000 feet, 18,270 were under deer. Young John Baird had taken over the property in 1876 on the death of his uncle, and had found it largely given over to sheep farming. There were five farms laid out on the lands of Knoydart, but two of them were vacant and he was soon forced to take over the stock of another two, due to the downturn in the profitability of Highland sheep farming.

Baird complained to the commission about the fall in wool prices and the consequent fall in rental-income. He said he was keen to extend his deer-forest operations, which could double his income from the land. Though there were 'considerable' signs of the remains of crofting populations on the estate, Baird thought that the introduction of crofters into these places – as there once had been – would be 'an injury to the property'. He also thought it would be much better for his remaining tenants to quit crofting for fishing: 'I had a good deal of annoyance with them some years ago. I was very much annoyed at their not fishing.'

They were, he claimed, not overcrowded and, being 'pretty comfortable', they had no complaints. In any case there were only fifty of them left on Knoydart, gathered in eleven families in one township on the shore beside the Sound of Sleat.

This land-use pattern on Knoydart, established under the Baird regime, outlasted the family's interest in the estate. Indeed, the Bairds had gone from Knoydart within a matter of years, and by the time of the Deer-Forest Commission the estate was in the ownership of the Bowlby family. However, when the commission visited Inverie in July 1894, it heard one labourer and four crofters from Airor; but not Bowlby, who instead sent his solicitor from Inverness. And by the 1920s, though still in the ownership of the Bowlbys, Knoydart remained an estate dedicated to deer, with some sheep and a residual population to tend them.

With the coming of Lord Brocket, conditions on Knoydart began to deteriorate in serious fashion. Brocket (family motto: 'the cat stroked is meek') was the second holder of a title created in 1921. Born in 1904, he was educated at Eton and Oxford. In 1927 he went to the English Bar, in the same year marrying; and in 1931 he was elected Tory MP for Wavertree until succeeding to his father's title in 1933. He also succeeded to a very great deal of money deriving from his family's investments in alcohol production. By 1939 he was able to list as his addresses Brocket Hall in Hertfordshire; Bramshill Park in Hampshire; a town house in Wilton Crescent, London; and Knoydart in Inverness-shire.

Popular disillusion with the new owner did not take long to set in. One resident later recalled:

> When he came to Knoydart at first it appeared that he was going to carry on the work of the man before him. But eventually things began to change, and he seemed to turn against the people. Then he started evicting, especially the older employees here and there, and restrictions were put on the movement of people. They weren't allowed near or around Inverie House where he lived, and things like that.

One of those evicted thus had left his ten-acre holding because 'the estate was allowing his house to fall into ruins, the house where he had been born and learnt the shepherding trade from his father'. In time he had become the breadwinner for his mother and sister. 'But when the only three houses beside them were allowed to go empty and it was plain that the estate was running down, the time had come when he must go.'

Another Knoydart resident recalled that it soon became a common sight to see boat-loads of furniture being ferried across to the railhead at Mallaig:

> As numbers of long-serving members of the local staff were paid off it became apparent that the object was to get rid of the local people. Even tourists, campers and hillwalkers were not welcome. The gamekeepers were instructed to see them off the land. Children seen walking or playing along the beach in the vicinity of the mansion were warned away.

Brocket, meantime, entertained mightily on his increasingly empty estate. Among his guests were Neville Chamberlain, Lord Woolton and the exiled monarch of Romania, King Peter. Others were rather more sinister, among them some rather important Germans. Hitler's ambassador to Britain, Ribbentrop, may even have visited the estate; there were at least 'a number of Nazi big-wigs visiting the place'. Central to these friendships was Brocket's involvement in the pro-Hitler fascist Right of pre-war Britain.

Brocket was not alone in this, of course. Hitler had many covert supporters beyond the ranks of Mosley's British Union of Fascists. They extended across industry, politics, the armed services and the press, to the churches (many Anglo-Catholics having spent the 1920s increasingly infatuated with the fascist experience in Italy) and land-owning circles and what was known generally as 'Society'. Not least of these socialite Nazis was, of course, Unity Valkyrie Mitford. Roughed-up by a proletarian mob in Hyde Park for wearing a swastika brooch, she would in due course shoot herself (romantically, if not immediately fatally) in Munich's Englischer Garten and be retired to Inchkenneth Island, off Mull – from where she was carried, in 1948, to die in Oban Hospital, at thirty-four years of age.

Somewhat more substantial allies of Hitler included the Bank of England's Montagu Norman, a staunch supporter of *rapprochement* with Germany. Thirty members of the House of Lords were members of the pro-Nazi Anglo-German Fellowship (AGF), including Brocket. The fellowship's leader was Major-General 'Boney' Fuller, the tank-warfare theorist, who was also a member of the British Union of Fascists (BUF) as well as a writer in *Fascist Quarterly*.

Significant elements of the press were also pro-German. *The Times* strongly supported appeasement; while the *Daily Mail* was violently pro-Nazi, its owner Rothermere (who would shortly invest in Hungarian estates in case Bolshevism should triumph in Britain) having described the 'sturdy young Nazis' as Europe's 'guardian against the Communist danger'. And if Mrs Ronnie Greville, daughter of the brewer William McEwen ('a fat slug filled with venom' in Harold Nicolson's phrase), was 'bowled over by Nazism', so too did the 8th Duke of Buccleuch remain (until 1939) a 'hard-core positive enthusiast'.

Not all the British 'enthusiasts' were themselves Nazis, of course. A legitimate distinction may be allowed between full-blooded fascism and an inclination to remain friendly with Germany at whatever cost, in the cause of preventing – or delaying – a rerun of 1914–18. (Not all of the enthusiasts were English, either. As any glimpse at the membership lists of the AGF will demonstrate, an interesting number were members of Scotland's landed and industrial élites).

But the links between the AGF and the Hitlerite leadership were strong. As a contemporary writer recorded:

> The Nazi Government must thoroughly approve of the Anglo-German Fellowship, for among the leading Nazis who have been guests of the organisation are such famous figures as Herr von Ribbentrop (on several occasions); Dr Ernst Woermann, Counsellor of the German Embassy; the Duke of Saxe-Coburg and Gotha; and Freiherr von Hadeln, SS Adjutant to Herr Himmler, head of the Nazi Secret Police and of the SS. Many members of the Anglo-German Fellowship have in turn been guests of leading Nazis. Lord Londonderry has frequently visited Germany where he has previously been guest of General Goering and Hitler. Herr von Ribbentrop has also been the guest of Lord Londonderry at his Irish seat, Mount Stewart, County Down. Members of the Fellowship who have met Hitler include Lord Mount Temple, Sir Barry Domvile, Lord Brocket, Lord Stamp, Lord McGowan, and Lord Lothian.

Among the activities of the AGF was the hosting of grandly formal dinners. One evening was held in London's Dorchester hotel in the middle of 1936, in honour of the pro-Nazi Prince and Princess von Bismarck. Those present included Barry Domvile, Lord David Douglas Hamilton, 'Boney' Fuller, members of the Guinness family, Lords Londonderry and Mount Temple, and Lord Redesdale, father-in-law of Oswald Mosley. (Not everyone in the Dorchester that night was a fascist. Another guest was one H.A.R. Philby – known to his friends as Kim – at that time working for the Fellowship's propaganda department, in which work he thoroughly impressed Mount Temple.)

In all of this, Brocket took a prominent part. In 1938, for instance, he was in Germany for the Nazi party rally at Nuremberg:

> The Parteitag is drawing to a close in an atmosphere of

indescribable tension. Herr Hitler today was speaking to 120,000 of his Storm Troopers and SS men, paraded before him. Sir Neville Henderson, the British Ambassador, remained here until the evening. He attended the parade of the Youth Movement yesterday morning, and in the evening was the guest of Herr Himmler, Reich Leader of the SS, at supper in the SS camp on the outskirts of Nuremberg, at which Herr Hitler had a friendly conversation over the tea-table with some of his English guests-of-honour. Among those at the Führer's table were Lord Stamp, Lord McGowan, and Lord Brocket.

Subsequent to this SS supper there was a second reception, hosted by Ribbentrop, at which Brocket sat next to Hitler. And a year later, in April 1939, the thirty-five-year-old Brocket was a guest of honour at Hitler's fiftieth birthday celebrations: 'All Germany is tonight celebrating Herr Hitler's birthday. Major-General Fuller and Lord Brocket, vice-president of the Anglo-German Fellowship, are the private guests of Herr Hitler.'

Within a matter of months, of course, both countries were at war. Overnight, the pre-war 'enthusiasts' were reborn as staunch anti-Nazis; or were otherwise interned, from May 1940, under the provisions of Defence Regulation 18b, with Mosley's wife Diana Mitford famously reduced to dining in Holloway on 'grocer's port and inferior Stilton'.

Brocket, perhaps on account of an alleged nervous breakdown, was not interned. But he had little opportunity during the war to visit his Highland estate, as Knoydart – and much of the surrounding district – was required for the training of Commando and Special Operations Executive (SOE) personnel. The two Czechs who assassinated Reinhard Heydrich in the centre of Prague were partly trained in the area, for instance. (The records of Gestapo interrogations relating to the operation are still extant in the appropriate archives in Prague and Berlin).

Knoydart, therefore, saw little or nothing of its owner during the war; and the estate was geared, for the duration of hostilities, to food production as well as special-forces training. But Colin MacPherson, who arrived as priest at Inverie in December 1942, recalled that even then there was a 'fair turnover of shepherds who came into Knoydart and shortly after coming there wanted to get away' – not because they disliked the area, but because they found that 'the conditions which they had been offered in the way of remuneration and perquisites when they were engaged were not being honoured by the estate'.

At this time, shepherds wishing to move required the permission of the wartime Agricultural Executive Committee. According to MacPherson, 'Many of these people, nearly all of them, when they wanted to write to the committee, landed on my doorstep and I had to write their letters.' He told of 'this consistent tale of failure by the estate' to honour its agreements with them: 'Reducing their wages after they arrived, for example. There may have been economic reasons for this, but this was the picture that was consistently thrown up.'

Post-war, however, the Brockets returned to Knoydart. Lady Brocket's first decree was that her employees dumped – with strict warnings that her orders be carried out to the letter – in the deep hole in the mouth of Loch Nevis, all the cutlery, crockery and water-closets of Inverie House, and the estate lodges, with which the trainees of SOE might have come in bodily contact.

The Brockets then turned their attention to the estate. At this stage, according to MacPherson, 'a pattern seemed to emerge that the policy was to curtail agricultural activity and turn Knoydart into a purely sporting estate. The corollary of that obviously was that there would have to be a reduction in the number of people.' And according to Duncan MacPhail, one of the land-raiders, who had served six years and four months, mostly abroad, during the war:

> It was very obvious what he was up to. It was a question of putting off all the sheep. All he wanted was the deer. People began to realise he had no interest in them, that he was going to force them out, bit by bit. There's no doubt about it, he wanted to get rid of all the locals, he just wanted it as a big estate for deer-shooting. I always thought that, and I always will think it. That was the whole thing, to get rid of the locals.

The farm manager in Knoydart at the time later recalled:

> I went there in the belief that Brocket wanted the estate to be one of the finest in the west, but shortly after I got there things didn't quite seem the same. Of course, the Highland Clearances were very much in the minds of the people there, I was very kindly lent the book on the Clearances [Alexander MacKenzie's history] which had a lot in it about Knoydart. The Clearances there were very vivid in their minds. The local people thought the estate should have been their own, that they had a right to the land, that it had been stolen from them, from the crofters. But Brocket was Lord Brocket on the estate, he made it very obvious who he was, he wanted all things on the estate just to suit himself, not for other people. He was running Knoydart all for his own personal benefit, not for the community there. The shepherds weren't allowed in the hills to look for sheep when he was shooting stags – maybe just as well, in case they got shot. He didn't like visitors about the place. But his standard of living was tremendous – even the piano was painted white, it was just a notion Lady Brocket had. She wasn't popular with the local people, I don't think she was popular anywhere.

And according to one of the Knoydart gardeners of the time, Brocket was a man who looked down on working people: 'In fact if there was one of them coming along the road smoking, he would stop them and tell them to put their pipe out. I left in November 1947, and inside the next year about fifteen families left the place.'

As another of the land-raiders, Archie MacDougall recalled:

> At the end of the war the military left, and once more the estate resumed its role as a sporting paradise for the Brockets and their guests. It soon became apparent that changes were imminent. Even the local children were prevented from walking on the beach in the vicinity of the mansion. Employees could be sacked at will, and Brocket did just that. One after another of the workers was made redundant. The reason given was heavy costs, and another excuse was the shortage of houses, as many held rented houses, and once their employment was stopped they could be forced to leave and go elsewhere. It could clearly be seen that the prime motive was to get the local people out.

Knoydart, therefore, in the immediate post-war period, was in a fairly explosive condition – not least because of a consciousness of the long Highland tradition of anti-landlord direct action; because of a radical Labour government making encouraging noises about Highland development; and above all, perhaps, because of a consciousness of the Napier Commission in the 1880s, the suggestions of the Deer-Forest Commission that followed it a decade later – and the subsequent legislation (most notably the 1919 Land Settlement Act).

As MacPherson said, the Deer-Forest Commission was set up to 'look at areas in the Highlands and Islands which might allow people to return to more spacious circumstances, and you'll find that there are areas of Knoydart scheduled as suitable . . . for settlement in the maps and in the text of the commissioners' report. This was known to the men'.

As a result, therefore, a development plan for the estate was drawn up by the land-hungry of Knoydart and presented to the Highlands and Islands Advisory Panel. It argued that the estate's 70,000 acres could yield £50,000 per annum, and increase the local population from 80 to 500 in five years. In a period of food rationing, it would mean Knoydart carrying 15,000 sheep, 200 dairy cattle and 400 summer cattle, with forty holdings of 1,000 acres each, including ten of arable and the rest grazing around 400 sheep. The plan also made provision for growth of inshore fishing and forestry, along with a ten-mile road to meet the railway at Spean Bridge. Underpinning the plan was the claim that a century earlier Knoydart had supported 1,500 people, 20,000 sheep and 200 cattle – while by 1947 there were only four landholders, with twelve usable houses lying empty.

Nothing, however, came of the plan. And thus, as Duncan MacPhail remembered:

> We put our heads together and thought, all this lovely ground and everything going off, Brocket kept putting off the stock, it was obvious all he cared about was the deer. We thought, why not have a crack at getting some of the land? I was very keen, it was dash hard lines that after all these years fighting, if you weren't going to get something out of it for yourself. Probably we all had the idea at the back of our minds that we were going to be put out – and we thought, well, we're entitled to a bit of our own land.

In the autumn of 1948, therefore, the Knoydart land-raid went ahead.

Soundings had been taken in the previous months by MacPherson with regard to resettling families from the Hebrides on the estate, as people from Harris had been resettled on Skye after the First World War. And he did find a number of people from his home area of the southern isles who expressed an interest in the idea. With the press invited to attend, and Brocket also on the estate, the raid took place on 9 November with the six raiders (the seventh would add his name later) staking out 65 acres of arable land and 10,000 acres of hill – each stake bearing the name of a raider.

The chief constable of Inverness-shire reported on the raid to the secretary of the Scottish Home Department a week later:

> On 9th November 1948, the lands of Kilchoan Farm, Scottas Farm and fields in the neighbourhood of the village of Inverie, all of which are owned by and in the occupation of Lord Brocket, were raided by six local people who 'staked' claims to the land. No offence under the Trespass Act appears to have been committed and the raiders were orderly. The raid appears to have been well planned, press reporters and photographers from far afield being on the spot in advance. It is understood that for some years the raiders have been agitating with the Department of Agriculture for occupation of land. The parish priest Father Colin MacPherson is playing a leading part in the effort of the raiders to draw public attention to their desire to obtain land. On complaining to the police Lord Brocket was advised that the only action possible at the moment is action in the Law Courts and it is understood that his Law Agents have applied to the Court of Session and have obtained Interim Interdicts against the raiders. It is believed that the raiders will persist in the raiding.

Public support throughout Scotland was instantaneous and widespread. The Inverie post office was quickly in receipt of telegrams of support 'flowing in from across the country', while the Lochaber Crofters' Union pledged full support and reaffirmed its policy that 'a bold and imaginative scheme of land settlement is required for the Highlands and Islands. They urge that full advantage should be taken of the existing powers of the Secretary of State for Scotland.'

A packed meeting of supporters was also held, appropriately enough, in Glasgow's City Halls. MacPherson told of 'the past 150 years on Knoydart, the depopulation there and the need for the repopulation of the Highlands'. Brocket, meanwhile, had left Knoydart almost at once for the mainland. Passing of necessity through Mallaig, he told an enquiring newspaper reporter that Knoydart was 'not suitable for many people as there is too much rain there'.

While the raiders cleared the land they had staked out, Brocket went at once to the courts with a petition for interim interdict:

> On or about 8th November 1948 the Respondents entered upon cultivated parts of the said farms of Kilchoan and Scottas to which they have no right title or interest whatsoever and staked out claims to smallholdings thereon. Each claim was pegged out and contained a post bearing the name of the person who alleged that he was the owner of that particular smallholding. As the action of the Respondents in staking their claim was well organised, carried out in concert, and with the press having been duly informed beforehand, the Petitioner believes that for some unknown reason some of the local people object to the Petitioner's ownership of the said estate of Knoydart and that further action may be taken.

(In the Closed Record of the case, dated 9 March the following year, Brocket affected to believe that 'the said priest Father Colin MacPherson . . . has induced and persuaded the Respondents to take the action they have taken and has persuaded them to trespass upon the said lands, and has since his appointment to Knoydart in 1946 [sic] consistently worked against Lord Brocket'.)

On 11 November a seventh raider joined the party, and its members announced that they were in the process of hiring a lawyer. On the following day, however, messengers-at-arms of the Court of Session arrived. The raiders debated at length a plan to accept the interdicts only to raise as a counter-bid an interlocutor or similar procedure against the Secretary of State for failing to recognise the land-settlement provisions of previous legislation. The stratagem was in the event dropped due to lack of funds. The raiders accepted the writs, and quit the land.

Meanwhile Brocket countered the raiders' proposals for the estate with an alternative development plan. Affairs on Knoydart were also drawing close attention from the government. Curiously – or otherwise – the government lost little time in commissioning a third report on Knoydart and its potential for development.

In the Commons on 25 November Arthur Woodburn, Secretary of State for Scotland, announced:

> In view of the conflicting nature of proposals for the development of the resources of the Knoydart Peninsula which have been submitted by different interests in the locality, I have decided, after consultation with the Highlands Advisory Panel, to invite Mr John Cameron, formerly of the Land Court, to examine the position and to advise on the best means of securing the full development of the resources of the area taking into account the social, economic and financial issues involved. Mr Cameron will be given details of the various proposals for developing the area which have so far been put forward, but he will be free to hear any representations and to suggest any alternative or modified proposals.

This may have been an understandable position for Woodburn to take in public, though his reputation as a man long concerned with the land question can only have encouraged the raiders to believe that their case would receive favourable attention from the government of which he was part.

In Woodburn's papers in the National Library of Scotland (oddly, there is no material specifically concerned with Knoydart) there is much on the land question in general, including a scrapbook of his time as election agent in the 1936 by-election in Ross and Cromarty, along with a brief diary of the campaign. In his draft (typescript) autobiography he notes, 'I saw the valley of Strathnaver filled with thriving farms which was the result of the land settlement schemes about thirty years before, and there is no doubt that a consistent and determined policy could change the face of the Highlands.' (He adds in manuscript at another point in the draft, 'Afforestation is the one hope for the Highlands. When trees went so did the people. As trees come back so will the people.')

There is also a press cut, dated 19 August 1948 (that is, just three months before the Knoydart raid), reporting a speech given by Woodburn to the Larbert Labour Party, during which he said: 'It is absolutely necessary that we should grow more food in our own country. Great areas of Scotland have been allowed to deteriorate by depopulation and the surrender of great stretches to deer and grouse.'

A month later, the *Inverness Courier* was reporting Woodburn as follows:

> There was a revival of interest in the Highlands for the redevelopment of the Highlands and the rehabilitation of the people throughout the countryside. Among ex-servicemen he found a certain impatience with what they felt was the delay in doing all things they considered should be done for the Highlands.

It was possible to increase the number of people who could live on the land in the Highlands, and so far as the government policy was concerned, they were anxious to see that the man who was getting to live on the land would have enough of it.

Also among his papers are 'Labour's Broadcast to Ross and Cromarty'. This was an election broadsheet for the 1936 election, in which the Labour candidate was supported by Malcolm MacMillan, MP for the Western Isles since the previous year. A further item, entitled 'The Land League Still Lives', notes:

> One of my most cherished memories is the part I took in securing the return to parliament for Ross and Cromarty of Dr Roderick MacDonald . . . Our first attack on the stronghold of landlordism in 1884 did not succeed. Nothing daunted, we returned to the fray in 1885 . . . let this victory be repeated in 1936.

Another item reads, 'From the glens and straths, from the western seaboard, from the islands, the tale has run these many years; the people go to the south, to the towns and to the cities. There is not a living for them in their own country.' And according to a third item, headlined 'What Labour gave the Highlands and Islands 1929-1931': 'At Luskentyre the land-hungry men raided and seized arable ground in the deer-forest. The Labour Government acquired the deer-forest under compulsory powers, took the crofters out of gaol, and settled them upon the land.'

In short, Woodburn was entirely aware of the historical background to the aspirations and actions of the Knoydart land-raiders of 1948; though, having announced the formation of the Cameron Inquiry, he could hardly be expected to pre-empt its findings.

That enquiry got under way before Christmas. Brocket did not come to a December meeting in Mallaig. He said he was sick. He sent, however, his factor who agreed that nothing had been done on Knoydart between 1939 and 1947 'to contribute to the country's food supply'. He retailed the information, presumably supplied by Brocket, that he could not furnish precise details as 'a great part of the estate records had been destroyed by enemy action in England' – which might be one way of saying that Brocket was not going to have the estate accounts open to any sort of public scrutiny.

The Edinburgh lawyer representing the raiders said it was essential to repopulate Knoydart in the national interest from the point of view of defence and food production, and also of improving social conditions. The Secretary of State had ample powers to repopulate Knoydart under the Small Landholders' Act and the Land Settlement Act. The only means whereby people had been kept on the land, he said, was 'by giving them holdings of an economic size with security of tenure, a fair rent, and compensation for improvements'. After stating that the population of Knoydart of 100 was much too small, he added that 150 years earlier there had been ten times as many people on the peninsula. By 1931 the population had dropped to 186:

> In view of these figures, and in view of the fall since 1931 by nearly 50 per cent, I do not think it can be disputed that something requires to be done very quickly to repopulate Knoydart. Otherwise any measures will be too late. From 1861 to 1931 the local population has decreased by 67 per cent, compared with a decrease of only 7 per cent in the county of Inverness during the same period.

Cameron issued his report the following March. Astonishingly, he found against the raiders' proposals and in favour of the development of Knoydart as a single unit, preferably under Brocket. Even more astonishingly, Woodburn agreed.

The raiders petitioned Woodburn, urging him to ensure that tenants on Knoydart be 'given the protection of the Small Landholders' Act. They submit that it is the statutory duty of the Secretary of State immediately to form smallholdings for them at Knoydart.' Woodburn, however, rejected the petition, and that, largely, was the end of the matter.

In retrospect it was an extraordinarily bad decision with catastrophic consequences for Knoydart. The appointment of the Cameron Inquiry had served splendidly as a diversion; and it cruelly damaged the impetus of the raiders' own aspirations. Spurned by the government, they would shortly be spurned by the courts too. Had funds been available, might they have won a case in the courts, forcing the government to apply the provisions of existing legislation? Should they have ignored the government and the courts, and simply taken and held possession of Knoydart by force of their own little number and extensive public sympathy?

Whatever the case, the damage had been done. Brocket was free to indulge such taste as he may have had for retribution – he had none, certainly, for development. He did his best to humiliate the raiders. One of them wrote to him on the last day of October 1949 asking for work. Brocket wrote back, 'If you send me an unqualified apology and undertaking never to repeat such acts as those on November 9th 1948, I will then give consideration to the question of your being employed again on the estate.' The raider in question met both conditions and withdrew his claim for a smallholding for good measure. Brocket, the millionaire brewer, replied: 'In view of your apology and undertaking never to behave in the same way again I have instructed my solicitors not to proceed against you, of course on the understanding that you pay your own costs up to date.'

Further: the report of Cameron, despite its major recommendation for single-unit control of Knoydart, had also suggested that the estate did give land to those men who clearly wanted it. Brocket, however, replied that he 'didn't intend to offer any land unless enjoined to do so by the government' – something, it was already clear, the government was quite unwilling to do.

The raiders, in their answers to the Court of Session lodged in the November of 1948, had argued that they had acted within their rights in terms of the Small Landholders' Act of 1911 and the Land Settlement Act of 1919. They argued that their actions, being for the purpose of assisting the Department of Agriculture for Scotland in the exercise of its statutory duties, were not an infringement of any rights of ownership. The interdict sought was therefore, in the circumstances, contrary to public policy. The Lord Justice Clerk, however, did not agree, in his opinion of February 1951:

> The justification which the respondents put forward is that they were within their rights in terms of section 7 of the Small Landholders Scotland Act 1911, which, as amended by the Land Settlement Scotland Act 1919, section 9, provides that when the Department of Agriculture are satisfied that there is a demand for smallholdings and that suitable land is available for that purpose, it is their duty to prepare a scheme for the constitution of new holdings under certain circumstances . . . I can only characterise this contention as fantastic.

In short, Brocket had won a magnificent victory and the raiders had suffered a terrible defeat. By 1951 people were drifting steadily away from Knoydart. Whether a criminal course of action would have been better is, with the benefit of hindsight, at least arguable. Duncan MacPhail, thirty-odd years later, argued:

> Well, I was in favour of sticking on the land like in the olden days they did. But this lawyer said that in these modern times these things wouldn't need to take place, that we should do it in the legal way and things would work out pretty good. But I am afraid that was our downfall. We would have been far better to have done what the old boys in the olden days did, stick on the ground till they put you to gaol. We all thought it was a very good idea, that it was going to be legal. But afterwards, when we saw the whole thing, and you look back on it, you realised it didn't pay to be doing it the modern way. Oh yes, it would have worked, if we had got the ground. I am sure we would have made a go of it. Anything was better than the way it was. It was getting less and less used, Knoydart – plenty of ground in Knoydart, and good ground, but all that Brocket was interested in was deer. That's all he lived for, to

come up and shoot the deer: and I always said, to get rid of the people.

Brocket did not stay long afterwards in Knoydart (though his taste for the Celtic fringe was undimmed and in 1949 he acquired a substantial property in the south of Ireland). He died in 1967 and eight years later the twenty-three- year-old Lord Charles Brocket, ex-Eton and the Hussars, inherited Brocket Hall. The mansion was shortly afterwards broken up into flats, as 'England's finest privately owned residence for executive meetings and incentive groups'. Its grounds were let for corporate conferences and motor-trade promotions. Later, Brocket was to serve a gaol sentence on account of an insurance fraud relating to his collection of vintage motor cars.

And by the 1980s Knoydart was largely empty. Between 1985 and 1988 thirteen houses were sold off as holiday homes. The original estate had been carved up and sold off as individual lots. Most of the peninsula was in the anonymous ownership of companies registered in the tax havens of the Dutch Antilles, the Bahamas and the Channel Isles.

In 1989 Knoydart was scheduled as the location for that year's Goose Run. The Goose Run, reported the *Oban Times* without a flicker of shame, was in aid of Survival International. And what was this Survival International? Why, it was 'an organisation which works for the rights of threatened peoples . . . and aims to ensure that they keep communal ownership of their lands, have facilities which are suited to their own needs, and are not exploited'.

FOURTEEN
THE LAND FOR THE PEOPLE

'I can see the proprietor here has no conscience and commitment as far as the people here are concerned. That's what you find with many proprietors in the Highlands and Islands. I think the people here have to take the initiative themselves. Things haven't got to stand still. People can shape the future if they have a will to do it.'

The Highland land question somewhat disappeared from Scottish politics in the 1950s and 1960s. This may have been connected to the renunciation, by the leadership of Labour in Scotland, of the party's long-standing commitment to Home Rule. This renunciation was, of course, reversed when Labour began to fear electoral obliteration at the hands of the Scottish National Party.

But the land question did not go away in these years, and – as we have seen – was an issue of continuing importance in the 1970s and 1980s. And the 1990s were witness to some modest change for the better in land-ownership in the Highlands – not least in Assynt, at Borve in Skye, and on Eigg in the Inner Hebrides. These are likely to be the first of many more changes, given the election of a land-reform-minded Labour government to Westminster in the later part of the decade and, rather more importantly, the rebirth of a Scottish parliament shortly afterwards. But research published in the middle of the decade emphasises the extent to which private landlordism continues to dominate the ownership of land in the Highlands, on a scale which would astonish any other European country (and many a former colonial nation in the Third World).

Andy Wightman's *Who Owns Scotland?* was published in 1996, as an updating of John McEwen's similarly-titled book from twenty or so years earlier. As Wightman says in his introduction, the ownership and use of land is 'one of the most fundamental issues in any society', but is a subject which in Scotland remains poorly understood. 'Not only does ownership convey significant and far-reaching privileges to those in possession of land, but the system and pattern of landownership has extensive economic, political, cultural and environmental impacts on the economy and development of the country.' And he goes on:

> How we as a society choose to define and distribute property rights
> and what obligations we place on their enjoyment has a profound
> bearing on not just economic activity but on the opportunities for
> the creation and distribution of wealth. Politically, land is
> important . . . Culturally, land and its ownership and use have
> shaped the outlook of the people of Scotland. Contemporary
> debates about land-ownership are a clear expression of a deep-
> seated feeling, unaffected by two centuries of urbanisation, for the
> land.

For the five mainland crofting counties (including the Hebrides as part of
either Inverness-shire or Ross and Cromarty), Wightman's research
identifies the extent to which large owners dominate the scene. For Argyll,
he lists the top five owners as: Robert Fleming and Trusts, with 88,900
acres; Trustees of the Duke of Argyll, with 60,800; Islay Estates Company
(Lord Margadale), with 49,500; John M. Guthrie, with 37,000; and the
Raven family at Patrick Sellar's old estate of Ardtornish, with 34,100.
Pension funds are also listed as large-scale forestry investors in the county,
with Eagle Star insurance possessing 10,000 acres; and the pension fund
of Gallaher, the major tobacco concern, having 4,254 acres.

Wightman observes that Argyll strikes him as 'rather a sad place, where
many of the local farmers have sold up and a new breed of wealthy
overseas buyer has moved in'. This is a feeling shared by many people in
Argyll who have 'seen the forestry plantations spread over the hills and
the farmers disappear. Argyll, as much as anywhere, convinces me that we
could do things better.'

As for the environmentally sensitive landscape of Caithness, Wightman
records:

> It has seen big changes in both the pattern of landownership and
> the people involved since 1970. The structural changes are
> associated with the frantic expansion of private forestry on the
> peatlands which caused a raging controversy in the mid-'80s.
> Fuelled by low land prices, a forestry company called Fountain
> Forestry went round London financial advisers persuading wealthy
> clients who had high exposure to income tax to invest in tree
> plantations against which tax could be written off . . . The
> environmental controversy, together with the publicity surounding
> the tax breaks, ensured that in the 1988 Budget, forestry was
> removed completely from the tax system and the mechanism
> which was fuelling afforestation in some of the most sensitive parts
> of the country was abolished . . . Land use changes of this
> magnitude could not take place without the unregulated market in
> land and uncoordinated land use policy which Scotland is still
> suffering from.

The five largest estates in the county were the 45,000 acres of Langwell and Braemore (principal interest, Lady Anne Cavendish-Bentinck); the 37,400-acre estate at Dunbeath and Glutt; Viscount Thurso's 36,800 acres; a 20,000-acre estate at Latheronwheel; and the 13,600 acres of Shurrey.

Inverness-shire too remained a county of big estates, though some well-known holdings had fragmented during the late 1980s and early 1990s. 'The most spectacular of these had been the virtual disappearance of the ancient lands of the Lovat family.' Simon Fraser died in 1994, leaving massive debts. He had sold the entire estate to one of his companies (Highlands and Islands Oil and Gas Co. Ltd.) for £6,005,966 and mortgaged the whole sum. After the sell-off of the Braulen estate in 1990, and the North Morar estate in 1994, 'the remaining 19,500 acres were sold in lots in 1995, with 6,500 acres being kept for the new schoolboy Lord Lovat'.

Another estate to have been broken up was the Knoydart estate which, after Brocket, passed through various hands including those of Lord Hesketh, (a Conservative spokesman in the House of Lords during the 1980s). He bought it for £250,000 in 1972, selling in April 1973 for £1.5 million. 'Philip Rhodes, who bought it in 1984, proceeded to split it up further, making a profit of over £1 million,' according to Wightman.

In Inverness-shire, the five largest estate owners were Alcan Highland Estates Ltd with 112,400 acres; South Uist Estates Ltd with 92,000 acres; Sir Donald Cameron's Lochiel Estates with 76,000 acres; the Earl of Granville's North Uist Estate Trust with 62,200 acres; and the Earl of Seafield and Viscount Reidhaven with 50,000 acres. In sixth place on the list was Jonathan and Lady Marcia Bulmer's North Harris estate, comprising 49,900 acres of land at Amhuinnsuidhe. Lord Burton's 31,000 acres at Dochfour and Glenquoich came in twelfth on the list. And at number 23 were the 22,400 acres of Gilbert M.H. Wills (Lord Dulverton).

Ross-shire, according to Wightman, is the 'county of the sporting estate. From east coast to west coast, the straths are empty and most of the owners are absentee. In Wester Ross alone, of a total population of around 4,000 in 55,000 acres, only between 250 and 300 people live more than one kilometre from the coast. No more than 300 people therefore live in 536,000 acres of land.' Wightman believes that Ross and Cromarty could be vibrant and dynamic, with its dramatic scenery, interesting wildlife and great outdoor recreational opportunities. All it lacks is a population. 'Comparable areas in Norway are packed full of villages and small farm forestry holdings. There is not one good reason why Ross and Cromarty should not develop in this way.'

The largest estate, the 81,000 acres of Letterewe and Kinlochewe, was principally owned by Paul Fentener van Vlissingen. The Stornoway Trust, deriving from the ownership of Lewis by Lord Leverhulme, had 69,400; while the third largest landowner, with 63,140 acres, was Sheik

Mohammed bin Rashid al Maktoum of Dubai. Captain Fred H. Wills was principal owner of 62,000 acres at Applecross, while the Gairloch and Conon estate comprised 56,900 acres.

Others owners included Jonathan Bulmer and syndicate with 45,000 acres at Uig and Hamanavay; and Richard Munro Ferguson, with 20,000 acres at Novar. The 23,600 acres of Inverlael and Foich were owned by H.J.E. Van Beuningen and others, through an investment management company. Lord Burton had 17,000 acres at Glenshiel and Cluanie through the Burton Property Trust. Edmund Vestey had nearly 16,000 acres at Assynt and Benmore through the Glencanisp and Drumrunie Deer-Forest Trust. Major Michael Wills had 14,800 at Achnashellach; Investments Bermuda Ltd had over 5,000 acres at Gledfield; and Fountain Forestry Ltd had 3,000 acres of Langwell Forest.

The pattern of land-ownership was broadly similar in Sutherland, an 'empty and lonely country' in Wightman's eyes. Here, in 1971, the newly constituted Highlands and Islands Develpment Board (HIDB) presented proposals for development to Willie Ross, the Secretary of State for Scotland (who had been responsible for setting up the Board). But these proposals failed to make headway due to lack of political will. As the 1970s came to an end, 'landowners sighed with relief'. In 1979 all such thinking was swept aside as a new body, Highlands and Islands Enterprise (HIE), took over. 'The land question had been discreetly dropped with barely a member of staff working on the subject.'

Trustees for the 2nd Duke of Wesminster owned 95,100 acres of the county, while the Countess of Sutherland controlled another 83,239. Edmund Vestey had 70,500 at Glencanisp and Inchnadamph. Lord Robert Iliffe and the Stone family had nearly 26,000 acres at Lochnaver, Syre and Rhifail, and Viscount Leverhulme 24,700 at Badanloch. The Hon. David Nall-Cain and friends controlled 6,600 acres at Gualin; while Fountain Forestry clients had land at another eight locations in the county. But there were, during the 1990s, a handful of developments in land-ownership that, in spirit at least, threatened this prevailing pattern of giant landholdings.

The first of these was at Assynt, in north-west Sutherland. In June 1992 the Assynt branch of the Scottish Crofters' Union agreed that it would attempt to bring into community ownership the North Lochinver estate, with a view to preventing it being broken up and sold off in small portions. The attempt followed the news that the estate, formerly part of the Vestey holdings in the area, was to be sold in seven lots. This sale came in the wake of the collapse of its owners, Scandinavian Property Services UK – a foreign-owned company which included in its important portfolio of socially-conscious investments a 'sauna club' in London. Crofters said that if the estate were to be sold separately, it would reduce crofting in the district to a state of chaos. The initial plan was that the Highland Regional Council would buy the estate – asking price £473,000 – and at once pass it over to a community trust, which would thereafter reimburse the council.

The existing crofts in the district derived from inland clearances dating from the early nineteenth century. At that time, towards the end of the wars with Napoleonic France, the evicted tenants had been driven to thin strips of poor soil by the coast, to crofts which they had to 'dig out of the bare hillside with their own hands' (in the words of the secretary of the local Crofters' Union).

There were futher major clearances in the 1830s. When the Napier Commission visited Lochinver in the 1880s, the Stoer cottar Kenneth Campbell told of forty-eight townships which had been cleared to make room for sheep farming. The last of these to be cleared was Ardvar, from which eleven families had been driven out. And in 1878, eighteen families had been removed from the farm at Clashmore. This was the spark that ignited the major disturbances in the area during the later 1880s.

In April 1887, a sheriff-officer sent from Golspie was met by a crowd of fifty or sixty men when he tried to serve summonses for rent arrears. The Clashmore men placed these summonses on a burning peat, forced the sheriff-officer and the landlord's local agent out of the carriage in which they had tried to shelter, and got them to promise never to return. (A fortnight later Michael Davitt addressed the tenants of the district at a pier-head meeting at Stoer, with the local Free Church minister as chairman.)

Later the following month a policeman returned with more writs. As the menfolk were absent cutting peats, the women assaulted him, took the writs by force, and burned them before him. They then threatened to throw him in the river, before driving him out of the village. One of the crofters later appeared in Dornoch Sheriff Court and got fourteen days in gaol.

That autumn there was further trouble at Clashmore. A week or so after the great raid on the Park deer-forest on Lewis, the tenants drove their cattle on to the sheep farm. The farm steading burned itself to the ground, and a few days later another property in the ownership of the Duke of Sutherland went up – or down – in flames. In early December the *Jackal*, which had been busy arresting the Park raiders, came across the North Minch to land forty marines and arrest one Clashmore tenant believed to be guilty of deforcement. But they failed, according to contemporary press reports, to get the man they really wanted: for Hugh Kerr had taken to the hills. A crowd shouting 'down with the House of Sutherland' later mobbed the marines as they marched with their prisoner to Culag House. Subsequently the soldiers were not allowed to leave their barracks 'on account of the unfriendly spirit exhibited towards them by the people. The officers too found it impossible to show themselves in Lochinver without receiving some unpleasant remark of the people's dislike.'

On the last day of that year, the authorities put in hand a middle-of-the-night raid on Hugh Kerr's house, in the expectation of catching him there for Hogmanay. At three in the morning under bright moonlight, six marines, a number of policemen and the intrepid Sheriff MacKenzie crept through rock and bog; but found that their elusive quarry was still somewhere in the hills. At the same time men brought into the district, to repair sheep-farm walls that had been knocked down by the Clashmore people, effectively struck work and went home. Hugh Kerr was not apprehended until August the following year.

It was therefore with some considerable sense of their own history and the story of their own community that the Assynt crofters, in the shape of the Assynt Crofters' Trust, launched in July 1992 an appeal for public support to buy the estate. A loophole in crofting legislation meant that the crofters could force the purchase of the land for no more than fifteen times the annual rental, if no agreement with the sellers could be reached. In so doing they would improve the social, educational and cultural environment of the crofting communities and of the natural environment of Assynt:

> We the crofters have resolved to band together to buy the estate, not for reason motivated by political or romantic sentiment, but because we believe that to give our crofting communities the best chance of surviving and prospering in the future, control of our resources – especially the land – will be our best chance. We have history, justice and the law on our side. With a little help from our friends, we will succeed.

A packed meeting in Stoer village hall heard the local MP, Robert MacLennan, recall:

> When I was elected twenty-six years ago, there was no worse example of absentee landlordism. At that time the feudal superior imposed upon the tenants heavy and unacceptable conditions on land use. You were not allowed to open a shop in competition to shops owned by the estate. You were not allowed to sell petrol in competition to the estate. You were not allowed to enjoy an extension of your lodging house beyond a very short period of seven years so that improvements could not be made.

In the first week, £15,000 was raised. By the end of August the appeal had raised £50,000. It had also secured a grant of £50,000, along with the promise of a loan of another £90,000. The HIE network (successor to the HIDB) had contributed the first sum, as a 'pilot project to collect information on the performance of a crofting estate owned and managed by local people'. The offer of a loan of £90,000 had come from Highland

Prospect, an investment company established by the Highland Regional Council. A further grant of £20,000 was forthcoming from Scottish Natural Heritage.

In September, with the closing date for the sale of the 21,000-acre estate just a fortnight distant, attention focussed on the extent to which the district had languished under the long reign of the Vesteys. It had been bought in 1937 by Ronald Arthur Vestey, father of the present owner and architect of the family's vast meat and shipping empire. But despite a staff of 22,000 and a turnover of £1,000 million in the financial year previous to that of the proposed buy-out, not much of this imperial wealth appeared to have usefully found its way to the Assynt community. Around fifteen years earlier, a child born in Clashmore had been the first baby in the Stoer area for over thirty years, for instance. And in the 1950s and 1960s, following decades of decline, it was thought likely that Assynt would soon be entirely empty of people: a curious if oddly resonant outcome, it might be thought, of twenty-five years' extremely wealthy and sporting stewardship.

Twice, the crofters' offer for the estate was rejected that autumn. But in December, after two weeks of tense negotiations with the principal creditor of the owners, the Assynt Crofters' Trust heard that their increased offer of £300,000 – rather than the £475,000 originally demanded – had been accepted. In the words of the *West Highland Free Press* report of the sale:

> Private landlordism in the Highlands and Islands was shaken to its foundations this week as crofters in Assynt heard that they had succeeded in breaking the lairds' stranglehold over North Lochinver estate, at last realising the dream of land for the people. The stunning breakthrough has been heralded by the crofters themselves, by public agencies and by politicians as the beginning of a new era in land use. And there have already been calls for crofters elsewhere in the Highlands and Islands to follow their lead and take their claim to the land. The atmosphere this week was electric, the air of hope almost tangible. Greeted by accordion music and rapturous applause, Assynt Crofters' Trust chairman Allan MacRae could not conceal his delight. But just as deep-rooted was his sadness, shared by many present, that others before them who had fought unsuccessfully for the land had not lived to see their aspirations realised. 'My immediate thoughts are to wish that some of our forebears could be here to share it with us'. Mr MacRae, whose own great-grandfather was cleared off the land at Assynt to make way for a sheep farm, said, 'There's no doubt that, in owning the land, crofters have struck a historic blow for people right throughout the Highlands and Islands.'

The second blow for popular ownership of the land was struck on Skye in early 1993, when crofters submitted a letter of intent to buy the 4,500-acre crofting township of Borve and Annishader. The tenants were to base their offer on the formula in the 1976 Crofting Act, in terms of which they were entitled to buy the land for fifteen times the annual rent paid without having to pay half the development value to the landlord. The proposal to transfer the land in question – unlike the Assynt buy-out – had come from the landlord himself, Major John Macdonald. The bid had followed the failure of the twenty-one tenants and the owner of the estate to agree the provisions of a proposed forestry project.

The crofters of the township had been set to become the first to benefit under the terms of the 1991 Crofter Forestry Act. This legislation allowed crofters, rather than landlords, to plant trees on common grazing land – and to retain ownership thereafter of those trees. But the Act required owner-consent for any such scheme. And at Borve the landlord was unwilling to grant consent, as it would deplete the value of the estate without depleting his running costs of it.

In early February, therefore, the crofters decided to proceed with an offer, which was to be of rather more value than the minimum stipulated by the 1976 Crofters' Act. Nevertheless, it was to be worth no more than a fraction of the open-market value of the land in question. According to the crofters' spokesman, Alastair Nicolson, the crofters were confident that they could raise the capital needed to buy the land as a crofting trust. But they were also prepared to consider forcing the sale in terms of the 1976 legislation if no deal could be agreed.

In the week that the Assynt crofters were celebrating the acquisition of their own district, Mr Nicolson said that while land remained in private ownership, there was always the possibility of it being sold over the head of local communities. 'We've now got a chance to be masters of our own destiny,' he said. 'To have control over our own township will let us know where we stand for the future.' The Western Isles MP Calum Macdonald, who had introduced the crofter-forestry legislation, added: 'In the Assynt case there was just a threat to use the legislation. If the Borve crofters succeed, it will be yet another breakthrough for the right of crofting communities to control their own destinies.' He hoped that the buy-out in Assynt, and the proposed buy-out at Borve, would represent a 'turn of the tide', leading to the formation of similar community trusts throughout the Highlands.

And just two months later, the crofters' attempt to acquire the 4,500-acre township was successful. In the middle of April, they heard that their second offer of £20,000 – £3,500 higher than the first bid – had been accepted. It included mineral rights, but not sporting rights, and was generally considered an amicable agreement with a co-operative landlord.

On the island of Eigg, however, the landlord was somewhat less than cooperative, and the historic buy-out less than amicable. The twentieth century had been one of continuous decline for this island's economy. During the First World War, twenty men left the island for military service. Ten were to die as a result (four of them from one family). After the war, the island crofters demanded more land under the 1919 Land Settlement Act. As a result, 150 acres of grazing land came under crofting occupancy. Still, in 1923, eleven islanders from the MacDonald and MacQuarrie families emigrated to Canada – a second terrible blow to a tiny insular culture already on the brink of extinction. By 1931 there were just 138 people left on Eigg, living in conditions of very considerable economic fragility. And in the Second World War, when sixteen men left the island for military and related service, only two returned to live there when the hostilities were over.

Still, the island at least enjoyed continuity of sympathetic ownership from the early 1930s until the mid-1960s. But in 1966, Eigg was offered for sale. A locally-connected consortium was outbid, according to Camille Dressler's *Eigg – the Story of an Island*, by a Welsh farmer called Captain Evans. And five years later Evans sold Eigg. Some of those involved in the earlier consortium again tried to get the island. But their detailed plan failed to persuade the HIDB to help finance the purchase. The Board was in the business of market forces, to which that old 'emotive and political thing' of land ownership was most safely left.

As a direct result, Captain Evans sold Eigg (for a profit) to the Anglyn Trust, which styled itself as an adventure project for handicapped boys. This 'non-profit-making Christian charity' enjoyed as a colourful figurehead one self-styled ex-navy officer by the name of Commander Bernard Farnham-Smith. The nineteen-stone Cockney arrived with his entourage shortly after buying the island. Chaos quickly followed. Not even the HIDB would give him money for his alleged development schemes. Quite quickly it became apparent that the man was a fraud, who had never commanded anything more grandiloquent than a fire engine.

He had formerly also 'commanded' a private school for handicapped children somewhere in Sussex. It had failed to reach government standards, and in 1968 the appropriate department stopped allowing local authorities to send children to the school. As a result it closed down. In 1974 Smith put Eigg up for sale, asking £200,000 – twice what he had paid three years earlier.

This time, the HIDB was shamed (somewhat unsurprisingly) into trying to buy Eigg. It offered that amount of public money to secure the island. Instead, however, the island went to Keith Schellenberg – the heir to a Yorkshire fortune in gelatine, a sort of cheap glue made from old bones and animal carcasses. He had bought Eigg jointly with his second wife, and they owned it in a limited partnership. The island, it was widely reported, had been bought specifically to keep it out of any sort of public ownership and to 'show what private ownership could do' in the Highlands.

Eigg was now to see just what private ownership could indeed do. Although Smith had wanted £200,000 for the island, and though the HIDB was prepared to pay this price, Schellenberg at the last moment offered £274,000. Smith pondered the social responsibilities of Highland land-ownership for about two seconds, grabbed the better price and bolted. Schellenberg said the Board should offer him a grant, or at least an interest-free loan, to match the difference in asking and selling price, claiming it was the intervention of the Board that had raised the price! The Board demurred; but would nevertheless spend a lot of public money to help finance the schemes of the new owner.

And so the private-enterprise development of Eigg – Schellenberg took over on April Fools' Day, 1975 – was once again under way. It may even have been a well-meant development at first: the island population quickly grew from thirty-nine to sixty and the school roll jumped from two to twelve. Schellenberg, meanwhile, imported a vintage car to the island's (very) few miles of (very) single-track road and hosted, from the island lodge, what he described as the Eigg Games. This insolent travesty, on the old Gaelic island of Eigg, concluded – according to the *Field*'s social diary – with a 'war game between the Hanoverians and the Jacobites'. Or, as one guest of the owner later told the *Daily Mail*:

> We spent our days as if we were Somerset Maugham characters, sunbathing or playing croquet on the manicured lawns. Or we piled on to the running board of the stately 1927 Rolls and made our leisurely way to jewelled beaches for long, lazy picnics or midnight games of moonlit hockey and football.

The remainder of the island's (permanent) residents went about their business, meanwhile. And if they had thoughts on the matter, neither the *Field* nor the *Daily Mail* saw fit to ask them what, precisely, these thoughts might consist of.

Within five years it was all going wrong. Schellenberg and wife divorced; the settlement resolved that she remained joint-owner of the island, as she had contributed half the money to buy it. Schellenberg devised a forestry scheme and grant-aid was approved for a 200-hectare planting on land surrounding one of the island's designated Sites of Special Scientific Interest. (The planting ruined its unique little bio-environment in the shadow of the Sgurr, that marvellously scenic volcanic plug that rears up above Eigg.)

Meanwhile, the new forester felt free to catcall the 'anti-enterprise environment which pervades the north-west Highlands'. At the time of the 1988 Games, one guest flew from the United States to London by Concorde. Another arrived on the island by helicopter in full Prussian army dress uniform with an entourage in matching ankle-length capes. On this occasion a swastika flew over the Lodge. Schellenberg's daughter,

Serena, explained this during the course of her father's failed libel action against *The Guardian* in 1999: 'A group of my father's friends called the Kaiser Team were coming and I could not find a German flag, so I put it up as a joke for them.' Serena's joke, it was reported, had made her father 'furious'. It was not reported how a swastika flag happened to be available on the Isle of Eigg.

A dispute developed later that day and one of the guests felt it proper to scream at some of the islanders, 'Scum of the earth, half-baked socialists'. Some of them, soothed the 'furious' glue millionaire by way of explanation, 'are not even British'.

The former Mrs Schellenberg remarried. In 1988, she took legal action against her former husband in the Court of Session. She accused him of 'mismanagement of their joint assets to the extent that the island was declining in value'. She now wanted the island sold, so that she could redeem her share. Schellenberg moved ownership of his share to a company of which he was a director. He appealed the court's decision, but lost the following year.

By 1991, it was expected that the island would be offered for sale imminently. The Isle of Eigg Trust launched an appeal for £3 million to remove the island forever from private ownership. But money was slow in coming in. In May 1992 Eigg was indeed offered for sale. Highland Regional Council asked the selling agents for an extension to the closing date, but was refused. And that July it transpired that the new owner of Eigg was – once more Schellenberg. He had bought it, in effect from himself, for £1 million. The exultant laird announced that he was going to take the Rolls on a triumphant tour of the island, and added that he 'could not sit back and watch Eigg become a sporting estate or worse still an example of collectivism'. A second honeymoon followed. By early in 1994 it had gone very sour once more.

On the night of 6 January – in as evident an intervention of the hand of God in Highland affairs as that which had hurled the contents of a stormy graveyard against a landlord's gable in Skye a century earlier – Schellenberg's vintage Rolls Royce spontaneously combusted. By the following morning there was little or nothing left of it but a pair of vintage and heavily singed axles. The next day Schellenberg himself arrived, accompanied by police (whose enquiries, forensic if not theological, proved inconclusive). He was, recorded an observer, 'quite scared actually; it was plain that he did not believe it was an accident and that he was wondering what would happen next'.

A month later, Schellenberg had recovered his nerve sufficiently to take part in a live radio debate broadcast from the island schoolhouse (in which the land-leaguers of the island had welcomed their Crofters' Candidate Charles Fraser-MacIntosh in the autumn of 1885). One of the guests was Allan MacRae, chairman of the Assynt Trust, who told the meeting:

I can see the proprietor here has no conscience and commitment as far as the people here are concerned. That's what you find with many proprietors in the Highlands and Islands. I think the people here have to take the initiative themselves. This is something that our European counterparts have taken for granted long ago. Here we are in Europe, and we are told to think like Europeans, and yet we still live under a feudal system in the large part of the Highlands and clearly there's got to be changes. Things haven't got to stand still. People can shape the future if they have a will to do it.

This broadcast was deemed to have had a cathartic effect on the islanders, whose efforts were duly enhanced to secure a solution to the problem of Schellenberg. For his part, he announced that he would never accept community control of the island and warned that he would sell it bit by bit to new-money outsiders. Two properties were offered for sale as holiday homes in the *Daily Telegraph*: 'The crofting township is at the other end, they are far enough away not to be a nuisance'.

According to Dressler, the islanders 'denounced this as asset-stripping', for they were concerned that 'selling Eigg into lots would turn it into an island of holiday homes, with disastrous consequences for its culture and traditions'. The islanders had 'more constructive ideas'.

Their central idea was a community buy-out, the first step of which was the handover of the Isle of Eigg Trust to the islanders themselves. An appeal for funds to buy Eigg was launched, with a target of £15,000. To this, their millionaire (and Lloyds 'name') landlord responded with obstructive derision. He would never consider 'anything so childish or pathetic as the notion of community ownership: I own Eigg and I will never sell it,' he said in August 1994.

By the following spring, however, Schellenberg was believed to be in financial difficulties, following separation from a third wife and big losses on Lloyds. It was also rumoured that an offer of £1.5 million had been made for Eigg. At Easter 1995 Schellenberg arrived; denied that the island had been sold; spent a long night at the Lodge shifting furniture; and fled at dawn. Later that day it became clear that he had indeed – with dazzling contempt for the islanders – sold Eigg. And he had sold it some considerable time previously, for £1.6 million, to a German self-proclaimed artist called Marlin Eckhart who styled himself 'Maruma'. Schellenberg had made a profit of £600,000 over just three years.

The Scottish press lost no time in exposing this new owner for what he was. His art professorship was fictitious; so too was his chair in architecture. He was completely unknown on the art market. Meanwhile the heavyweight German news magazine *Stern* checked his credit rating and found it unsatisfactory. Further, he had taken out a bank loan equal to the value of Eigg, and had used the island as security against a loan of £300,000 from a company in Hong Kong. Very soon, wages were being unpaid and it was clear that Maruma's connection with Eigg was going to be a short one.

At the end of July 1996 Eigg was back on the market. The asking price was £2 million. A month later the islanders announced their plan for the community to buy the island, in partnership with local government (the Highland Regional Council) and conservation interests (the Scottish Wildlife Trust). By the end of November £1.2 million had been raised and, on the basis of a professional valuation of Eigg as a property, offered. The selling agents announced, with what might politely be described as magnificent insousiance, that £1.2 million just wasn't enough; but that Mr Maruma had been kind enough to 'leave the island on the market to enable those who offered, and anybody who might also wish to do so, more time to raise the necessary funds to meet the asking price of £2 million'.

Meanwhile, one of Maruma's creditors acted. In March the Hong Kong businessman who had loaned Maruma £300,000 on the day Eigg was purchased got a court order in the cause of getting his money back. The creditor could now force the sale of the island – to the highest bidder – within twenty-eight days. On Friday, 4 April, the creditor's lawyers accepted the islanders' offer of £1.5 million (much of it made possible by the anonymous contribution of an English woman). And so the Isle of Eigg was at last free from the sort of landlord who had bothered it for so long.

Given the shameless circus of greed, idiocy and obstructionism that had preceded this move, it might be thought well within the bounds of realism to describe the takeover of the island, by the people and in the name of the people, as an improvement of some due modesty.

There were other developments in the Highlands during the 1990s, in terms of the erosion of the dominance of private landlordism. At the end of 1997, Skye and Lochalsh Enterprise took ownership of the 4,600-acre Orbost estate on Skye. And in the autumn of 1998 the conservationist John Muir Trust bought the 8,400-acre Sconser estate on Skye, two months later trebling the common-grazing hill land of the local crofting community.

There was also, throughout the decade, a growing awareness of and interest in the Highland land question as a matter of economic and cultural significance for both the Highlands and Scotland as a whole. This was reflected powerfully in a string of publications, conferences and the policy resolutions of most of the political parties. In time, it was even reflected in the activities of HIE.

During the early years of the decade, certainly, the land question was ignored by HIE: its reports until 1997–98 scarcely mention land, and dismiss the Assynt buy-out in a couple of sentences. But with the new Labour government in place after the general election of 1997, and the obliteration of the Conservative party in Scotland and south of the

Border, HIE – without a blink of embarrassment – was able to report a great, new, 'fresh impetus on land'. According to its annual report for 1997–98:

> Access to land as a vital resource in the development of sustainable rural communities received substantial impetus from the new Government. This followed the successful acquisition of land by communities in Assynt, the Island of Eigg and at Borve in Skye. Following a request from Brian Wilson MP, then Scottish Office Minister for State, HIE set up a Community Land Unit in July of 1997.
>
> The unit's objectives are to promote community-led land purchase or management initiatives, provide technical advice and support, including financial assistance, and to contribute to the research and development of land policy.
>
> Main achievements during the year included the purchase by HIE and Skye and Lochalsh Enterprise of Orbost estate on Skye, with the intention of creating a new rural settlement based on a mix of housing, smallholdings and workspaces.
>
> We made a successful application for European Objective 1 funding to create a technical assistance programme and gave technical and financial assistance to the Knoydart Foundation and its fund-raising appeal, and to some 20 smaller community land initiatives including Balmacara, Lochcarron, Achmore, Eigg and Laggan.
>
> Financial assistance helped Abriachan Forest Trust to purchase 540 hectares of woodland on the side of Loch Ness from Forest Enterprise – the first such transfer to a community group in the UK.
>
> Research projects included an audit of existing community land initiatives, an evaluation of the Laggan community forestry project and the formation of a digitised land ownership map and register in the Highland Council and Argyll and Bute areas.
>
> We assisted a series of community land training seminars and approved funding for four major conferences on land-reform issues.

This extraordinary *volte face* serves as something of a grim reminder of how – at times – politics really are a matter of immense importance in the Highlands, as elsewhere.

But it also underlines the extent to which, as Scotland enters the twenty-first century, there is at last a legislative and financial framework in place for an expanded and radical reform of land-ownership in the Highlands. After all, in the Wesminster and Edinburgh elections of the late 1990s, all the parties in Scotland – excluding the Conservatives – were committed to land-reform; and the early years of the parliament in

Edinburgh are likely to be distinguished by legislation in this cause. That, after all, is what the majority of its members were elected to do. And indeed that new Scottish parliament moved very quickly indeed on land-reform: it was formally opened on 1 July 1999; and just eight days later the new administration published its first Scottish White Paper – on land-reform. This was launched, appropriately enough, at Abriachan above Loch Ness.

According to the terms of the White Paper, around £10 million of lottery funds could be available to help communities throughout rural Scotland buy the land on which they live and work. There was, in addition, the threat that powers of compulsion could be available against obstructive landowners.

A community body wishing to buy its land must, for the legislation to apply, have first registered its interest. If the land in question then comes on the market, the community will have thirty days in which to signify a wish to buy. A government-appointed valuer will then set a price for the property. Thereafter, the community will have six months in which to raise monies to match the valuation. According to the Depute First Minister, Jim Wallace:

> Our proposals on community ownership and right of access will create in Scotland a modern and fair approach to land ownership and represent a long-awaited and significant change. But this is only the beginning. There will be an integrated programme of action and legislation over the next four or five years.

John Murdoch and Alexander MacKenzie – among many others – would surely have wondered why it had all taken so long. But they would – surely – have approved.

FVRTHER READING

Very many books have been published in the last twenty or thirty years on Highland affairs, as casual inspection of any competent bibliography or well-stocked bookshelf will demonstrate. A handful of the best titles from the last decade might include the following.

The standard history of the economic formation of Highland crofting is, deservedly, James Hunter, *The Making of the Crofting Community* (second edition, Edinburgh, 1991). The same author's *The Claim of Crofting* (Edinburgh, 1991) very usefully covers the political and administrative framework of crofting between 1930 and 1990. For a detailed description of land-ownership in the Highlands to the mid-1990s, see Andy Wightman's wonderfully impressive *Who Owns Scotland?* (Edinburgh, 1997). For a judicious but stylishly critical portrait of selected major estates in the modern Highlands, see Auslan Cramb, *Who Owns Scotland Now?* (second edition, Edinburgh, 2000). For a historical portrait of a Highland community (and one that should serve as a model for portraits of other communities), see Camille Dressler, *Eigg – the Story of an Island* (Edinburgh, 1998). Joni Buchanan, *The Lewis Land War*, (Stornoway, 1996), is an excellent study of land-centred agitation. David Craig, *On the Crofters' Trail* (London, 1990) is also well worth reading. Very recent titles include: John MacAskill, *We Have Won the Land* (Stornoway, 1999); Eric Richards, *Patrick Sellar and the Highland Clearances* (Edinburgh, 1999); Catriona M.M. Macdonald and E.W. MacFarland (eds), *Scotland and the Great War* (East Linton, 1999); Krisztina Fenyö, *Contempt, Sympathy and Romance* (East Linton, 1999); and Denis Rixson, *Knoydart* (Edinburgh, 1999).

Readers will also find the following titles of interest. John Prebble, *The Highland Clearances* (London, 1969) is a still-influential book, easily available in paperback. The text of the play *The Cheviot, The Stag and The Black, Black Oil* is contained in John McGrath, *Six Pack – Plays for Scotland* (Edinburgh, 1996). Colin Kidd, *Subverting Scotland's Past* (Cambridge, 1993) and T.M. Devine, *Clanship to Crofters' War* (Manchester, 1994) are also worthy of inspection. Ian Richardson, *One for the Pot* (Laggan, 2000) is an excellent account of the methods and opinions of Highland poachers.

Readers may wish to explore government material relating to land-agitation. They can do no better than start with the report of, and minutes of evidence to, the Napier Commission, and the Deer-Forest Commission, before moving to slighter (or at least shorter) material such as the official report relating to the despatch of marines to Skye. Parliamentary debates are often worth reading in full: they were also, of course, covered at great length in the principal newspapers.

As for the various journals which concern themselves with Highland affairs there is none better than the *Transactions of the Gaelic Society of Inverness*. As for manuscript sources: estate and government-department material is available in the appropriate archives. Much of it has been turned over, and much of that has appeared, in one shape and interpretation or another, in published form. But there is still plenty of material to be examined. For instance, the logs of the various naval vessels involved in crofter repression might make interesting reading. The collections of private papers of many of the urban leaders of land-agitation remain unexplored. And someday, someone might find the papers of Charles Guernier, the French writer who published in the 1890s material on the Highland land struggle, and which is clearly based on very close contact with Land League leaders of the period.

Newspapers remain an essential source. Indeed, for a popular perspective on events, they are far more important than the covert and self-serving material of landlords and their various agents. Reporters generally had magnificent shorthand, and their newspapers would publish their highly-detailed verbatim reports at great length. The *Glasgow Herald* and the *North British Daily Mail* gave much space to Highland affairs. The *Oban Times* and the *Invergordon Times* were wonderfully radical local weeklies in their day. John Murdoch's *Highlander* and Alexander MacKenzie's *Scottish Highlander* were radical weeklies of the highest quality. So too was *Forward*. For all of these, the published index to the *Glasgow Herald* (and to a lesser extent, that for *The Times*) can serve, albeit in an approximate way, as an index. The *Stornoway Gazette* has, in the last twenty or so years, carried masses of valuable memorial material relating to land-centred conflict in the Hebrides, and especially Lewis.

Last, but never by any means least, is the *West Highland Free Press*, whose quality of news reporting has been unmatched by any Scottish newspaper in the last quarter-century. From its inception it has echoed in quality and strength of purpose *The Highlander*, the *Scottish Highlander*, and *Forward*; and it may be said to have bettered any of them, at least in that it has retained its radical focus longest. Certainly, it is the single most essential guide – of any class of record – to Highland affairs for the last thirty years of the twentieth century. It has also published vast quantities of material relating to Highland and crofting history from a radical perspective, often drawing on hitherto unpublished archival or private manuscript material, or on hitherto unrecognised oral sources. The Scottish Parliament has a cultural responsibility; it should arrange for the complete run of the *West Highland Free Press* to be made available, in page-image format, to students at home and abroad via the Internet.

240